Politics for Everybody

Politics for Everybody

Reading Hannah Arendt
in Uncertain Times

NED O'GORMAN

The University of Chicago Press
Chicago and London

The University of Chicago Press, Chicago 60637
The University of Chicago Press, Ltd., London
© 2020 by The University of Chicago
All rights reserved. No part of this book may be used or reproduced in any manner whatsoever without written permission, except in the case of brief quotations in critical articles and reviews. For more information, contact the University of Chicago Press, 1427 E. 60th St., Chicago, IL 60637.
Published 2020
Printed in the United States of America

29 28 27 26 25 24 23 22 21 20   1 2 3 4 5

ISBN-13: 978-0-226-66502-3 (cloth)
ISBN-13: 978-0-226-68315-7 (paper)
ISBN-13: 978-0-226-68329-4 (e-book)
DOI: https://doi.org/10.7208/chicago/9780226683294.001.0001

Library of Congress Cataloging-in-Publication Data

Names: O'Gorman, Ned, author.
Title: Politics for everybody : reading Hannah Arendt in uncertain times / Ned O'Gorman.
Description: Chicago : The University of Chicago Press, 2020. | Includes bibliographical references and index.
Identifiers: LCCN 2019027818 | ISBN 9780226665023 (cloth) | ISBN 9780226683157 (paperback) | ISBN 9780226683294 (ebook)
Subjects: LCSH: Arendt, Hannah, 1906–1975. | Political science.
Classification: LCC JC251.A74 O46 2020 | DDC 320.5—dc23
LC record available at https://lccn.loc.gov/2019027818

♾ This paper meets the requirements of ANSI/NISO Z39.48-1992 (Permanence of Paper).

For Graham, upon college, tolle lege

When a people loses its political freedom, it loses its political reality, even if it should succeed in surviving physically.

—HANNAH ARENDT, "Introduction into Politics"

When the facts come home to roost, let us try to at least make them welcome. Let us try not to escape into some utopias—images, theories, or sheer follies.

—HANNAH ARENDT, "Home to Roost"

CONTENTS

Preface / xi

INTRODUCTION / Prodigal Politics / 1

ONE / Untwisting Politics / 16

TWO / Phenomenal Politics / 35

THREE / Judging Politics / 55

FOUR / Lies, Damned Lies, and Politics / 76

FIVE / Why We Need Rhetoric / 92

SIX / The Political Imagination (or, Freedom!) / 114

CONCLUSION / Politics Reborn / 136

Acknowledgments / 143
Artist Statement / 145
Notes / 147
Bibliography / 165
Index / 171

PREFACE

This is a book about happiness.

You've no doubt heard the phrase "the pursuit of happiness." This phrase was, and is, revolutionary. For the signers of the Declaration of Independence and those on whose behalf they spoke, *happiness* was the goal of political life. This is a startling claim—at least, to twenty-first-century ears. We are not accustomed to connecting politics to happiness. Indeed, we are much more likely to link politics to negative feelings of misery, depression, apathy, outrage, or anger. Yet, when Thomas Jefferson wrote "the pursuit of happiness," he wasn't being flippant. He was echoing an age-old commonplace. The ancients put "happiness" or "flourishing" as the end purpose of political life. They argued that the best way to secure our everyday contentment is to invest in the constitution and maintenance of our collective life.

Writing in the middle of the twentieth century, the German-turned-American political thinker Hannah Arendt observed that, with the crucial exception of civil rights movements, Americans had largely forgotten this founding truth. "Happiness," to be sure, was a major pursuit for many Americans in the 1950s and 1960s. But it was a private happiness, a happiness sought in new kitchen appliances, television comedy shows, and Betty Crocker recipes in the 1950s, or in sex, drugs, and rock 'n' roll in the 1960s. Americans, Arendt noted, had substituted such private affairs for the age-old pursuit of what people in Jefferson's time unabashedly called "public happiness." It was for public happiness, not bigger paychecks or more stuff, that people had emigrated to the New World from England and elsewhere in the first place, she observed; and it was for public happiness that the American Revolution was fought.

When Arendt wrote, the replacement of public happiness with private happiness was not seen as a problem by most Americans. What's the big deal? they asked. They were confident of a wealthier future for themselves and their children; many saw good reason to prioritize their economic lives and their personal well-being above civic participation; and they saw in consumer goods, entertainment options, nice houses, and nice cars ever-expanding means of private happiness. To them, it seemed like public life was at best a kind of extracurricular activity, reserved for those with particular public or political ambitions. During this time a kind of new American credo took hold: "We hold these truths to be self-evident, that all men, women, and children are created equal, that they are endowed by their Creator with certain unalienable Rights, that among these are the right to be left alone by Government, to despise Politicians, and to focus on making more Money." This was the credo that Ronald Reagan brought to the White House in the 1980s, and it has been an American orthodoxy ever since.

Or until quite recently. As I write, our desertion of civic life and our relegation of politics to an after-school club is coming home to roost. Aided by social media, our long-neglected political culture is encroaching on our private spaces, causing family fights, ruining friendships, and making many of us personally unhappy, depressed, or deeply outraged. Moreover, the world's big problems—from climate change to growing economic inequality to information warfare to refugee crises—are hitting home (sometimes quite literally) for many of us and can't be ignored any longer.

Hence, the basic point of this book: *sustained and widespread private happiness depends on public happiness*. This is the premise the American republic was founded upon, imperfect though that foundation was; and it is no less true now than it was then. The quality of our public life shapes the quality of our private lives. Politics forms some of the essential conditions for our private pursuits, rather than being the hobby of those odd birds who are "into" politics.

The project known as "liberalism," which was the guiding philosophy of the second half of the twentieth century in North America, has long suggested otherwise. Liberalism is related to, yet quite different from, being "liberal" in one's political positions (conservatives subscribe to liberalism too); it can be defined as the belief that protecting the private pursuit of happiness is the primary obligation of society. Liberalism is rooted in some very important truths: individuals matter; individuals need protections; and individuality is a good thing.

Yet liberalism can put such a premium on the rights of individuals to pursue whatever they see as leading to their private happiness that it can neglect the broader social, political, and environmental issues that, as a matter of fact, set the conditions and circumstances for those private, personal pursuits. Liberalism teaches us that if we just focus on pursuing our private interests without encroaching on the private interests of others, happiness is ours for the taking. The extreme version of this approach is called "libertarianism."[1] But this is simply not the way the world works for most of us: as we are now seeing, our private lives, not to mention our economic lives and the very health of our bodies, are not walled off from the political dynamics of neighborhoods, communities, countries, and climates—they are directly affected by them. Politics is a *quality-of-life* issue—a matter of happiness.

This is a "republican" claim. Republicanism, like liberalism, should not be confused with the political party or particular political ideologies; it is simply the idea that the quality of your private life cannot be neatly separated from that of public life, that private happiness depends to some degree on public happiness, and that the means of public happiness are both by nature constitutional (for example, the "separation of powers") and practical (for example, active citizenship). Republicanism predates liberalism, and there is good reason to conclude, as some scholars have done, that the latter is but a trimmed-down version of the former.[2] Regardless, whenever committed liberals (again, we are not talking about left-wingers versus right-wingers here, but rather those who in their guts or minds subscribe to the tenets of liberalism laid out just above—many of whom are political conservatives) take to the streets or to the airwaves to get something done, they are reviving the republican spirit of speech and action in the public sphere for their liberal cause.

So too, this book channels the republican spirit. It was written in the context of political circumstances and crises that came to a head in the second decade of the twenty-first century. It argues that we need to revive the republican spirit as a matter of course, and not just during election cycles or during times of crisis. This means that, though I teach at a university, I wrote this book as a citizen more than an academic. Our main topic is *politics*, and this book argues that politics is for *everybody*.

More specifically, this book is a defense of politics written for people who have lost faith in it—people like my friends, neighbors, students, fellow church congregants, and those I hang out with at the coffee shop and gym. As a general rule, they seem to fall into one of two camps: those who are sick and tired of politics, and those who are anxiously preoccupied with it. For all the talk of partisan polarization, the pole between those who are "checked out" and those who are "amped up" is, I believe, the most consequential form of political polarization today. It is the infrastructure on which partisan polarization is built. My goal, therefore, is to argue for a political middle ground that has nothing directly to do with political parties or ideologies, but with the worth, value, and importance of politics itself.

What follows is hardly a neutral case for politics, or a case for neutral politics. In keeping with its guiding spirit, Hannah Arendt, this book provides a case for republican democracy. John Adams quipped two hundred years ago that "the word *republic*, as it is used, may signify any thing, every thing, or nothing"—and he'd be as right now as he was then. Nevertheless, he continued, when you put the word *democracy* alongside *republic*—or as he wrote, "democratical"—you get something very specific indeed, and very special: a political order where the government is of the people, by the people, and for the people, rather than of, by, and for the privileged, rich, or scheming.[3]

Hannah Arendt is the most knowledgeable defender of republican democracy in the last century. Her learning was erudite and bookish, but it was also immediately practical and personal. She was a political refugee, a German Jew fortunate enough to escape the Nazis in the 1930s. Her thinking about politics, therefore, was rooted in her own experiences as a refugee who eventually made a home in America. Perhaps the intensity of this experience contributed to the rigor and acumen of her writings, which many find different and difficult to grasp; as the teacher who first introduced me to Arendt years ago, Stephen Browne, writes, "Even her most astute students confess to struggling to decipher just what she means."[4] One of my goals for this book is to show that Arendt's political thinking is in fact rooted in common sense and everyday experience. That is, her approach to politics is grounded, sane, and realistic. For Arendt scholars, the questions and issues I raise in the pages that follow will be familiar; they will find little in these pages that is surprising or new, other than perhaps some of my interpretations of Arendt.[5] For other scholars, I hope this book might serve as an introduction to Arendt (the endnotes, I expect, will be particularly helpful).[6] Still, this is less a book about Arendt and more an Arendtian book. It stands somewhere between an introduction to her work and that of other important political thinkers, and an introduction to the political arts themselves. It is the product of a decades-long conversation I have been having with Arendt's writings and the traditions she engaged, and of many other conversations I've had with teachers, friends, family members, students, and even strangers.[7]

Speaking of strangers: while I was writing this book, a stranger became a priceless participant in its production. In its pages you will see a series of drawings by the talented Chicago-based artist Sekani Reed. I did not know Sekani until pretty late in this project. When I saw her paintings displayed at a local art show and then again on Instagram, I was struck by her remarkable ability to bring the human face and the human hand to life. After mulling it over, I got up the nerve to ask her if she would be willing to do a series of drawings for this book. After some conversations, she agreed. Working with Sekani ended up offering a small taste of the possibilities for politics: we were strangers to each other; we came from different places; we represent different generations. None of our "identity" categories align: we look different, talk different, act different, and listen to (mostly) different music. Not surprisingly, we did not always see eye to eye. Still, we *talked* with each other—sometimes at length face-to-face and sometimes in fits and starts via text messages—about matters (or as Arendt would say, "objects") of common concern. Out of our conversations came more than the drawings you see in these pages. Some of the very words and ideas of this book emerged, as I learned them in conversation with Sekani. Needless to say, the arguments in this book do not necessarily reflect her point of view; likewise, her drawings are not simple "illustrations" of points I'm trying to make. Rather, they are in visual discussion with the themes and arguments of the book—capable, like the democratic citizen, of both standing on their own and joining in conversation with other voices.

INTRODUCTION

Prodigal Politics

I begin with a parable, a political parable, the parable of the prodigal son. Told in the Bible, my slightly embellished version of it goes something like this: A rich father has two sons, older and younger, each guaranteed a large inheritance. The older son is dutiful and responsible, patiently waiting for the day when he will inherit his half of the family estate. The younger son, by contrast, is ready to cut out on his own as soon as he can, asking for his inheritance while he is still quite young and his father still healthy. Perhaps to the young son's surprise, his father agrees to go ahead and give him his portion of the inheritance, even over the older son's protestations.

Gobs of money in hand, the younger son ventures out into the world, only to spend all his wealth in a short time on loose living. Now penniless and pitiful, he first serves a stint as a farmhand before crawling back home in shame, ready to ask his father for a job on the family farm, where at least he won't have to sleep with the pigs. Before the younger son can even get a word in, the father runs to him, embraces him, and calls for a party. The older son, aghast at the father's show of extravagance, complains to his dad that, though he has worked dutifully and faithfully for years, he's never gotten a party. The father responds by saying, "Look, everything I have is already yours!"[1]

The parable of the prodigal son has long been taught as a lesson in unconditional love, but there is every reason to read it as a political parable as well. In the ancient world, like today, venturing out from home was a way of growing up. In giving the younger son his inheritance and letting go, the father says to his grown child: you are now free from the restrictions, as well as the protections, of our home. You are my equal. Upon his humiliating return home, the younger son is ready to become a family servant in exchange for protection and provision. Instead, the father refuses the offer and insists on the ongoing freedom and equality of his son through embrace and celebration. There will be no return to the old ways of paternal supervision and restriction, the father says: we are still equal, and you are still free. The older son resents this. He thinks freedom and equality need to be earned rather than freely given, reserved for the best behaved. The father's response—"All that is mine is already yours!"—is him saying, "You too are my equal, and like your younger brother, you are free! Though you have never left the house, I have let go of you too!" For both sons, therefore, the basis of the relationship is no longer one of obligation and command, but of freedom and equality; and every matter is negotiated as such, including matters of jealousy, injustice, foolishness, and prodigality.

I will be arguing in this book that politics, like the father's love, begins with the art of letting go, of giving up control, of relating as equals rather than as masters and servants. We are accustomed to thinking that equality and freedom are the end goals of political activism. I will be arguing that they are the *beginning* of politics, that without them politics is not possible. Moreover, I will be arguing that this is a matter of fact, not wishful thinking. There will be little idealism in this book, no Pollyanna promises of a perfect political world. On the contrary, I start with three realities.

First, people have and do relate to other people as equals. Not all relationships happen this way; we might even conclude that most do not. Nevertheless, *equality happens*. Second, when people relate to one another as equals, they relate in freedom. Of course, this freedom is not total or absolute. Nobody is absolutely free—that's a Pollyanna idea if ever there was one. Our bodies and minds are limited. We are frequently forced to meet the basic necessities of our bodily and social lives: making something to eat, getting enough sleep, showing up on time for work, caring for family members in need, and so on. And there are plenty of people and powers out there that actively work to control and even exploit the rest of us, limiting our freedoms. Nevertheless, just as equality happens, so *freedom happens*. Freedom, I will be arguing, is not a state of being, it is a *quality* of being with others—a quality of relationship. Third, equality and freedom, like the relations between the father and his two sons in the parable above, is a matter of ongoing human choices and practices, not nature, society, or market economies. While freedom and equality are facts of human life—human phenomena—they also need to be repeatedly chosen, for they are not the only facts of life; there are plenty of oppressive or just plain necessary ones as well. Freedom and equality therefore need to be purposeful matters of choice. This is what so many political struggles in human history have been all about.

Politics is ultimately the art of living in freedom and equality with others. Political relationships are very special: they happen whenever two or more people relate to each other as equals and in freedom. This in turn produces the form of human power called political power. Such relationships are not automatic. They have to be intentionally pursued, as one pursues a craft or an art. There are all kinds of injustices and distortions that can twist politics into something other than the art of relating in freedom as equals, and that can mistake the power of the gun for political power. The parable of the two sons is in part a story of one such distortion: resentment. The older son resents the freedom of his brother. He wants his father to lay down the law, to punitively enslave or otherwise indenture his brother. Resentment, to be sure, is a commanding force, but it is one that damages politics, twisting it into something other than the art of relating to others in freedom and equality. Under the sway of resentment, politics can be distorted to become a way of getting revenge, forcing one's way, or pitting "us" against "them."

Therefore, this book is about the difference between authentic politics and twisted politics. I explore, explain, and argue for this difference, defending authentic politics over and against its many abuses and abusers.[2] Of course, the evidence is everywhere that twisted politics is winning the day. During the last decade, the United States, for one, has seen a dramatic increase in political polarization, and many people are *stuck*—either stuck in their little political cocoons, unassailed by doubts, differences of opinion, or data to the contrary; or stuck not knowing what to do about the fact that so many are stuck. Political scientists and media scholars are inventing new phrases to try to get their heads around the phenomenon—*filter bubbles, affective polarization, expressive partisanship,* and so on—but only to say the same basic thing: a perverse partisanship rules (one, I should add, that is very profitable for certain media and social media companies).[3] Many of us are unable to see the worlds of others, let alone the world itself, apart from our partisan perspectives. None of us are fully free of the myopia. And education is not the panacea you might think. In fact, a 2016 Pew Research Center study concludes the opposite: the more educated you are, the more likely you are to insist on your way of seeing the world.[4] Factors like media consumption, rural versus urban residency, or one's tax bracket each make a difference in the nature of the political myopia, but not in the basic fact of the myopia itself. And other studies show that the more you actually care about politics, the more likely you are to be stuck in your bubble.[5]

It is no wonder that many of us have decided to ignore, escape from, or otherwise avoid politics. Political arguments have ruined innumerable friendships and family gatherings. If you want to get along with your

Thanksgiving.

coworker, avoid talking politics. If you want a peaceful Thanksgiving meal with family, don't talk about politics. If you want to keep things cool in the classroom, stay away from politics. The *New York Times* told the story of someone who lost all her friends because she voted for Donald Trump: "Friends I've had for 40 years," she exclaimed. "It's insane, that's what I'll tell you."[6] Indeed, "insane" is a good description for the distorted politics of our time. It is not just the broken friendships and disastrous family gatherings, but the insane appetites of cable news and social media for drama, outrage, and faux debate; the crazy amount of money in the electoral system; the ridiculous wall-to-wall political ads during election season; and the bizarre maps of voting districts, engineered to keep the party-in-power in power. So many of us are justifiably fed up with politics.

Despite all that, this book is a defense of the dignity of politics in the age of its infamy. It argues that politics is the quintessential everyday art of relating in freedom as equals and that rather than being the problem, it is part of the solution to our political myopia, malaise, and malevolence. It argues that we need to do more politics, not throw out politics; to take politics more seriously, not write it off; to give politics a thinking chance.

It does so by exploring the works of the most articulate defender of politics in the twentieth century, Hannah Arendt (1906–1975), a German-born

Jew who fled the Nazis in the 1930s, ultimately taking up residence in the United States.[7] Over the next thirty years, Arendt would write a trenchant analysis of totalitarianism, the five-hundred-page-plus *The Origins of Totalitarianism*, as well as a host of other books and articles on topics ranging from revolution to the nature of human responsibility in caring for the world. She also became one of the most controversial writers of her day by arguing, in a series of articles that first appeared in the *New Yorker* and later appeared as the book *Eichmann in Jerusalem*, that Adolf Eichmann, one of the administrators of the Holocaust, exemplified "the banality of evil"—a phrase that critics took to mean "bland" or "boring."[8]

On the contrary, Arendt's infamous phrase, the "banality of evil," was meant to designate the way in which evil—particularly, modern evil—is so often done by people whose most conspicuous sin is simply *not thinking*.[9] The massacres and genocides of the twentieth century, Arendt noted, as well as a host of less spectacular forms of human cruelty, were by and large carried out by people who were less diabolical than they were thoughtless, be it in the form of groupthink or a heedless commitment to duty, loyalty, or obedience. Indeed, Arendt was careful to stress that "not thinking" has nothing to do with intelligence. It is something *everybody* is susceptible to, just as everybody can stop to think:

> Thinking ... is not a prerogative of the few but an ever-present faculty of everybody; by the same token, the inability to think is not the "prerogative" of those many who lack brain power but the ever-present possibility for everybody—scientists, scholars, and other specialists in mental enterprises not excluded.[10]

Politics, for Arendt, is not the be-all-and-end-all solution to such thoughtless evil, but it was a major antidote if for no other reason than politics calls us to speak with, and thus potentially think with, others who are different from us. Political solutions, Arendt argued, are never automatic; they are never a matter of strict conformity or obedience. They are always made by taking into account the perspectives, voices, and concerns of others, and they culminate in judgments and actions rather than thoughtless prejudices or instinctive reactions. And this political enterprise, Arendt insisted, is ultimately for *everybody*.[11]

The Curious Case for Politics

The curious case for politics that Arendt made begins with the paradoxical fact that, on the one hand, we need to work to practice and cultivate politics, and yet on the other hand we cannot escape politics, no matter how we might try. Arendt noted that for several centuries now humans have tried to escape the world of politics by believing that some other power—the economy, science, technology, religion, race, or individual self-actualization—will burst the bounds of our political condition on Earth and lead us into ever-expanding heavenly horizons of progress. Met with the arbitrary decisions and disastrous consequences of monarchs in past centuries, eighteenth- and nineteenth-century Europeans and Americans conceived of things like "the laws of history," "the designs of providence," "the benefits of industry," "the secrets of biology," or "the magic of the markets" as ways of building a world beyond politics. The twentieth-century results of this would-be world without politics were absolute, and absolutely catastrophic. Claims for the historical destiny of the Aryan race gave us the Holocaust; the demands of Soviet collectivization gave us the gulags; the priority of physics over politics gave us the Bomb; and "capturing markets" gave us civil wars in Central and South America, colonial and postcolonial wars in Africa, and sweatshops in Asia.

Arendt suggested that these catastrophes had the form of a boomerang effect. Whereas each of them—Nazi Germany, Soviet statism, nuclear terror, or economic imperialism—began from the desire for a world beyond politics (in the form of social orders premised on racial identity, dialectical materialism, defense science, or profit maximization, respectively), they each bounced back to perversely "politicize" everything, from one's genetics to history to science to sweaters and bananas. Arendt further suggested that they each began from a position that was not so much devoid of politics as characterized by the severe concentration of politics within a singular destructive dynamic. A distorted and oppressive politics, in other words, could not even be escaped by those who wished to overcome it. They could only take hold of it and further twist it toward their own self-serving purposes.

Indeed, as long as "men, not Man, live on the earth and inhabit the world," Arendt argued, someone somewhere is going to be doing politics of one form or another. (Arendt, writing in the middle of the twentieth century, used the word *men* to refer to all humans, irrespective of gender.) Politics, she argued, is part of our human condition by virtue of the fact that "we are all the same, that is, human, in such a way that nobody is ever the same as anyone else who ever lived, lives, or will live."[12] We are plural, and the fact of our "plurality" requires us to work out our sameness and differences in a political manner of one kind or another.[13] The essential question for us is as old as political philosophy itself: Who gets to participate in what kind of political processes, toward what ends, and by what means? We cannot escape politics. We can only work to make it better or worse, more constructive or more destructive, more democratic (where politics is the prerogative of the people) or more oligarchic (where politics is the privilege of the few).

Arendt argued for an authentic, democratic politics. Her arguments at times seem idealistic. But they are not. On the contrary, her approach to politics was *more* real than those taken today in TV's *House of Cards* style, presenting politics as a zero-sum game of power full of backstabbing, corruption, lies, manipulation, and ruthless acts of domination. To be sure, there have been plenty of people in positions of political responsibility who, to put it mildly, do not work well with others. And such people can exert major power, either through coercion or destruction.

But here's the thing: piracy, tyranny, and destruction are not authentic expressions of the art of politics. They are perversions and exploitations of it. This is something that Arendt seems to have learned from St. Augustine (354–430 CE), the subject of her graduate thesis.[14] Augustine saw evil, wickedness, and crime as but twisting what is good into something malevolent. Piracy, tyranny, and destruction are parts of the art of theft, not politics. And while many thieves have occupied the halls of government, occupying the office does not make any of them any less a thief. If your interest in reading this book is in this sort of thing, you'd best put this book down and go read one on the art of theft.

The art of politics is *more* real than these arts of theft because thieving, like a parasite, depends on politics for its sustenance. In order to steal, there has to be something there to steal. In order to manipulate, there has to be something there to manipulate. In order to lie, there has to be a truth. In order to kill, there has to be a life. My point here is that just because something is more shocking, grotesque, or depraved does not make it more real. There are plenty of daily instances of *House of Cards*–style politics, far too many to recount; corruption is so often the norm rather than the exception in contemporary government. Nevertheless, corruption is always the corruption *of* something, and much of what we call politics today is but the corruption of politics. It is this primary phenomenon, the phenomenon of politics, that is the focus of this book.

Twenty-first-century populism—seen in Brexit, in the election of various "strong men" to positions of political power, and in brewing racial and nationalist crises in North America, the European Union, and parts of South America—has depended on a lot of lying, manipulating, and theft, yet it has had one redeeming quality: it reminds us that *we live in a political world*. There is no escaping it. Politics is our lot. The question is, What will we do with our lot? We need better politics, not less of it. Politics is an art in need of defense and democratization. A revival of and reeducation in the meaning of politics and the political art could weaken the ideological, partisan hyperventilation that is paralyzing us. It could help us get in touch with our own inner political animal in ways that would enhance neighborliness, enrich communities, and strengthen the competency of government rather than tear us further apart.

At present we are suffering from something like an autoimmune disease: in attacking the very real sickness of the political system, we have also been attacking the principal means of its health. Or perhaps the better analogy is psychological: we are projecting onto politics the causes for problems that are a result, in essence, of the weakening of politics, and this can only be addressed through strengthening it. We need a reintroduction to basic politics, so as to reclaim the means of some collective health and sanity.[15]

We must, for example, take seriously the politics of our economic lives, regarding the economy not as an autonomous, uncontrollable force in our collective life, but something we can address together. We must make civic leadership meaningful again, so that words like *honor* and *respect* are not reserved strictly for soldiers and flags but unadorned civilians. We must keep engineers from gaining a monopoly on political power by further entrenching their algorithmic powers in our global digital networks. And we must, as everyday citizens, relearn the arts of persuasion, debate, dialogue, deliberation, and difference-making, turning these from pieties into everyday practices.

Hannah Arendt's Course in Basic Politics

Arendt's course in basic politics revolves around six facts we can grasp with our five senses and our common sense. She begins by asking us to refocus our attention on our basic human situation, the first and primary fact: the fact that you, I, and others live together on Earth. This is what Arendt calls "the human condition."[16] It is quite significant that Arendt starts her thinking about politics with the human condition, not "human nature," for so many other influential political philosophers of the modern age have assumed that politics is in one way or another a response to, and a means of dealing with, the problem of "human nature."

Part of what I will do in this book is explore not only Arendt's thinking, but where some of the ideas she challenged come from. The idea that politics is a means of managing "human nature" is very old, but it got major support at the dawn of the modern age from John Locke (1632–1704). Locke helped lay the philosophical groundwork for what is known today as "political liberalism," a position that has been shared by many people on both the conservative and liberal sides of the ideological spectrum. Locke argued that human nature is acquisitive, avaricious, and grasping. We are possessive individuals. We are all grabbers. We want to *own* things—above all, ourselves and the means of our survival and sustenance. Therefore, Locke envisioned a society built on property rights and contractual rules that would guard "me" and "my stuff" against the grab game of society. He thought guaranteeing the rights of those who meet certain qualifications—specifically, being a male and owning property—was the way to do this. As such, his was a political theory that would have pleased the older son in the parable of the prodigal son: only those who are entitled get rights.

Since Locke, political liberals have revised over and over again the "qualifications" for getting rights, but they have never given up on the basic Lockean game: political liberalism is a politics for *anybody*—anybody, that is, who meets the proper qualifications. Once you're "in," the main benefits you get are protections against the ways others might try to grab what's yours. As I said, this has been the consensus position among conservatives and liberals alike. While different parties have disagreed on who qualifies for protection and on the nature and extent of various rights and rules for society, they have agreed that the essential political questions come down to the rights of possessive individuals and corresponding laws.

Arendt criticized this position. She thought politics was for *everybody*, not "anybody who meets certain qualifications." Moreover, she thought it ridiculously reductive to conclude that one picture of "human nature" should guide society. She thought human nature is too complicated and variable to function as a steady foundation for politics. In fact, she worried that theories of human nature tend to result in our efforts to make others what we theorize people to be in the first place. If we believe human nature is malleable, subject to conditioning and behavioral control, we will try to make people into the equivalent of glorified dogs. If we believe that human nature is good and noble, we will try to force people to become saints. And if we believe that human nature is acquisitive, we will try to turn everyone into buyers and sellers of stuff.

So Arendt began her approach to politics not with human nature but with the human condition—above all, the fact that to be human is to live with others on Earth. "That's obvious," you might say. In fact, taking what is obvious and making it meaningful was at the heart of Arendt's work—as was questioning what we so often take to be obvious. All human activities, she argued, are conditioned by the essential fact of our life together on Earth.[17] We can't escape this, no matter what forms of exclusion, exploitation, and oppression rule the day.[18] What do we do with the fact of our coexistence? Now, *that* is the quintessential political question, she argued.

In taking up this question, Arendt stressed a second fact: that in general all people on Earth share a set of basic human capacities—the capacity for thought, the capacity for communication, and the capacity to do things, or for "action." We all generally have the capacity to use our minds to form ideas, assertions, opinions, and judgments. We all generally have the capacity to communicate with others, to use words, gestures, or images to make statements, ask questions, express feelings, or just plain remind ourselves and others that we exist.[19] Finally, we all act, be it in ordinary ways like picking up a piece of trash from the sidewalk, or heroically, like pulling a child from the road before a speeding car. Thinking, speaking, and acting are the basic means by which we navigate the earth, our communities, and the world of cultures and civilizations.

We now have two observable facts: we coexist on Earth, and we each have some basic capacities that help us steer through our lives with others. Here we come to a third fact: there are particular objects, issues, and events that become matters of common concern among a diverse group of people. This fact starts with the observation that each of us tends to care about things— not each and every thing, but some things. To really care about something is to put yourself into it. When more than one person cares, they inevitably make that thing a "common" concern. And as we organize around matters of common concern, we begin to make what Arendt called a "common world."[20] A common world is not identical with that bright blue sphere called Earth that we see in NASA photographs. Rather, it is the collection of all the various things we care about *with* other people, be it trees, dolphins, taxes, tasers, stereotypes, or sidewalks.

As we care about such things with others, we will very likely find ourselves seeing the matter differently from some others. My neighbor, for example, wants to get rid of a messy tree that stands between our houses. I want to keep it because it offers shade for my porch. We see things differently not because we are members of different political parties, but because we are different people with different standpoints. The tree forms a sticking point, you could say, between me and my neighbor. But Arendt would say that, more fundamentally, it is a *connection point* in my common world with my neighbor. At the same time, the various microbes in and around the tree are not part of our neighborly common world because neither of us has thought much about them or been persuaded to care about them. For the city arborists, by contrast, those microbes might be objects of care, and thus part of a common world.

Difference is therefore the fourth fact in Arendt's basic course on politics. Sometimes our differences are slight; other times they are major. Either way, we should not expect to see things in exactly the same way or have exactly the same standpoint. We all stand differently in the world. If a bunch of people see things in exactly the same way, it is because they have let go of their individual perspective and individual thinking for the sake of a group. Sometimes, the surrender of one's standpoint to a general viewpoint can be harmless—say, with fans of a pop group. Sometimes it can be necessary, as with soldiers fighting in the field of battle. But other times it can be quite dangerous—especially when we start to think and act like cogs in an ideological or political party machine before many-sided issues that are best approached through a plurality of perspectives.

Hence, a fifth fact, *freedom*. For people to freely use their capacities for thought, speech, and action in addressing matters of common concern is qualitatively different than for people to be *forced* to do things. We all act under pressures and constraints of various kinds. There is no such thing as absolute freedom. Nevertheless, there is a qualitative difference between marching in step as part of dance troupe we've joined and marching in step under the gun of a prison warden. Freedom for Arendt is seen in the *quality* of human action; it is a matter of conviction and context. And when it comes to caring about things together, caring freely is qualitatively different and qualitatively superior to "caring" because one is forced to or because everyone else does. It is the difference between simply moving along in life and *acting* (see chapter 6).

Finally, the final fact: for people to freely use their capacities for thought, speech, and action to address matters of common concern, they need a space to do so. We need a space where we feel like there is space *between* people, where we can speak and act in the plural, not as a big singular blob. Arendt somewhat enigmatically called this a "space of appearances."[21] The space is a space of "appearances" because for anything in the world to appear before you, you need some distance between you and the object. By seeing something even at a slight distance from you, you intuitively realize that the issue is "not just you"—it is part of the world outside your head.[22] Therefore, it can be a matter of common concern, something others can also see. If what worries me can't be seen by anyone else, it cannot become a political object. Likewise, if I can't put any distance between an object and myself— let's say me and the tree—then whatever others say about the tree will feel to me like they are saying it about *me*. I, therefore, become a political object, so to speak. While there is nothing inherently wrong with this (I may justifiably feel so strongly about the tree that I see it as part of myself), it is good to be aware that when we enter into a space of "appearances"—be it an online forum, a living room, a school board meeting, a local bar, a political convention, or a street corner—the things we care about, including ourselves, can appear to different people in different ways.[23]

There we have it. Six basic facts that shape our basic political existence. These six facts can be summed up in one very Arendtian statement: *Politics happens when people freely come together as equals to speak about, or act on, matters of common concern.* Freedom and equality here are fundamentally ways of relating to one another, not just legal categories or ideological slogans. They do not depend for their essence on law or national identity, but on the choices we make about how to relate to others. In your workplace, for example, you are not, in one manner of speaking, a free equal to your boss. Nevertheless, you can speak to your boss *as a free equal* about something that concerns you both—let's say school shootings—and when you do, you enter into a political relationship.

Note how Arendt's basic approach to politics is free of so many of the words we associate with politics: *politicians, government, campaigns, parties, media, elections, conservatives, liberals, independents, radicals, right-wing, left-wing, socialists, libertarians, authoritarians.* It is not that Arendt did not care about these things—on the contrary. Nor is it that she lacked a recognizable political perspective; though she was not much of a Republican or Democrat when it came to American political parties, she was very much a republican democrat in the historical sense that emphasizes the power of the people, the rule of law, and the importance of what she called "public freedom."[24] Rather, at the heart of Arendt's approach to politics is the insistence that politics is a basic human capacity, and that it can be done more or less authentically. We are, among other things, she argued, *political beings.* Every time we speak, act, or otherwise interact as equals with others, we showcase the remarkable potential we humans have for things like cooperation, confrontation, trust, making demands, listening, expressing viewpoints, articulating opinions, making judgments, apologizing, and forgiving. These capacities are at the heart of forming and preserving political communities.

Arendt argued that these capacities are the bases of genuine political power. Political power is not wielded like a gun or a sledgehammer; it is constituted, formed, and coproduced by people as they come together around matters of common concern to exercise their capacities for communication and action.[25] Moreover, she pointed out that these capacities constitute the only viable basis of what we call "human rights" and "human dignity"— which she tended to characterize, more precisely, as "political rights."[26] Because you, as an individual, are endowed with the political capacities for communication and action, Arendt would say that you have a right to a community that respects those capacities as much as you do, just as a fish has a right to water. She also suggested that the only kind of community that can fully respect your capacities as an individual (and not merely as a member of a family, social group, or identity category) is a free political community of equals, or a democracy. The market will not protect your right to speak and act; technology will not respect your dignity; "history" does not care for your individual human life; and, as we have learned over and over again in the last century, states or governments, when they grow authoritarian, are quite willing to disregard your rights and dignity in the name of their administrative power. Democratic political communities are the only kind of community that can fully respect someone's capacities for communication and action. Therefore, in giving up on democratic politics, Arendt argued, we surrender far more than the ideals of individuality and freedom—we relinquish our dignity, and as such a degree of our humanness.[27]

This argument is not pie-in-the-sky. On the contrary, it is rooted in the six basics of the human condition discussed above, even as these facts are also "normative" or ideals to fight for and pursue. Moreover, these facts do not in the least bit exclude other realities of human existence like violence, exploitation, or danger. In her day, Arendt was one of the more prominent critics of the oppressive and restrictive tendencies of twentieth-century modern society, including in the "free societies" of the world. She thought we moderns were not nearly as fond of freedom and equality as we claimed, that we were often better at building cages for ourselves and others than at constituting free communities. Too often in times of crisis we turn to *technological* and *economic* solutions, when what we really need are *political* ones. While these technological and economic fixes may be efficient, effective, and perhaps even rewarding in the short term, they fuel long-term crises, for they neglect our political capacities in favor of conformity to the machine-like motions of economy and society. Moreover, they often result in a mismatch, as engineering or market approaches are applied to what are essentially nontechnical and noneconomic problems like mistrust, hatred, exploitation, or corruption. At some point, Arendt suggested, people will begin to resent being treated as grist for the mills of systems run by economists, lawyers, defense planners, and engineers. That point, I think it is fair to say, is upon us.

Living during the horrors of the twentieth century—Nazi Germany, Soviet show trials and gulags, Vietnam, Cold War nuclear standoffs—Arendt wrote like someone trying to pick up the pieces of war-ravaged ruins not to rebuild the ruins as they once were, but to build something new for all of us. Arendt herself drew heavily from the history of political thought so as to think politics anew for the future. In a similar way, in the pages that follow I will consider some of Arendt's major insights, along with those of other political thinkers, to think through the challenges and possibilities for politics for the twenty-first century.

Several challenges are central to Arendt's work, and to the defense of politics in the chapters that follow: differentiating authentic politics from twisted and distorted views of politics (chapter 1); the difficulty we have appreciating politics (chapter 2); the challenge of political judgment (chapter 3); the problem of truth in politics (chapter 4); and the role of persuasion in politics (chapter 5). My goal in all of this is not only a defense of politics, but to somehow stimulate and stir your political imagination, at the heart of which is the imagination of freedom (chapter 6). This means seeing politics in a more positive light, as well as learning to recognize politics in both its authentic and distorted forms.

In reading this book, I invite you to temporarily put aside your preconceived notions about politics and consider alternate ways of thinking about it. If you are a skeptical reader, I simply ask that you treat this book as a thought experiment and see where it takes you. If you are one who is intrigued by the prospect of a defense of politics, I ask you to pay close attention in the pages that follow and judge for yourself what it is about politics that is worth defending. And if you already see yourself as a friend of politics, I would ask you, as much as the skeptic, to check your preconceived notions of politics at the door and see where this book takes you.

This book, I need to say at the outset, offers no airtight argument; no such defense is possible. Nor is it a defense of all of Arendt's various thoughts and positions. Arendt has had more than a few critics over the years, and she was guilty, as am I, of oversights, moments of obliviousness, and periodic wrongheadedness.[28] And while probing the limits of Arendt's thinking is a worthy and important task, this book does not do that either. It is more like the drawings that appear in these pages: sketches meant to stimulate your political imagination.

At the heart of this book is the continuation of Arendt's courses in political education. Political education, or what the ancient Greeks called *paideia*, has been a critical part of various societies all across the world and throughout history. But in order for us to want a political education, we first have to believe that politics is worth it. Therefore, this book participates in another tradition, spanning from Moses to Machiavelli, Mozi to Martin Luther King, and Isocrates to Arendt, of defining and defending the dignity of the art of politics. I aim to persuade skeptical and sympathetic readers alike that (1) politics is possible wherever two or more meet; (2) politics, as a means of living in our common world, is superior to technological and economic solutions with respect to freedom and equality, if not efficiency; and (3) democratic politics is nothing but an attempt to broaden the scope of politics among people. Along the way, I will introduce or reintroduce you to a range of thinkers from the distant past: Plato, Aristotle, René Descartes, John Milton, Thomas Hobbes, and others.

Arendt wrote, "The thread of tradition is broken, and we must discover the past for ourselves—that is, read authors as if nobody had ever read them before."[29] While to some readers what follows will not seem entirely new, I nevertheless invite you to work with me to see politics anew, as if for the first time.

ONE

Untwisting Politics

On October 9, 2016, two US presidential candidates squared off in a televised debate. Donald Trump and Hillary Clinton had been going at it on the campaign trail for months, but this early-October debate seemed potentially decisive, with the election only a month away. The stakes were particularly high for Trump: not only was he trailing in most polls, but on October 7, two days prior to the debate, a videotape surfaced of Trump boasting to the television host Billy Bush about the ways in which he forces himself sexually on women, grabbing and groping. The debate, it seemed, was sure to bring more than its typical share of awkward moments to candidate Trump. And it did. Remarkably, though, the most awkward moment for Trump was not the topic of the salacious tape but rather a simple and indeed all-to-common word, *politician*. Early on, perhaps for the first time, Trump found himself publicly calling himself a politician, admitting with incredulity, "I cannot believe I'm saying that about myself."[1] How could this label get such a bad name that a man could feel more awkward about calling himself a "politician" than being caught on tape boasting about sexual assault? Politics is indeed in a bad state—at least, electoral politics.

Unfortunately, much of what we think about politics we learn from the world of cable news, talk radio, social media, fictional television shows, and reality TV. I call it the "electoral-entertainment complex." This world makes being a politician the equivalent to being a predator. It is a world where politics is big business and the politician is a virtual reality TV star—or an actual one. It is a world where sensationalism trumps substance, and where power is measured ultimately in profit. It is also, like the military-industrial complex that President Dwight D. Eisenhower once warned against, a clear and present danger to any republic inasmuch as it is a gross form of "unwarranted influence" on our political lives.[2]

Nevertheless, this world has an alluring power. Some of us find ourselves intently watching contrived political takedowns on cable news, obsessively reading the politician's latest tweet, or fearing The End at the latest political news. For others of us, the electoral-entertainment complex is not so much compelling as it is generally persuasive—it gels with our cynicism about politics. We know that electoral politics in the age of corporate media and big-money lobbyists is cultivated to satisfy our taste for drama more than our capacity for thought. Nevertheless, we are drawn in to the productions of sensationalistic, conspiratorial, or just plain stupid political coverage if for no other reason than it is the only way politics is served up to us. Of course, there are those of us who don't tune in it all. For us, politicians might as well be on a different planet. We have other things to do, other celebrities to follow, and other cares to pursue.

No matter where one fits in this spectrum, the electoral-entertainment complex makes us all antipolitical in attitude, if not in actual conviction. We despairingly or cynically float among a range of attitudes about politics that I will explore in this chapter: politics as business; politics as a game

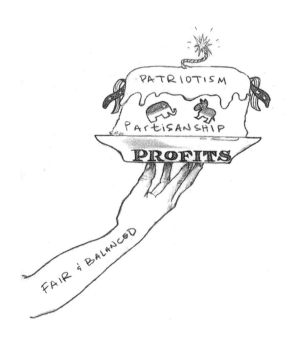

Politics on a platter.

of winners and losers; politics as war by other means. Positively, of course, some of us hold fast through it all that politics would ideally be about rational debate and consensus building. But faced with a void of such an approach to politics, we become depressed or just plain numb.

Of course, we don't need a political theorist like Hannah Arendt to tell us that politics in the age of the electoral-entertainment complex is twisted. However, she can help us see the tangles more clearly. Therefore, in this chapter I offer a study in contrasts. In the first half, I focus on the distorted views of politics that reign over us with an addictive, sometimes deadly intensity. In the second half, I turn to Arendt's vision of politics as the art of living freely with others who are inevitably different from us. By pitting the electoral-entertainment complex against Arendt's vision of politics, I want to get us to think more than anything else about our *attitude* toward politics. This is more than an intellectual exercise. Our attitudes are shaped by our experiences, and our experiences have an economy: we value some experiences more than others by *how* and *how much* we pay attention to them. My goal, frankly, is to invite you to restructure your attention economy when it comes to politics—to pay more, not less, attention, to politics; but at the very same time to pay a different *kind* of attention to politics.

Politics as (Show) Business

Several decades ago, Neil Postman, a popular professor at New York University, warned that television was catapulting America out of the grounded, rational world of reality into the fantasy skies of entertainment. He saw presidents John F. Kennedy and Ronald Reagan, who each fused politics with show business, as risking the trivialization of politics, its reduction to staging, spectacle, and soundbite. According to Postman, Americans in the age of television were in danger of making celebrities out of their politicians and politicians out of their celebrities. Thus, the title of his book announced Americans were *amusing themselves to death*.

But show business is *not* what politics is all about, Postman insisted in his lively prose. For him, authentic politics is inspired by the Enlightenment of the eighteenth century, an intellectual movement that centered on rational conversations among reasonable parties about real-life matters. Real politics, Postman suggested, has little to do with show, and certainly nothing to do with popularity and celebrity. It is all but a branch of philosophy: solemn stuff for solemn people. He argued for a nation of educated citizens capable of working out their differences through reasonable, enlightened conversations and disciplined public discourse.[3]

Indeed, the argument that genuine politics has to do with reason and reality whereas fake politics has to do with mere popularity and show is as old as the Greek philosopher Plato (c. 424–347 BCE). But it is not the argument you will find Arendt making, or that I will pursue in this book. Rather, Arendt argued that philosophy—especially philosophies that claim to be "enlightened"—could be as antipolitical as anything show business might throw at us, precisely because philosophy can try to escape or remake the constantly changing political world in favor of unchanging, eternal truths. Philosophy can become a kind of escape art, but Arendt was not an escapist.[4]

Rather, she argued that because politics is an art of and for everyday life, its proper place is the very world in which you and I live every day, a world where we have to rely on our five senses and a good deal of common sense just to get by. Philosophers and other learned experts, Arendt said, too often ask us to forget the everyday world and make austere principles or transcendent ideas, rather than common sense, the means of living with and working out our differences. Philosophy therefore risks restricting the practice of "true" politics to an educated, enlightened, and out-of-touch elite. Arendt felt so strongly about this that she refused to be called a political philosopher, though many people consider her one. She was happy to be called a political thinker or a political theorist, but not a philosopher.

Therefore, while Arendt shared Postman's worry about politics as show business in contemporary capitalist culture, she did so for different reasons and would clearly scrap his philosophical alternative. It's true that politics has quite a bit to do with talking, conversation, and making arguments; however, it has never conformed to the Enlightenment model of rational citizens debating points according to the rules of reason and verifiable knowledge alone. Even enlightened sages—here you might think of our ideal picture of the founders at the constitutional convention, debating the finer points of creating a new nation—have been shown to have been blind to their unreason (most obviously, a nation that begins with the declaration that "all men are created equal" institutionalizing chattel slavery). No, politics is not a branch of philosophy, and never will be. The Enlightenment certainly helped us take more seriously the role of reason, liberty, and equality in political life, but in insisting that the only people at the political table who count are the ones who talk "rationally" it became a means of excluding those who don't talk, act, or think like refined, highly educated white European males.

What, then, of politics as show business? Unlike Postman, Arendt argued that the problem with politics as show business is not really the "show" part.[5] It cannot get away from an element of show, for politics necessarily takes place in what Arendt called the "space of appearances." When we watch politicians, listen to pundits, consider referendums, petition for a speaker to come to campus, or express our support for (or opposition to) union workers on strike, we have to rely on how things *appear*. Even if we work to get underneath the surface appearance to figure out what is really going on—a necessary and crucial political skill—we still are best off relying on our senses and good judgment, rather than some grand "theory" that comes to us out of the ether or the internet.

So, the problem with politics as show business is not "appearances." Rather, the problem is when it becomes *only* about show—which, not coincidentally, is the point where it frequently becomes only about business, about serving the interests of money and power. Postman was right to insist that the world of commercial show business circulating through our small, and now even smaller, screens has twisted our understanding of politics in profound ways. It can do so by making politics almost exclusively about show. As Arendt observed of the decades in Europe leading up to the rise of the Nazis, when big business took hold of state power, "The theatrical quality of the political world had become so patent that the theater could appear as a realm of reality."[6] Today much of what we think we know about politics comes from the commercial productions of our media channels. But more than this, much of what we take to *be* politics happens onscreen and through the networks of our media channels, making it conform to the logic of the entertainment industry—a logic where you matter ultimately as a consumer.

When politics becomes business or a mere extension of business, not only does it revolve around the financial bottom line, but it gets incorporated into the unending, limitless quest for money and wealth that capitalist economic expansion demands. It values us, as citizens, only inasmuch as we are useful, participating "positively" in society by contributing to the growth of the economy measured by the stock market or some other metric; otherwise we are burden to society. To look at politics from a "business perspective" is to see everything, including *ourselves*, through a cost/benefit lens. Arendt argued that such utilitarian thinking, especially in an age of growing automation, leaves most of us superfluous.[7]

Moreover, in business, "scarcity" is the rule. As a letter writer to my local newspaper put it, "Politics is about who gets what."[8] There's not enough for everybody; therefore, you have to compete for your piece of the pie, your share of the market. Finally, business turns us into buyers and sellers, consumers and capitalists, rather than fellow citizens.[9] The writer Marilynne Robinson notes that when citizens become nothing but taxpayers, public goods like schools, highways, and clean water become public burdens. "While the Citizen can entertain aspirations for the society as a whole and take pride in its achievements," she continues, "the Taxpayer, as presently imagined, simply does not want to pay taxes."[10] In sum, politics as business leaves us either misers or paupers.

By contrast, *your life matters*. Arendt argued that politics is a life-affirming art. One of Arendt's most eloquent biographers, Julia Kristeva, writes, "Arendt sings an ode to the uniqueness of every birth and praises its capacity to inaugurate what she does not hesitate to call 'the miracle of life.'"[11] As long as we live, we matter to the world we inhabit together. Politics is the art by which we say that we matter, others matter, and the world itself matters. It is a way in which we can *show* ourselves to others, appearing before them, speaking and acting with them to try to keep something going or start something new. Nobody can monopolize our share of speech and action (though the powerful can try to force the rest of us to stop speaking or acting through threats and violence, and loudmouths can try to drown us out). Politics is for *everybody*. When politics becomes the servant of business interests, it becomes weapon wielded for the few engaged in the unending quest for more money. Indeed, as Arendt noted, it becomes downright imperialist. And when politics becomes imperialist, it becomes violent. And when politics becomes violent, it transforms into something quite other than politics, as it takes flight from the world in which we freely speak and act with others to become a market, a machine, an army, or a fist.[12]

Winner-Takes-All Politics

In fact, show *business* has meant that many of us, wittingly or not, have a strong sense that politics is ultimately about the exercise of coercive force by the "winners." Reality TV teaches as much. Take *Survivor* as a prime example. The first megasuccessful reality TV show, *Survivor* originally featured about twenty contestants dropped in a remote jungle or island where they formed tribes and figured out how to survive together, even as they competed with the other tribes and each other to be the last person standing. At the end of each episode, someone would be voted out of the tribe by their fellow contestants, to the point where, after numerous episodes, eventually someone would be left all alone as the victor, the "Sole Survivor."

Survivor began as a British TV show in the early 1990s. Its British origins are apparent inasmuch as its approach to politics is a fusion of three of the greatest British thinkers of the last five hundred years: Thomas Hobbes (1588–1679), John Locke (1632–1704), and Charles Darwin (1809–1882). With Hobbes, *Survivor* treats politics as an art of power and survival;

with Locke, it relies on the egalitarian "democratic" means of voting as the procedure for determining who gets to survive and who does not, as well as how to distribute scarce resources; with Darwin, *Survivor* is about the survival of the "fittest," with the "weaker" members of the species being eliminated first.

Survivor performs a winner-takes-all view of life. It represents a widely shared view of politics as essentially about determining who wins and who loses. *Survivor*, of course, puts a democratic face on this process—the contestants at least get to vote. Shows like *American Idol* or *The Voice* put an aristocratic face on the process (the etymological meaning of *aristocracy* is "the power of the best"), as famous entertainers, the "best," get to decide who will join their noble ranks. And *The Apprentice*, now forever a part of world history thanks to Trump, puts an authoritarian face on the process: the magnate, and the magnate alone, gets to decide who will get a piece of his real estate empire. More than any other form of contemporary entertainment, reality TV has taught the world to see politics as a process of picking winners and losers in a fight to the bitter end for scarce resources, privileges, rights, and more stuff. But this, again, is really the business of business, not politics. Indeed—and this is a point that was not lost on Thomas Hobbes, of all people, let alone Arendt—a nation of winners and losers will soon become a nation of enemies, and a nation of enemies leads inevitably to gross expressions of political power.

If we are going to recover and rehabilitate politics, we need to start by jettisoning the idea that it is essentially about determining winners and losers. (The common saying "Elections have consequences!" can be one of the most undemocratic things you can say.) Arendt argued that if politics is approached as a game of survival of the fittest, it can degenerate into tyranny or, more catastrophically, totalitarianism. The thing about treating politics in this way is that it necessitates, like *Survivor*, that every person be seen first and foremost as a potential enemy, and only provisionally as a friend. The problem here is that living with enemies, or potential enemies, is ultimately part of the art we call not politics, but war.

Politics as War by Other Means

It was the nineteenth-century Prussian strategist Carl von Clausewitz who said, "War is politics by other means." He had a compelling point: war, to keep from being interminable, requires a political or diplomatic end point of one kind or another. But Clausewitz's maxim has been twisted head over tail to become the idea that politics is a form of warfare—with the goal to defeat, and indeed even destroy, the "enemy," even if that enemy happens to live just a few blocks away. Steve Bannon, a prominent American political consultant, once bragged that when he was leading Trump's campaign, he never went on television. Why? "Because politics is war," he told the *Wall Street Journal*. "General Sherman would never have gone on TV to tell everyone his plans." This view of politics is the logical outcome of believing, as so many do (maybe even you?), that politics is ultimately about determining who wins. If winner takes all, then winners will want to win at all costs; otherwise they justifiably fear that they will be left out to hang, literally or metaphorically. And so, they will approach politics as war.[13]

The milder version of this approach to politics is the idea that politics is essentially about parliamentary tactics, palace intrigue, or electoral maneuvering. This view of politics is willing to grant the other "contestants," so to speak, something like the right to survive or get by in life, but it essentially sees them as competitors for power and influence—competitors that must be held back, outmaneuvered, or otherwise excluded. This is what many mainstream politicians, political consultants, and political insiders make politics to be. It is an approach to politics that is quite old, rooted in the palace intrigue of ancient monarchies (and replayed in the still-all-too-common crony politics of both purportedly democratic and explicitly authoritarian regimes). It is a view that accurately captures the fact that politics always calls for flexibility and foresight, and often means difficult negotiations, uncomfortable compromises, and tactical maneuvers. But in a winner-takes-all mindset, this often becomes nothing more than politics as cold war, a bipolar conflict where everyone who is not for you is assumed to be against you.

Indeed, what is consistent across these twisted views of politics is that they each ultimately assume that we are enemies before we can ever provisionally be friends. They also assume a world of scarcity, that there are limited goods to be had, and that some will get them and others will not. This leads quite naturally to the exercise of force and manipulation in order to win for oneself or one's group the limited goods available. As such, we all end up either as victors or as casualties of war.

In the United States in the age of the "culture wars," this is exactly where we've ended up. In our so-called "civic" life, we are enemies first, friends only secondarily, suspiciously, and provisionally. This approach, it needs to be said, was the explicit position of the Nazi "crown jurist" Carl Schmitt (1888–1985), who noted that true politics is based on a fundamental distinction between friends and enemies. Politics is about facing off against enemies, and if "necessity" dictates—if one party cannot vanquish the other party by other means—it can always end in violence.[14]

Politics as Rule

There is one other view of politics that people often take for granted that is problematic: politics is about rulership. How could it be otherwise? As Noëlle McAfee writes, "In the dominant imaginary, politics is what *governments* do."[15] And what do governments do? They rule us; they tell us what to do; they command us, threaten us, and occasionally reward us. Politics-as-rulership is a dominant view of politics in part because it is how politics is often served to us on the screens of the electoral-entertainment complex, where politics is about politicians. Admittedly, it is hard to imagine an approach to politics that does not have something to do with ruling and governance. Yet, making rulership the essence of politics is, in Arendt's words, "profoundly untrue."[16] In understanding why this is so, we begin to transition to Arendt's positive case for politics.

The notion that politics is essentially about rulership, we might say, is to hit the general range of the target but to flat-out miss the bull's-eye. The ancient Greeks, Arendt frequently recalled, saw human life as moving among three distinct realms: the realm of necessity, the realm of contemplation, and the realm of freedom. As animals, we all have bodily necessities: food, water, shelter, and so on. As mindful animals, we also often seek to contemplate, understand, or otherwise appreciate the world in which we live. But as *political* animals, we do more than care for our bodies and minds: we also speak and act in freedom with others. Strictly speaking, rulership better describes the way we deal with life's necessities than with our mindful contemplations, let alone our free relations.[17] In the ancient Greek world, the head of a household, the god of a temple, and the authoritarian ruler of a people shared the same name: *kýrios*. Whether in the household, the temple, or the kingly realm, what set the *kýrios* apart was his power or authority to command. Athenians therefore saw monarchies and chiefdoms as the equivalent of giant households where the king or chief bossed around everyone else for the sake the survival of the realm.

But in a democracy, there was no *kýrios*, save in the assembly of citizens themselves.[18] In democratic Athens, the difference between those in government office and everyday citizens (*politês*) was not the difference between ruler and the ruled. Rather, everybody was first and foremost a citizen, and as such, they were obligated to lead by means of persuasion, not command.

As the historian Josiah Ober points out, whereas the suffix -*archy* in *monarchy* means "rule," the suffix -*cracy* (*kratos*) in *democracy* means "the capacity to do things."[19] To rule in a democracy, citizens have to rely on their individual and collective capacities to do things—especially capacities for debate, argument, advocacy, dialoguing, judging, and, Arendt would add, forgiving.[20] If a citizen at any point comes to command another citizen, their relationship is no longer democratic in character. Arendt would say it is not even political, but is of another type: parental, economic, military, or police-like. In other words, politics for the ancient Greeks—as well as the citizens of the ancient Roman Republic, as well as us today—is the art of how to do things together *apart* from one person commanding and coercing others. It is the art of free cooperation, coordination, and compromise.

Rule is a necessary but limited human activity. To see politics as essentially about "rulership" is to risk turning politics into a mode of command and control. This, Arendt suggested, is really an elitist form of politics, where authentically political experience is reserved for or limited to the ruling elite, who in turn get to tell the many what they must do. In other words, it is a monarchical or oligarchic view of politics, a politics for the "one" (*mon-*) or "few" (*oligo-*) over and against the many. In essence, it means that only a few get to experience the freedom to do politics and to do things by political means. The notion that politics is essentially about ruling is a way in which elites have frequently constructed for themselves "an island of freedom" in the world: they get to live freely in political association with other elites while the rest of us are subjected to their domination.[21] Hence, they monopolize not only politics, but also freedom. The most extreme version of this view of politics is authoritarian. It's no wonder that many of us are either jumping from the body politic or looking to climb and topple it.

The Art of Living Freely

Arendt argued against political elitism and authoritarianism of all kinds. Rather than reducing politics to rule, she saw it is a form of human action and interaction in conditions of relative freedom, equality, and what she called "plurality." It is a form of human relationship, one that emerges among people in certain situations under particular conditions. This is what I will refer to as Arendt's "phenomenal" conception of politics.

Arendt calls us to look at the world: "The world men are born into contains many things, natural and artificial, living and dead, transient and sempiternal, all of which have in common that they *appear* and hence are meant to be seen, heard, touched, tasted, and smelled."[22] Looking at the world,

The twenty-first-century body politic.

you can see all kinds of things, including *politics*. Politics, like lightening, is something that can appear before you; and, just as whenever lightening appears it entails many tiny particles of ice bumping into one another to create an electrical charge, so politics, wherever it appears, involves a collection or plurality of persons bumping into one another as relative equals and in relative freedom. Both are "phenomenal," in the technical sense that they come to "appear" and in the more everyday sense that they are quite amazing.

Politics is a phenomenal realm, Arendt further argued, where reality and appearances are distinguishable and yet always interacting. This is what we might call Arendt's "Heisenberg principle" of politics: because politics, like science, is a human activity, political reality cannot be neatly separated from human observation and participation. So too with political knowledge. Political "realists," past and present, argue that *reality* is the basis of political action. Arendt wholeheartedly agreed with this. Still, she argued that "appearances" are *part* of our political reality—that is, the political world is a phenomenal world, a world that we engage with and through our senses, even as it cannot be reduced to simply what we see, hear, feel, taste, or smell. In politics, there is no escaping either reality or appearances.

Politics therefore "appears" in our life as we bump into others. It appears whenever we find ourselves engaging with others about matters of common concern to shape our common world. And this represents a distinct form of human power: as Arendt wrote, "authentic politics" is "different peoples getting along with each other in the full force of their power."[23] The sort of "getting along" that politics aims at, admittedly, is quite strange. It does not require intimacy, companionship, or even affection. It can happen across great distances. And it need not involve any specific intention to be buddies with a particular person. That is, the "getting along" power of politics can happen—and most often does happen—among perfect strangers.[24] It only requires that we be willing to (and know how to) speak and act cooperatively with others with whom we are not intimate. The reason we would want to form such alliances is because through them we can enjoy "common goods" not in the sense of commodities or consumer goods, but rather "goods" that serve our public happiness or what sociologists call our "quality of life."[25]

Let me get right to one such quality-of-life good. What would it take for you to enjoy taking long evening walks on city streets? For most of us, a sense of safety would be a priority. We do not want to have to actively work to be safe or have to hire a security detail. We just want *the streets themselves to be safe* and to be able to walk them freely. Safe streets are a great example of a common good in that they can be achieved cooperatively, and once had, they are there for all. Of course, they are built on an infrastructure of other common goods: quality sidewalks, ample street lighting, crosswalk signals, relatively clean air, not too much noise pollution, friendly people, adequate but not overbearing policing, and a lack of prejudice or racism or other kinds of harassment. For cities where the streets have such qualities, politics may be the art by which alliances were formed to achieve such goods. For cities where the streets lack such qualities, politics is the art by which they might be achieved.

There are, to be sure, antipolitical ways to achieve safe streets. First, you can buy them. In fact, many people in the United States have settled for buying safety, or at least the feeling of safety. Gated communities, far-out suburbs, country clubs, and retirement resorts all sell safety. Many city councils in America function as de facto country club boards, setting up building codes and neighborhood regulations designed to keep "undesirable" people out and their well-off residents snugly, and smugly, comfortable. The second way you can have safe streets is through heavy policing. Surveillance states like Singapore have safe streets. If all you are concerned with is safety, with little care for neighborliness, you might be comfortable being the subject of a government with maximum authority to surveil and police its people. In fact, the difference between a gated community in the United States and the safe streets of Singapore is only a matter of degree: both get their safe streets by prioritizing surveillance and policing, and both are low on the quotients of neighborliness, community, and active citizen participation.

What's wrong with this essentially authoritarian means of achieving safety? For some people, frankly, nothing. The ends justify the means. However, from the perspective of a defender of politics, what's wrong is pretty simple: the means by which we achieve goods often matter as much to our quality of life as the goods themselves. Getting your groceries at the local grocery store is a different means of shopping than having them delivered to your door through a digital service. The latter might offer you a better selection and more competitive prices, and you might save some time. But the choice between the two is not just a matter of efficiency, it is a matter of community. By going to the grocery store, you help keep jobs in your community; you make yourself available to run into an old friend (or avoid an old boss); you can chitchat with the cashier; you can request a new product from the grocer; you can weigh an apple in your hand and smell the cantaloupes.

Politics is a means as well as an end—the arrow *and* the target. This is a central claim of Arendt's work. Politics is for her a way to achieve objectives, but it is also a goal in and of itself. To live politically is to live freely and cooperatively with others, where neither force nor necessity apply as the final principles of our common existence together. Living freely, Arendt held, is therefore living politically. The ultimate question she asked was, Who gets to live politically?—a question whose answer is identical to the answer to the question, Who gets to live freely with others? An authoritarian society is not without politics. Rather, it is one where the ruler or ruling class gets to live politically, and thus freely, and the people don't. Arendt, again, argued for an antiauthoritarian politics for *everybody*.[26]

A politics for everybody happens only as every person who cares to show up actively shares in caring for common concerns and relates to others in relative freedom. Many Americans talk all the time about freedom: they fly the flag, sing the song, honor the troops, and wear the colors. But many in this supposed "republic" have to buy their way into good neighborhoods, good schools, good parks, and good jobs. Some may want to defend such a society as consistent with free markets. Fair enough, as long as we do not confuse free markets with political freedom or a democratic republic (something, frankly, we did not start to do until the 1970s!). A gated community has nothing to do with the flag, other than the flag as a commodity that can also can be bought and sold. Common goods, and the alliances on which they depend, cannot be bought and sold. They can only be freely made together, in common. And politics is the art of freely making such goods.

The Original Three-Dimensional Art

Like any great art, politics is multifaceted. Aristotle, to whom Arendt was indebted, thought of politics as a three-dimensional art, or as a single "master" art comprising three sub-arts.[27] First, there is the art of writing constitutions and setting up towns, cities, states, and nations. What are the basic laws, rights, and obligations of citizens and those in government, and how do we ensure the system works? Second, there is the art of day-to-day governing. There are all kinds of matters that cannot be "constitutionalized" or reduced to the letter of the law, and addressing these matters is what government is for. And third, there is the art of citizenship. For Aristotle, citizenship is more than having the legal status of a citizen. Citizenship is a practice, something one does as much as a status one has. It involves how you relate or do not relate to fellow citizens, those in government, and even foreigners and strangers. As we will see, while these three dimensions of politics are interrelated and interdependent, citizenship is the one art that can stand alone, and the one art that is the foundation of politics.

In considering politics as a three-dimensional art, let's return to reality TV. In some respects, creating a political society is like creating a reality TV show. Reality TV shows are essentially staged games. As disconcerting as it may seem, so are political societies—though, let's be clear, politics is a deadly serious "game," and one aimed at something much, much greater than ratings and profits. Still, the analogy is helpful. In creating a reality TV show, the creators of the show first need to design its blueprint, come up with its structures and rules. Then they need people—in the case of reality TV, typically offscreen directors and writers—who govern, police, and refine the day-to-day operations of the show. Finally, you need a setting and participants who know how to play the game well and don't work to sabotage it.

Just as a successful reality TV show depends on all three dimensions, so does a successful political society. Let me elaborate further. For the ancient Greeks, "lawgiving" or constitution making was the most revered of the political arts, such that when Aristotle penned his treatise *Politics*, he focused it almost exclusively on constitutions and laws. The Greeks saw constitutions as more than political blueprints; these were founding documents representing founding moments. Like the architect in a construction project, constitutions get the political project going; as such, they require a great deal of foresight, expertise, and practical wisdom. Constitutions create the look and feel of a polity. More important, constitutions set the terms for the structure and scope of alliances among the people included within a political society: they construct a "system of power" and edifices of authority as they determine the broad rules of the "game" of political action and interaction.[28]

Arendt argued that constitutions, like virtually all political phenomena, can be understood as a form of speech. Specifically, she argued that constitutions are essentially *promises*—promises by which a group of people bring a degree of permanence to their shared political world. Political constitutions are promises to one another and to future generations: "Just as promises and agreements deal with the future and provide stability in the ocean of future uncertainty where the unpredictable may break in from all sides, so the constituting, founding, and world-building capacities of man concern always not so much ourselves and our own time on earth as our 'successor,' and 'posterities.'"[29] In a strange way, therefore, constitutions are the manner in which we speak and relate to strangers—people who are foreign to us not by geography or culture, but by the fact that they are not yet born. So too, those of us who are on the receiving end of this particularly powerful form of political speech are able to converse with, interact with, the dead. Constitutions, in sum, bring a durability to our political, worldly existence by transcending the limits of our own mortality.

But constitutions cannot carry themselves out. They need "directors," so to speak. These directors or governors interpret the meaning and intention of the constitution and apply it to present circumstances. They make the constitution relevant to the present as well as formally enact the political virtue of promise keeping. Governors, legislators, and judges make judgments about what is lawful, permissible, and best for the people within the bounds of the constitution. They also write additional laws to further direct the political society. And they "execute" laws, promises, and judgments.

The ancient Greeks compared the governing dimension of politics to steering a ship at sea. Towns, cities, states, and nations are always seeking to get somewhere (or, as the case may be, to not get somewhere). The conditions for getting or not getting somewhere can sometimes be calm and pleasant, and other times quite stormy. Governing, like constitution making, takes great skill, expertise, and practical wisdom. It is not for the faint of heart, or the lazy. It also depends invariably on alliances. No one can govern alone, not even kings, for governing is a social act: one always governs others, and one typically governs with others. Governing hinges on the ability of people to cooperate in order to reach a destination. This is why governing is never a matter of strict "rule." It takes far more than authority. It takes art.

Unlike reality TV show directors and writers, democratic societies—especially republics—have usually wanted their governors "on screen," in full view of all, as republican citizens have been suspicious of behind-the-scenes meetings and machinations. (Here again, to be clear, I am using *republican*, like *democratic*, to refer to political approaches rather than political parties.) Republican societies work very hard to resist the seeming gravitational pull toward governing from behind closed doors, pulling the strings, and manipulating the people. By contrast, other types of constitutions—monarchic, oligarchic, dictatorships—structurally allow for ample behind-the-scenes governing. It's built in to the blueprint, part of the script. Moreover, as Arendt repeatedly argued, bureaucracies too often do the same, but rather than governing from behind the scenes, they govern from the position of a nameless "nobody" as opposed to a distinct "somebody" with a name, face, and personality. To be sure, not all bureaucracies are anonymous and impersonal, and there are many conscientious people who work in bureaucratic institutions; but even these good citizens recognize, and resist, the bureaucratic pull to anonymity, impersonality, and invisibility.

These first two dimensions of the art of politics—constitution construction and governing—are formal and official. Those of us who have grown up in relatively stable political societies have had the luxury of taking such matters largely for granted. Most of the peoples of the earth in the last century, however, have not been so privileged. Since 1914, hundreds of constitutions have been written worldwide, and many more governments formed. Constitution making and day-to-day governing are therefore heavily used contemporary political arts, not just things of the past. Indeed, even in the

United States the constitution has been repeatedly reinterpreted over the last century, and formally amended numerous times.

The third dimension of the political art is citizenship. It is the most informal and common political art, as well as the most important. Citizenship, we tend to think, is essentially a legal status. People are born citizens, or they have to legally earn their citizenship. Ideally, citizen-as-legal-status is a guarantee that you get to participate in the "game." In fact, many legal citizens have been kept from full participation in political life by other citizens. And there are noncitizens, in a legal sense, who are great contributors to our civic life. This is because citizenship is more than a legal status; it is an art of getting along and getting things done together.

The art of citizenship shapes *how* the political game is played. If a group of reality TV show contestants were to simply refuse to play along, they would ruin the show. Of course, contestants who act like this would also be kicked off the show. Most democratic constitutions don't allow for uncooperative citizens to be kicked out of the country. On the contrary, democratic constitutions grant extraordinary privileges to citizens, including the right to opt out of the practices of citizenship with impunity (the exceptions in the United States have been military service and jury duty). Nevertheless, the quality of a democratic society depends on the quality of citizenship among its citizens. Citizenship entails a whole range of practices and habits, from how we talk to one another to how we educate ourselves and others, how we hold those in government accountable, how we agree to disagree, how we make sacrifices for one another, and how we allow ourselves to be ruled by those in government office (especially in a democracy, being ruled is as much an art as ruling).

Citizenship is the most important of the political arts for two reasons. First, it is a form of friendship. If politics is about getting along and getting stuff done with all our differences, then citizenship, as both Aristotle and Arendt argued, is really a kind of friendship, albeit a friendship premised on a mutual commitment to common quality-of-life goods rather than intimacy. Fellow citizens must be friends first, and enemies only provisionally, if they are to live together politically. Second, the practices of citizenship precede as well as follow from constitution making and governing. No constitution is written apart from people coming together, and when they come together they will have to use the same skills and practices that are required for everyday citizenship within an already constituted political society. (In the blockbuster musical *Hamilton*, Alexander Hamilton is presented as a great *citizen* at a time when the US Constitution had not yet been written!) Citizenship, not constitution making, is therefore the foundational political art.

It is citizens who make constitutions, govern day-to-day matters, and relate to one another. While I may conceivably be able to live with my close kin off the grid in some remote part of the world in a place with no constitution or government, the minute I come upon a stranger is the very minute my citizenly art will be tested. (For that matter, my political skills might be tested by my close kin!) It will be tested all the more if that stranger wants to stay and make a home alongside mine. If yet other strangers come along, we may have to set up laws and start a government. But the nature and quality of those laws and that government will depend on the nature and quality of our citizenship.

It was Aristotle who said that humans are political animals, and while Arendt was not an advocate of an old Aristotelian "political naturalism," she did think there is something spontaneous about politics.[30] We "do" politics all the time, including in places and situations where we are not prone to see it or understand it as politics. By contrast, the sites and spaces of politics that are recognizable to us—twenty-four-hour cable news, political campaigns, social media feeds, the punditry—can be downright antipolitical. What we take to be politics is often a weapon against people coming together "in the manner of speech and action" so as to address in common the concerns of the common world that they each inhabit together.[31]

So while we may have thought politics is easy to see (It's on TV!—or billboards, yard signs, bumper stickers, YouTube ads, and the latest headlines that pop up on our phones!), in the age of the electoral-entertainment complex, politics has become very hard to recognize. In the introduction to this book, I suggested that we suffer from something like an autoimmune disease, as the very thing that can help us, politics, is the very thing we are prone to attack, or at least dismiss. But we also suffer from nearsightedness: we see politics when it is standing right in front of us—when, for reasons of power, profit, or protest, it screams, "See me!"—but we have a hard time seeing the politics that is just down the street or just behind the screen, in the boardroom or in the algorithms that run the chatrooms.

This is in part because we mistake a particular kind of political system—electoral politics—for the whole of politics, as if politics comes down to partisan maps and campaign slogans. If we think all politics is electoral, we will have a hard time recognizing politics because we assume that it is so easy to see. We might even think that the biggest challenge we face is not seeing politics at all, but rather tuning out the political system.

However, it is even harder to see politics because, as we will explore further in the next chapter, politics is primarily a *phenomenon*, and a system only secondarily. This is a central insight of Arendt. Writing in the middle of the twentieth century, she argued that powerful central governments, large-scale bureaucracies, national security regimes, global capitalism, and partisan political systems each threaten to crowd out politics, or at least hide it from our view. When coupled to the popular prejudices against politics, "the danger," she wrote, "is that politics may vanish entirely from the world."[32] Hers was not an argument made from nostalgia, as if prior to the twentieth century there had been some golden age of politics.[33] Rather, as we will continue to explore, Arendt understood "politics" to mean something very specific, even while it was necessarily indefinite. She held that those paying attention can directly experience and recognize politics as though it is a steady breeze: it is noticed, even if you can't precisely point to it. The problem, she warned, is that in the modern age of massive winds of change, we rarely notice a breeze.

TWO

Phenomenal Politics

Ohtani. As I write the name, I have no idea if it will go down in baseball history or not. What I do know is that Shohei Ohtani is the baseball equivalent of a miracle. In 2018, his debut season in major league baseball, the 23-year-old Japanese athletic wonder burst onto the American sporting scene as a top-tier major league hitter *and* a top-tier major league pitcher. This is simply not supposed to happen in modern professional baseball. Not since Babe Ruth—a full century before Ohtani—had the baseball world seen such a hitting-and-pitching-double phenom. But Ohtani's feat was in some respects greater than Ruth's, for he appeared on the scene after the overlords of professional baseball had surrendered virtually all their decision-making capacities to MBAs and systems engineers with their computers. "Moneyball" was the new name of the game. Every swing, every throw, every catch, and every sprint made by every young prospect was being compressed into "data" and run through a bunch of algorithms to predict the overall future performance of the player, their "wins above replacement" value to the organization. The problem with Ohtani was that there were no data, no "comps," no proxies for processing a two-way player. He could not be triangulated. His very existence broke the analytics, rendered them mute, ineffective, and stupid. And boy, was he extraordinary![1]

We are all, in fact, system busters. We are all ultimately unpredictable. The builders of the computerized models that fund social media companies, hiring agencies, and college admissions committees may say they have some "comps" (comparisons) for us, and they might try to triangulate those proxies around us; but the fact is that *you* have no true comparison.[2] You are one in 7.5 billion. Every comparison used to stand in for you is at best like a stand-in actor, a mere substitute body used for technical purposes. But every movie director knows that stand-ins are not the real thing. And every director also knows that once the real actors arrive on set, no matter the script they've been given, there's no telling exactly what's going happen. They are *actors*, after all, not bots. If only the directors of data sets acted like they knew the same thing!

Hannah Arendt was well aware of the spell computational systems would cast on us. Writing after World War II—the heyday of early computing—she witnessed the earliest rumblings of the seismic shift from a turbine-based industrial society to a computer-based "postindustrial" society. She saw, as did many others, that "prediction" would outpace "production" in the new economic machine, and that bit-based calculations would become the means of the automation of everything from factory production to news production. In fact, Arendt argued, the postindustrial turn to automation (or "automatism," as she sometimes called it) was a kind of sideways *return* to nature. Humans have always been surrounded by automatic processes. The rotating of the planets, the rising and setting of the sun, the turning of the tides, organic decay, bodily death—these are the most predictable systems we can imagine, utterly reliable in their overall consistency. Moreover, the human animal is itself an automatic system in essential ways: we breathe automatically, digest involuntarily, and even dream uncontrollably at night. Automation is what makes us animals in a world of animals; it is what makes us creatures of nature.

And yet, we are possibly the most unpredictable of animals. It is the nature of the human actor, like the good Hollywood actor, to be improvisational. While our stomachs are predictable, our actions are never fully so. "Every act," Arendt wrote, "is a 'miracle'—that is, something which could not be expected"; the whole of human historical existence, at both the individual and the cultural-civilizational level, is a kind of "infinite improbability." Human history is a "chain of miracles," inasmuch as it could never have been fully predicted.[3] Each moment of joy, each act of love, each form of sacrifice, each promise kept is a kind of marvel, if for no other reason that it is done freely. Of course, it is true that we have done great harm with our freedom too. We have exploited one another, destroyed one another, stripped the earth, and built the Bomb. Indeed, in the twenty-first century, more than any other time in human history, we are living with the consequences of our free actions as the very rhythms of climates, ecosystems, and migrations are also becoming, as if in our likeness, more uncertain and unpredictable.

What is the way forward here? Be warned: there are some who argue that the answer to our systemic problems is to be found in engineering these systems. They believe that large-scale problems require large-scale solutions, and that we have to take a controlled, objective, and systemic approach. Others argue for market solutions; others for strong government action; and yet others for ambitious technological solutions. But while some of the major problems we face are indeed systemic, their remedies are not ultimately the stuff of systems—at least, not technological and economic systems. A systems approach to systemic problems can be a de facto strategy of avoiding the real problems, one where we pit system against system—for example, markets against governments—but fail to address the core challenges, the *political* challenges, that lay at the heart of twenty-first-century crises. If our actions are responsible for our challenges, our actions are essential also to their remediation.

The recent rise of demagoguery across the globe—Big Men with their Big Promises—is an expression of a widespread sense, especially among the dispossessed, that the systems of modernity are failing us and that concrete human action is needed. Whereas the economists and engineers have said, "The systems can fix it," the demagogue comes along to say, "No, I alone can fix it!"[4] Indeed, the bipolar swing from big systems to authoritarian leaders is a distinctly modern quandary. Modernity—the epoch in history that took off with the rise of large-scale industrial society in the 1800s and led to radically ambitious endeavors in science, technology, and global markets in the 1900s—is fundamentally systems oriented. Everything that happens is supposed to happen *bigly* and *systematically*. That is how "predictability" works. This is the meaning of "efficiency." It is the modern meaning of "reason." This is the magic of modernity.

But the modern world, for all its big systems, has been far from predictable, far from efficient, far from reasonable. And so we have looked on more than one occasion to Big Men to come and rescue us from the systems. At the extreme ends of this bipolar swing are totalitarian formations, either in the form of totalizing systems or totalizing leaders. Indeed, in her *Origins of Totalitarianism*, Arendt argued that totalitarianism is not an exception to modernity, but built into it. Given the power of technology; given the scale of economic markets; given the bureaucratization of state power; given the distinctly modern claims that even "history" itself is a kind of systemic force; and given large-scale social pressures for unity and conformity, we moderns turn from Big Systems to Big Leaders, bouncing from allegiance to impersonal powers to highly personal ones, all in the tragic hope of getting a hold of processes that seem to escape our control.

What can we mortals do to break this seemingly automatic cycle? Politics. For Arendt, this is the beginning and the end of the matter. Indeed, for all the horrors of the twentieth century, there are also remarkable examples of powerful and genuine political movements that broke cycles and defied oppressive systems. The struggle against apartheid in South Africa, the sit-ins for civil rights in the United States, the efforts to rebuild communities wrecked by war or economic exploitation, heroic resistance to totalitarian powers, the fight for child-labor laws, and movements on behalf of clean air and clean water—each of these efforts, and many more, depended neither on the supposed powers of automatic systems nor on power-hungry leaders. Rather, they depended on "different people getting along with each other in the full force of their power," as Arendt conceives of authentic politics.[5] In a modern world of big powers, be they Big Systems or Big Men, politics appears and reappears in small and big ways as a means of unexpected and improbable new beginnings.

This chapter looks at this, the miraculous art of politics, by pitting it against the magic-like power of Big Systems and Big Men. In its distilled form, magic is a means of *force*. When Harry Potter goes at it against his archenemy Lord Voldemort, witchcraft and wizardry function as means by which to summon formulas (spells) to control the elements in a battle for the future that will ultimately be won by force rather than political power. Likewise, when we work by means of science, engineering, or technology to control the elements—be they radio waves, electromagnetic currents, fossil fuels, or atomic energy—we wield our own kind of modern magic to control the future. And we have been, generally speaking, enthralled by these magical modern powers—that is, until we discover that their power is not just *for* us, but *over* us; a thing to be feared as much as it is revered.

A *miracle*, however, is an altogether different kind of phenomenon than magic.[6] There is no hocus pocus for a miracle, no formula, program, or code, but only one-of-a-kind actions. Every miracle, Arendt argued, is an interruption of causal chains and automatic processes, a disruption of what "must" be or what "always" is. They are unexpected because they happen freely: a Ku Klux Klan member renounces his ways through conversations with a black man; a small, homogenous rural community embraces and educates undocumented immigrants; poor farmworkers campaign for, and win, legal protections.[7] Therefore, miracle is at the heart of Arendt's "phenomenal" conception of politics. Politics, she argued to the consternation of political cynics and political scientists alike, is essentially unpredictable, and for this we ought to be grateful. To be sure, we political animals *can* be predictable animals, but we need not be—and this "need not be" is what gives us our miraculous political powers, our always renewable freedom to act anew.

The Spell of Systems

Technology, *History*, the *Economy*, the *State*, and *Society*: Arendt suggested that these are like modern gods, seemingly controlling our fate and determining our fortunes. Or better, these are modern magical forces that, like the powers of the wizard in the Depression-era movie *The Wizard of Oz*, promise to grant our wishes—as long as we bring the right offerings. Arendt frequently discussed the allure these seismic systems have over us. They leave us with the feeling, as she wrote, "that no one is a free agent, and hence the doubt that anyone is responsible or could be expected to answer for what he has done."[8] Indeed, there is something decidedly abstract and impersonal about these globewide powers. And yet each is undeniably human in origin and effect. They are, to be sure, bigger than any one individual, but they are not autonomous, let alone automatic. Though they feel like immovable forces, they are but the artifacts of our modern, all-too-human ambitions.

In the film *Modern Times* (1936), Charlie Chaplin plays the part of a factory worker busily trying to keep up with the pace of the assembly line. From time to time, the factory's managers—ever eager to achieve faster and faster rates of production—turn a dial in a control room to speed up the pace

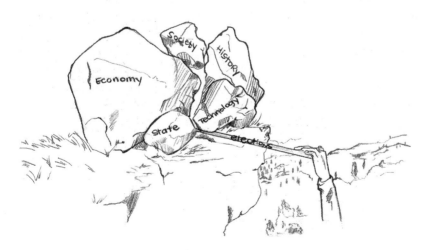

Making room for politics?

of the assembly-line belt. Chaplin's character is forced to work ever more frenetically, until he can no longer do so. Overwhelmed by the furious pace of the modern machine, he has a nervous breakdown that sends him to the hospital and onto a series of other unfortunate adventures.

Modern Times was a funny look at a situation in the Great Depression that was not at all funny. The speed of technological change and the increasing velocity of the technological systems operated by industrial barons in the early twentieth century left millions of people in the lurch economically, emotionally, and existentially. But at least in *Modern Times*—which was as critical as it was comedic—it was obvious that humans were operating the machine. The film clearly points the finger at the greedy factory owners. In the twenty-first century, technology and technological change are just as rapid as they were in the 1920s and '30s, but we tend to point the finger at "technology" itself as the cause, as if it were a self-running system.

Technology is an obvious example of a modern power we deify, and thus allow to defy us.[9] We modern worshippers of the machine hold as self-evident that technological developments are inevitable and we can't really stop them; that every problem (including the problems brought by Technology) must be approached and solved as an engineering or "design" problem; and ultimately that any new innovation or scientific finding is a sign of "advancement" or "progress." Technology is not just the control room of modernity; it is its *sanctum sanctorum*, its holy of holies.[10]

For Arendt, the dominance of Technology was felt in three twentieth-century innovations that remain profound problems today: mass media, industrial automation, and nuclear weapons. In each case, she wrote, particular technologies stand in "rebellion" to the human condition: mass media by turning us into targets for propaganda and other forms of malign mass influence; industrial automation by making it harder and harder for humans to work for their livelihood; and nuclear weapons by immediately threatening human existence itself.[11] None of these innovations, Arendt suggested, came as the result of a broad range of people saying, "We want this!" Rather, they were justified by a few powerful men, an oligarchic elite, saying, "These things are inevitable and must be done!"—leaving the rest of us feeling helpless to stop them. (I recently overheard a group of veterans at a coffee shop going on about how a Veterans Administration Hospital has replaced people with robots to transport supplies from room to room—this at a time when the unemployment rate among veterans is a major problem.)

Technology therefore takes on something like the force of History. We are now in a curious position with respect to History.[12] Maybe most of us wouldn't mind "making history" in some way, but nearly all of us live as though we were at best participants within it, or simply spectators of it. For example, Barack Obama's 2008 presidential election was celebrated as "historic," and it was—but not for the reason many people claimed. In the wake of his election, many of his supporters spoke as though the election proved that History was on the side of racial progress. Things really were getting better, they said; it was just a matter of time. Pundits started writing about a "postracial" US society, and others about the "browning" of America. Given the ensuing years, these progressive witnesses to History must have felt like those in the decades after the failure of the French Revolution—both "fooled by history" and "the fools of history."[13] Clearly, we have to learn over and over again that history is what we make of it, that it has no laws of its own, progressive or otherwise.

The intellectual genealogy of political progressivism—a strange fusion of philosophy of history, evolutionary theory, utilitarianism, and revolutionary thought—makes it especially prone to deferring to History as the engine of political change, often with the naive assumption that political progressives are on the "right side" of history.[14] But political conservatives can be equally wed to History, nostalgically attaching themselves to an ideal past that needs restoration.[15] History is a force we all want to be "on our side." It is invoked across the ideological spectrum, summoned to justify all sorts of acts, from moon shots to military missile launches to antidiscrimination laws to white supremacist violence to new shopping malls.

History, of course, is also something we fear. We worry that it, like the machines in Charlie Chaplin's factory, might move too fast, leaving us unable to keep up. Our relationship to History is therefore ambivalent, if not downright contradictory. It is a force we want to marshal, and yet we often see it as something ominous and alien. Even powerful political actors, Arendt noted, often behave as though they are mere role-playing actors in the pre-scripted drama of "historical destiny," as if their responsibility is simply to "accept their part in History."[16] The rest of us, in turn, watch them like people watched *Forrest Gump* in the 1990s. In the film, Forrest finds himself carried along by History, moved from becoming an All-American running back at the University of Alabama to a soldier in Vietnam to a founding investor in Apple computers. And all along, Forrest acts as though *he*, like us, is nothing but an accidental spectator to the historical events that so powerfully defined his generation.

The Economy is no different in this regard. Economists—many of whom would shun notions of "historical destiny"—nevertheless tell us that the Economy is a self-running progressive system; that while it touches everything in our life, from what we eat to what we do for a living, it is beyond our control and ultimately "efficient." Many economists argue that any attempt we might make to control or otherwise direct the Economy is bound to create more problems than it solves. They therefore argue that we need to make as much room as possible for the Economy to move, minimizing administrative intervention, because "free markets" are best for the Economy and ultimately (always "ultimately") for most people (always "most" people—someone has to pay the price of economic development). Indeed, for most of us the Economy is a large-scale system that we experience like a great but fickle wizard, blessing and cursing us at will for reasons that ultimately remain mysterious to us.

For others, of course, the Economy should not be left to itself. They argue that government has a role in directing it. Here the State becomes a vast instrument of control. Arendt criticized the modern conception of "the state" as exclusively mechanistic; it is seen by us as a kind of technology, a giant battleship for navigating the sea of human concerns, especially economic and security concerns. Our relationship to the State can therefore be either as passengers on a friendly ship or captives on an enemy ship, depending on how we feel about the government and its actions. We might simply seek to sway the captains of the ship of State to better serve our interests; or we might work in fierce opposition to them to resist or even eliminate them. Regardless, if we approach government as if it were no more than a technical apparatus, we will see politics as no more than a means of grabbing hold of State controls to serve our own individual or group interests.[17]

The arena in which we often feel ourselves to be vying with Technology, History, the Economy, and the State is "Society." Society is the biggest and most nebulous of the large-scale systems we moderns face, and seemingly the most ubiquitous.[18] We are accustomed to reading or hearing, and perhaps even saying ourselves, "In today's society . . . ," as if everything that characterizes our age—be it technological changes, historical developments, economic realities, or the machinations of government—is in some way ultimately a product of Society. Arendt was particularly concerned about our deference to Society, for "society" comes nearest to substituting for political community altogether, as Society, unlike Technology, History, or the Economy, makes us feel like we belong to a *human* community. It's like being a part of one big "super-human family," Arendt wrote.[19] We belong to this family not by virtue of our individuality or our equality, but by some genetic common denominator that makes us all "one." And we don't choose our family; we are born into it. So too we don't choose our Society, but are born into it.

Society, therefore, exceeds our sense of power to influence or change. Think about it: you don't likely say that you belong to *a* society, but to "society" as such; you don't write "In my society," but "In today's society." Indeed, this is part of the power of *social* media. None of us feel in control of social media. Social media makes us all but members of some singular transcendent, the "social network." Arendt suggested that in the modern world, Society and notions of "the social" have become the means of getting many different people to see themselves as ultimately but part of one undifferentiated mass of people. Thus, while we might feel ourselves "watching" technological progress, historical events, economic fluctuations, and government actions, we feel ourselves part of—maybe even trapped by—Society and its ways.

The Populist Predicament

These large-scale systems can each function as rivals to politics and political community. The free exercise of our human capacities for thought, speech, and action cannot be readily realized through a machine, the march of History, free markets, state power, or being part of the One Big Family we call "society." Technology, History, the Economy, the State, and Society therefore can leave us feeling powerless, subtly or bluntly stripping from us our sense of freedom and human community. And so we grow scared.

Fear, according to Arendt, is more than having a sense of impending danger. It is rooted in a more profound feeling of helplessness before an impending danger. We become fearful when we feel as though we are no longer able to *act* so as to make a difference:

> Fear as a principle of public-political action has a close connection with the fundamental experience of powerlessness that we all know from situations in which, for whatever reasons, we are unable to act. . . . Politically speaking, fear (and I am not talking about anxiety) is despair over my impotence when I have reached the limits within which action is possible. . . . Therefore fear, properly speaking, is not a principle of action, but an anti-political principle within the common world.[20]

Fear is how we feel when we feel incapable of fending off a threat—this is why fear is an antipolitical emotion. It would make us powerless. The irony here is that because fear is an antipolitical emotion, it can be a very powerful force in the political realm. Indeed, fear is in the emotional throne room of authoritarian power, an emotion stirred by autocrats so as to exploit us.[21] Ap-

Citizenship?

peals to fear by powerful people are designed to make us feel powerless, such that the only logical solution, from a feeling perspective, is an authoritarian one. Met with the conspiracy of large-scale systems that seemingly exceed our power to control, we look to a Big Man to come and save us.

That this is the emotional and political logic of twenty-first-century demagoguery is not difficult to see. Demagogic politicians announce the dangers! They use the dangers to stir fear in us. They stress how helpless we are apart from their great "leadership." They ask us to pledge loyalty to them, to become one with them, to virtually worship them in the way a manipulative abuser demands absolute fidelity from his victim. They stir in us a feeling of weakness, allowing us to feel the full force of our power only as we attach ourselves to them. They rage with us against the machine, but not to empower us—rather, to empower themselves.

The demagogue's political crimes go even further. He or she politicizes everything, from the press to the judiciary, to the police. Demagogues, to be sure, make a kind of "politics" visible again. In them people can see a form of political power (albeit a malign one) and are reminded, and perhaps heartened, by the fact that the world is a political world. Yet, even as demagogues make politics visible again, they invalidate its democratic expression, offering an authoritarian model as the only truly effective and authentic form of politics. They therefore magnify the appearance of politics only to jealously guard it as their lone rightful possession.

This is exactly what authoritarian leaders have always attempted to do. They don't seek to rid the earth of politics, but rather make it their prized possession. Indeed, part of the reason that we have been so deferential to large-scale systems like technology, the economy, or certain forms of government bureaucracy is because they appear to be alternatives to authoritarian personalities. The choice to be ruled by systems rather than by humans is arguably what makes us "modern" in the first place. Technology, markets, and some forms of bureaucracy don't appear authoritarian, because they seem to be *impersonal*. An authoritarian has a face; a machine or a market does not. But these systems are not without their faces—they are full of them. They are just typically hidden.

In our running in horror from authoritarian leaders to impersonal systems like bureaucracy, markets, or technology, we leave the fundamental problem unaddressed: namely, the political powerlessness of we the people. We simply replace one master with another. When we suspect that these "impersonal" systems that rule us are really being operated by and for the interests of particular people, our thrall gets transferred to the "great leader," who tells us she will fight for our interests. So, the bipolar swing becomes, like an assembly line, an incessant cycle. In the wake of authoritarian abuses and evils, a new crop of engineers, economists, or liberal-minded politicians come along to argue that we need to turn our collective fate over to impersonal objective systems that are, supposedly, free of authoritarian potential.[22] But, once we are given over to these systems, they also act like tyrants, demanding from us our jobs, our education, our neighborhoods, and our health. So, we look anew for a Big Man to come along and save us. And the machine turns again.

If this seems disorienting, even Chaplinesque, it should. Underlying Arendt's sober writings about the spell of systems and the hexes of "great leaders" is an underlying sense of the absurdity of our modern condition. We moderns, she suggested, are more deferential, more reverential, and more tragicomic in our willingness to surrender responsibility for Earth, for each other, and for ourselves to "higher powers" than ancient religious people ever were, our modern prejudices against the ancient past notwithstanding. To be sure, ancient peoples sometimes surrendered responsibility for their fate to the gods of the clouds, sun, and moon; but we surrender responsibility to things we can't even see: technological forces, historical progress, economic markets, government metrics, or "society." And when these modern magical forces fail us, we look for a new grand wizard, who tells us that the problem is *those [black, Jewish, gay, immigrant, religious, etc.] people*.[23]

Here we need to return to what Arendt called the "human condition." Here we humans are, walking on Earth. Neither we nor Earth needs to be propped up. Here we are standing on Earth with one another. This is our basic human condition. And yet, when it comes to our life on Earth together, we defer to Big Men or to the wizards of Technology, History, the Economy, the State, and Society who, as long as we prop them up, promise to rule over us and determine our individual and collective fate and grant us our wishes. Yet, we end up like Dorothy and her companions in *The Wizard of Oz*: when we pull back the curtain, we find nothing but middle-aged men at a battery of machined controls.

This is why we need to stop walking down the yellow brick roads of modernity's big systems and make our way back to *politics*. There are many forms of human power: technology, labor, science, erotic love, knowledge. But political power is rooted in individuals freely acting among others toward goods that can be enjoyed in common. The necessary condition and only true mode of operation for political power is freedom—the capacity to act and to take responsibility for your actions.[24] We suffer from an insufficient attachment to freedom and an overattachment to fear.[25] If we the people are to act freely and responsibly, then we need to not just see politics anew, but to exercise and experience the miraculous form of human power that is political power.

The Phenomenal Life of Politics

Ever since the Greeks began writing about politics two and a half millennia ago, democracy has been conceived as one form of government among others. Whereas a monarchy is a rule of "one," an aristocracy the power of the "best" (by name at least), and an oligarchy the rule of the "few," a democracy is rooted in the capacities of the people (or the *demos* in Greek). In each of these forms, those who get to rule are identical with those who get to act freely. For this reason, from Arendt's perspective, democracy is more than just one form of government among others. For her, there is a special kinship between politics and democracy in that democracy potentially widens the scope of politics to everybody, such that we all can freely share in political life as we come together "in the manner of speech and action" to address the challenges of the common world that we inhabit together.[26]

The core faculty of politics, Arendt argued, the means of its actualization and recognition, is *speech*: "Wherever the relevance of speech is at stake, matters become political by definition, for speech is what makes man a political being."[27] What is it about speech that is so central to politics? To begin with, speaking is something that we do *with others*. Speaking, we'd say, is a social activity. While we may "talk to ourselves," even then we are addressing ourselves as an "other." But drinking, playing games, roasting marshmallows, and a host of other activities, you might respond, are also social activities. Are they also political activities? Speech is distinct from these other activities in that it is addressed *toward* others, calling for a response of some kind or another. Moreover, speech is *about* things—typically, objects or events in the world and ideas about them. Finally, speech is a form of *action* that is oriented toward getting others to act too, typically in a cooperative venture of one kind or another. In interacting with others about common ideas, objects, or events, we have the basics for a social life, and in addressing these ideas, objects, or events from different perspectives, we have a basic condition for politics.

That politics is a basic human capacity rather than "what governments do" means we can address all kinds of topics politically, from work wages to human reproduction to racism to transportation. In the words of Linda Zerilli, topics become political when they "are brought into a relationship as the object of a dispute, that is, the occasion for speech and action with which people create the common world, the space in which things become public, and create it anew."[28] Anything can become political if it can be disputed among people in a common space.

Still, there is a big difference between engaging a topic politically and "politicizing" it. To "politicize" a topic is to transform it into a wedge, dividing "us" from "them." To politicize everything, is to turn the whole of life into a means of dividing and destroying. As Bernard Crick writes in his classic *In Defense of Politics*, "The attempt to politicize everything is the destruction of politics. When everything is seen as relevant to politics, then politics has indeed become totalitarian."[29] By contrast, to engage a topic politically is to claim that it legitimately concerns both *us* and *them* and, as Arendt wrote, seek to "act in and change and build a common world."[30]

Politics is therefore a type of cooperative human community. Cooperation can be structured and even institutionalized, but it can never be forced. It can happen only as people willingly work in concert with others. The ancient Romans called their political community a "republic" because it was seen as "the people's thing" or, in Latin, the *res publica*. Even the Latin word *civitas*, from which we get words like *citizen* and *city*, was seen by Romans as describing a phenomenon more than a particular geographical place, as seen in the fact that St. Augustine could write of the "city of God" (*civitas dei*) alongside the "earthly city" (*civitas terrena*), neither of which was a particular place but rather phenomena that appear in the world when people act in concert toward particular loves and aspirations. Politics was above all a form of life that emerged among humans as they came to speak and act with one another about matters of common concern.

Politics is also, then, in a qualified sense, "anarchic," or without rule (*an-archê*).[31] While political communities can be founded on, and can even center on, the question of "rule," politics is not reducible to constitutions and government. It is simply something that happens among people. "Politics arises *between men*, and so quite *outside of man*," Arendt wrote. "Politics arises in what lies *between men*, and is established as relationships."[32] To enter political life is to participate in a form of rule-lessness with persons who respect one another as equals.[33]

This means, in opposition to so many of our assumptions about the nature of politics, that politics is necessarily nonviolent.[34] Nonviolence is not a mere political strategy or tactic; it is a condition of politics because freedom from force is a condition of politics. But this is not "negative freedom," understood as the right of an individual to be free from the interference of others.[35] No one is politically free who is only free of "interference." Nor is one free if they are subject to the power of impersonal forces. On the contrary, political freedom is realized only interpersonally, only *with* others, and is in this sense always "positive." To be politically free is to act with others without resort to force or violence. This is the reason nonviolence as a political tactic is politically powerful: politics, to restate the formula so often used on behalf of the modern state, has a monopoly on the legitimate use of nonviolence.[36] The claim of the state to possess a monopoly on the legitimate use of violence, as well as the state's frequent resorting to violence, while not in itself necessarily unjust or wrong, is necessarily antipolitical. Inasmuch as the state would want to rest its legitimacy on *political* grounds, it risks compromising its legitimacy every time it uses violence.[37]

On this ground, not only the state, but markets and machines stand in opposition to politics, as they each depend on forms of force. As Arendt argued, the word *economy* is derived from a space of rule: it comes from the Greek *oikos*, meaning "household," and in Greece the household was a space where men gave orders to women, children, and slaves. Indeed, our twenty-first-century global economy extends over Earth as a form of dominion, forcing the means of life from Earth and its inhabitants, and transforming inanimate and animate things into means of sustenance and, even more, the monetary wealth of some. The economy depends on forcing the elements—

and indeed, people—to obey a logic that is not of the people; technology is the means by which that force is so often exercised. Together, economy and technology really are conjuring arts, our modern means of calling up forceful spirits.

The Miraculous Art of Politics

Politics is not magical, and it does not pretend to be. It is phenomenal. If politics has always had an intimate relationship to religion, it is not because politics is or even looks like an art of conjuring, as does magic. Rather, as Arendt argued, politics has the form of a miracle, full of the unexpected: "Whenever something new occurs, it bursts into the context of predictable processes as something unexpected, unpredictable, and ultimately causally inexplicable—just like a miracle."[38] Politics produces *new* things, events, and ideas in the world as people come together to speak and act: "The miracle of freedom is inherent in this ability to make a [new] beginning."[39] The practice of the Greeks to consult the oracle at Delphi was a tacit acknowledgement that political wisdom cannot simply be conjured up or mined from the earth. It must be consulted, and often waited upon, as in expectation of a miracle.

Politics therefore also has the form of a gift. What is exchanged in the political transaction—thoughts, words, promises, pronouncements, sentiments—works not by means of the mechanisms of industrial production but by "trust production."[40] What is given in the political act, and what is received, is not a thing to which we can attribute a "value" to be stored for use another day in a barter or market economy. Rather, what is ultimately given and received is *trust*. "Trust enables agreement," Danielle Allen writes.[41] Trust also enables productive disagreement, argument, and difference, for trust is more than agreement—it is a *quality of relationship*.[42] Paradoxically, trust is at once an infinitely renewable social resource and always a precarious one, as the conditions for trust can be hard to sustain. They depend on widespread virtues of respect, goodwill, self-restraint, and self-sacrifice, as well as structures of responsibility and accountability.

Politics, more than anything else, is an *art*. The ancient Greeks categorized the arts according to how they are realized, completed, or "perfected." Some arts are realized in things you can touch and keep. Think of painting: it is hard to conceive of someone practicing the art of painting without producing a painting, even if it is a bad one. The end or purpose of painting is an object, the painting, not the idea of the painting or the painter. The ancients called arts like this "productive" arts. They contrasted productive arts with what they called "theoretical" arts. The purpose of theoretical arts is to produce not things, but knowledge about things. Astronomy is a classic example of a theoretical art. It does not produce stars, of course; it produces knowledge about stars. You could say the same thing about psychology—it doesn't produce human psyches, it produces knowledge about them.

The third type was called the "active" arts. These are a special case, for their purpose is neither things nor theories about things. Rather, they realize their "end" or purpose *in the act itself*. Think of dancing. The art of dancing is realized in the dance. It is not just that you can't be a dancer if you don't dance; it's that to dance is to fulfill the purpose of dancing. Of course, you might fulfill it more or less well, with varying degrees of passion, art, or agility; but the quality of your art is seen only in the activity of dancing itself. It is possible, to be sure, to produce theories about dancing, but such theories in no way would realize or bring to a kind of perfection the art of dancing itself. To do that, you have to dance. So too, it would be possible for a dancer to produce something in the world for others: a performance, a recording of a performance, a choreographic script, an experience. But for a dancer, none of these "things" represent the perfection of dancing (though they may entail the proper recognition of that perfection).[43]

While political actions have all sorts of consequences and produce definite things (for example, laws), and while it is possible to theorize about politics endlessly, politics is more like dancing than painting or astronomy. It is mostly an active art, a mode of ongoing action and interaction. In politics, it is not enough to simply produce a law—you have to justify it, enforce it, tweak it, and sometimes repeal it in ongoing actions. Politics would be, ideally, a continuous collective performance, an improvisational play with many actors that never ends, an always evolving musical performance. Of course, it is often more like steering an armada through a stormy sea: we have to not only act, but react; we have to be aware of and responsive to the outside conditions; we have to communicate with the other ships alongside us; and we need crews, not just captains, to navigate.

Prioritizing the active and reactive qualities of the political art is, admittedly, flipping politics on its theoretical head. As we have already begun to see, for eons two closely related concerns have dominated political theory: constitutions and rulership. Ever since Plato, philosophers have organized political philosophy around arguments about what should be the foundational laws of society and its constitutional principles. That's why they've spent so much ink drawing out the distinctions among democracies, monarchies, aristocracies, and so on, as if what was most at stake in politics is the type of constitution. To be sure, constitutions are critical; they delimit in a solemn promise the nature, extent, and quality of political authority and power. But what matters as much is the *quality* of political life within a given nominal or actual constitutional regime. It does not matter what is written if the people perish. Furthermore, a constitutional democracy can be repressive; a monarchy can be liberal.[44] The preoccupation of some political philosophers with constitutions turns politics into clockwork, as if we need only to build the clock, wind it up, and let it run. Arendt taught that we need instead to ask questions in the neighborhood where politics actually lives—namely, questions about action and freedom, communication and community, power and possibility. We need to think of politics as we think of dancing: an art of coordinated action.

A Political Miracle

Consider what happened in a church basement in the poor and historically marginalized neighborhood of Roseland on the South Side of Chicago.[45] There, one spring evening in 2003, official representatives from the Chicago Area Transportation Study (CATS) showed up for what they thought would be another perfunctory meeting about long-neglected public transportation needs in the area. The majority-black area was a transportation desert, devoid of public transit services the rest of the city enjoyed. This made it very difficult for the residents of the area to get to places of employment, training, and education—therefore exacerbating high unemployment rates and disinvestment in the area.

In the early 2000s, Chicago's leaders began to plan for a new generation of transit projects in the metro area. Nearly all the planned projects focused on better serving the wealthier residents of the suburbs, leaving the people of the South Side to continue to fend for themselves. Given the poverty of the area, city leaders had no immediate interest in better serving it. People in greater Roseland, however, had a different idea. They desperately wanted the transit authority to extend the "Red Line" rail—which runs north and south from downtown Chicago—some thirty blocks further south into their neighborhood. The cost for such a project would be astronomical, eventually estimated at $2.3 billion—one of the biggest infrastructure projects in Illinois history. And it would take decades to complete. Poor people asking for such a big thing seemed like a flight of fancy.

Nevertheless, several community leaders in greater Roseland asked representatives from CATS to come meet with them in a local church. To the surprise of the CATS officials, two hundred community members showed up at the meeting. At the meeting, Developing Communities Project, a community organization, asked for an extension of the deadline for public input, so as to better gauge community interest. CATS agreed to hold off. In the next two weeks, Developing Communities Project gathered some 1,500 signatures supporting the extension of the Red Line and compiled reams of evidence and arguments for engineers, experts, and community members to work through. CATS agreed to consider the matter further.

For the next year and a half, the people of greater Roseland worked to persuade the city, state, and federal governments to approve and ultimately fund the project. They were reminded repeatedly of how improbable the feat was. Still, they persisted. They met with legislators and city council members. They developed contacts with journalists, who began writing stories about the initiative. And they partnered with a local university to run studies to measure the economic impacts of the project for Chicago and the state of Illinois.

In November 2004, a nonbinding ballot referendum was held on the Red Line extension. Nearly thirty-nine thousand South Side voters turned out—a record. Soon after, the Chicago City Council, the Illinois state legislature, and the federal government got on board. In May 2005, two years after the meeting in the church basement, President George W. Bush came to Aurora, Illinois, to sign the Federal Public Transportation Act. Among its many provisions, it designated the Red Line extension as a priority transportation project, and as I write, the project is underway.

For the people of greater Roseland, politics offered possibilities that neither markets, technological innovation, governments, nor "progress" had offered the community for decades. By making rail transportation a political topic and by using the political means of speech and action, they opened a new place for themselves in Chicago's future. The miraculous result was not only one of the largest public transportation projects in Illinois history, but a new beginning for greater Roseland.

History is full of such miraculous political stories and countless other less obviously miraculous but still phenomenal stories. Indeed, what we call "history" is nothing but the product of political stories of all sorts. So many of the great technological innovations, economic transformations, revolutions in governing, and transformations in society that historians study have vital political dimensions, for anything that is truly *new* in human history is the result of human action. And most new things in human history, whether of great or small consequence, have been the result of humans speaking and acting together in the full force of their freedom and power.

The critical question has been, and continues to be, who gets to so act, and toward what ends.

In a Gallup survey done during the 2016 election season, a full 90 percent of citizens agreed that "most politicians are more interested in winning elections than in doing what is right." Seventy-three percent said, "Most elected officials don't care what people like me think." And 63 percent agreed that "people like me don't have any say about what the government does."[46] A great many of these same citizens casted their votes for Trump, and this makes sense: they already felt themselves to live an apolitical existence, unable to act except through an electoral act that could only, at best, destroy the status quo in favor of a radically uncertain future. Trump, unlike his rival Hillary Clinton, at least allowed them to vicariously experience a new kind of political being.

This crisis has been a long time coming. In the 1970s the German social critic Jürgen Habermas, who learned much from Arendt, saw it as a kind of three-headed hydra.[47] The first head is the capitalist economy. Capitalism is powerful—so powerful that it can make you rich or send you into destitute poverty; it can give you lots of stuff, or stuff you with mass-produced food; it can move you with other migrants en masse from the country into the city, and from city centers into the slums; it can give you a nice house in the suburbs, and leave you unable to make your mortgage payments. Capitalism can even move mountains (in the form of mining and other "land development" projects) and all but walk on water in the form of new technologies.

But there's one thing capitalism can't do: create a stable society. The nature of the market is mercurial, disruptive, even destructive. It's full of ups and downs, booms and busts, bubbles, fits of depression, inflationary pressures, and debt crises. Therefore, the state steps in. Better yet, the state is always stepping in to manage its volatile partner. The state is the second head of the hydra. The state manages the money supply, measures gross domestic product, messes with the tax code, spends to stimulate, or to provide social safety nets, and bails out the banks or farmers so they don't go bankrupt.

But there's one thing the state can't do: make it all make sense. The state can't make *meaning*. That is something "we the people" have to do ourselves. It's a job for everybody. Meaning—real meaning—can't be manufactured or dictated. It's the stuff of culture, community, and communication. So here we are faced with a crisis of *meaning*, the third head. We live in this big, globalized society of money, markets, manufacturing, and ubiquitous information, with governments trying variously to manage or manipulate the mess, and it all seems grossly illegitimate because so little of it makes sense; so little of it conforms to our expectations of the way things are supposed to be, the way we'd want things to be. We can't consent to this mess not because we can't understand it, but because we understand all too well that it is not working well for most people—this is what Habermas called a "legitimation crisis."

Enter politics. Poor, feeble, much-maligned politics. The stuff of *politicians*. (There was an ad for a cigarette tax hike in a midwestern state, a constitutional amendment where the revenues would be specially designated to fund early childhood education. The ad's villain? Not the cigarette industry. Not lobbyists. Rather, *politicians*. Keep our tax revenues out of the hands of politicians, the campaign says. Make the tax and the distribution of its revenues *constitutional*, a matter of fiat from here on out. Free us from the politicians!) Politics is in a sorry state, not the least because politicians have done so little to help it. Many politicians are as cynical about politics as the public is, and would just as soon get rid of politics and turn things over to the market. And many politicians are in fact power-hungry bastards.

But here's the catch: *politics is the only way out that does not sacrifice our freedom*. The fix for the three-headed hydra of our legitimation crisis is a political fix. If the problem is that we can't together make sense of it all—even worse, if the problem is that the system simply does not, and cannot, make sense—then it follows that "making sense" or "making something that makes sense" is the solution. Otherwise we are stuck with the status quo, or something much worse than the status quo.

This is not to say that we "just need to come together" and fix these problems, as is often said. Nor is it that we all need to become political activists. Rather, it is to say that if we are going to live freely together, we need to learn to see the phenomenal power of politics and relearn its ways.

THREE

Judging Politics

In the summer of 2017, a small group of paddle boarders was enjoying the water in Southern California, having a good time, as Southern Californians are enviously prone to do. They were on the Pacific Ocean, of course, with its great variety of sea creatures that, no less than Californians, live in a world of their own with their own needs, pleasures, and desires. The Pacific, as you probably know, includes among its vast number of creatures the great white shark—that beautiful but horrifying creature seen in heart-stopping films like *Jaws*, *Unbroken*, and *The Shallows*. Biologists tell us that as far as food goes, great whites prefer seals, sea otters, and fish. Nevertheless, in certain circumstances they will attack humans, and when they do it is rarely playful and can be deadly. In any case, on this particular day in sunny California, no fewer than fifteen great white sharks found these paddle boarders (or, at least, the space in which they were moving about). The problem for the paddle boarders was not only the sharks, it was that they were unaware of having such dangerous company. Several hundred feet off of the beach they blithely played about, laughing and jesting, maybe even cracking jokes about dangerous sharks.

Thankfully, a sheriff's deputy was on patrol in a helicopter over the beach. As the deputy flew over the area, he saw the paddle boarders below and the horde of great white sharks circling. Alert to the danger, he got to work. Sort of. Radio in hand, rather than getting on his loudspeaker and telling the paddle boarders to calmly paddle to the shore as quickly as possible, the deputy deemed that he needed to get proper authorization before warning the paddle boarders. It turns out—who would have known?—that the public beaches of Southern California are under the jurisdiction of lifeguards, not the sheriff's department. So, the deputy judged he had to get permission from the lifeguards to notify the paddle boarders that their lives were in imminent danger. And as things turned out, the lifeguards were hard to reach. The deputy had to go through the emergency operator, who had to figure out which lifeguard station to contact, and so on. This took some four excruciatingly long minutes while the paddle boarders frolicked and the sharks circled. As the fifth minute approached, the deputy got the authorization he sought and, at long last, got on his copter loudspeaker to warn the paddle boarders, instructing them to leave the water calmly but immediately. They did.[1]

The sheriff copter's onboard video of this episode got widespread attention on web-based news sites across the world. It was every bit as suspenseful as *Jaws*, except even more nail-biting, given that it was real: you can see the sharks circling as you hear the deputy repeatedly trying to get authorization to warn the paddle boarders below. While the video was widely offered as a human interest story, a viral video to draw you in to a bit of drama, I hope to convince you in this chapter that this story should have appeared on the politics page—or, at least, that the event was every bit as political as a speech on the floor of the US House of Representatives. As is clear by now, I am working to persuade you that politics is something more than party politics, voting, or even protests on the streets. It is, Arendt argued, a basic human phenomenon where we address others in speech and action about matters of common concern. Certainly, sharks circling paddle boarders constitutes a "common concern," and one that can be addressed through speech and action.

Let me sketch out here three particular ways in which the deputy's encounter with the paddle boarders and sharks was political, starting with a peripheral sense of politics and moving to the central concept of politics that drives its defense in this book. First, and most obviously, we can see that the deputy's care to make sure he got proper authorization from the lifeguards was a product (in part, anyway) of interagency politics. No doubt there had been some back-and-forth in the past between the lifeguards and the sheriff's department about who has jurisdiction where and in what situations. In this respect, the deputy's lengthy authorization procedure was akin to "office politics." He was making sure he didn't step on anyone's toes (despite the vulnerability of the toes of the paddle boarders!). This is a most generic sense of "politics": making sure you play the power structure just right so as to either stay out of trouble or get the advantage.

And it is a perfectly acceptable way to think about politics, as long as that's not *all* we think about politics. For there is a second sense in which the story of the sharks is a political story: it is a story of the controversial actions and inactions of government actors and agencies. Indeed, the episode was ripe with bureaucracy, procedure, and protocol—the stuff we tend to associate with "government." Rather than immediately *act*, the deputy proceeded according to a preset script written who knows where, and one we presume he would have followed regardless of whether the crisis concerned life-threatening sharks or a violent surfer. These protocols are "political" not so much because they are the product of government, but because they can and do periodically become objects of public debate. Bureaucracy is the way modern democracies have standardized governing, trying to make it fairer; or if not fairer, more efficient; or if not more efficient, at least predictable. And so bureaucracy can be tedious and controversial, and when it garners public attention as an object of frustration or contention, it becomes political. In this case, a lot of people reacted strongly to the deputy's actions, such that it became a political story in this second sense.

But the heart of the political matter here goes much further. Because it is the heart of the matter—the nut we have to crack, so to speak—I devote this chapter to it. Let me put it here as straightforwardly as I can: this shark's tale is a political tale because it involved particular *judgments* about how things should go among people, especially people who don't know each other well, or at all (the deputy, after all, was a perfect stranger to the paddle boarders).[2] If for Arendt speech and action are the most political of human capacities because they are the essential means by which we freely interact with others, *judgment*, she would argue, is the most political of our mental abilities because it is the means by which we think through and decide when and how to speak or act with others.[3] Therefore, wherever and whenever we find stories about people making judgments about how things should go among fellow humans—some of whom are, or might as well be, strangers—the story belongs on the politics page. This is especially true in moments of *crisis*, big or small, when the future is exceptionally uncertain.[4] In fact, the ancient Greek word for *judgment* was *krisis*, from where we get our word crisis.[5] This makes sense if for no other reason that crises call for judgment. In moments of crisis we make consequential decisions, and the quality of our judgments will set the course of the crisis.

The Art of Political Judgment

How do we make judgments? Let's take an everyday scenario. You are driving down the street and come to a crosswalk where a pedestrian is waiting to cross the street. What do you do? Do you drive on by? Do you slow down and carefully drive through? Do you hesitate, stop, and then go without letting the pedestrian cross? Do you stop and just sit there? Do you stop and

How you stop . . .

wave the pedestrian on? Do you stop and honk? Do you drive on through and honk? Do you drive through, honk, and make a gesture? There are at least a dozen different ways you could approach the situation.

How do you come to do what you end up doing? Your judgment could be based on some quick logical thinking. For example, you may deduce that stopping and letting the pedestrian cross could make you late for work. Or it could be a matter of how you're feeling at the moment. You may already be angry about having to get up so early to get to work and therefore in no mood for niceties. It could be a matter of respecting the law that gives pedestrians the right of way. You are a law-abiding citizen and always seek to follow the law. Or it could be a moral matter for you. You live by the Golden Rule and want to do to others as you'd have them do to you. Just as there are a dozen different ways that you could approach the crosswalk, so there are a dozen different reasons you could decide to do what you do.

Does it matter what judgment you make? If you were to collide with the pedestrian, most definitely. Does it matter why you made the judgment? In the court of law, not as much as you might like. Your motivation or reason for driving through the crosswalk might help determine the kind of crime, but not the fact of the crime. Does it matter how you come to make your judgment? Arendt would say yes, most certainly, for in fact *how* you come to make judgments is more closely related to *what* judgments you make than *why* you make judgments.

Motive—the why of judgments—is morally important and politically significant.[6] Motives tell us, in part, what kind of people we are. But they are often hidden and difficult to discern.[7] Indeed, sometimes our motives are inscrutable to even ourselves. We often don't know why we do what we do, and when we do, our motives are rarely straightforward.[8] But *how* we come to a judgment is something we can explain both to ourselves and to others—and the explanation of this "how," Arendt has suggested, will do more to shed light on the quality of a judgment than will any account of motives. "I didn't think about it" is a more illuminating explanation than "I was angry," for there are a dozen different things you could do with your anger but only one way to make sense of your thoughtlessness: it was thoughtless. Likewise, to say, "I thought about how I would want to be treated if I were in that situation" reveals a good deal more about the nature and quality of your decision to stop and wave the pedestrian across than simply "I want to be a good person."

In our political lives we make all kinds of different types of judgments—not just how to vote, what position to take on an issue, and what political candidate to support, but also what to do with the piece of trash on the sidewalk, whether to call the cops when we hear gunshots, or whether to stop at a crosswalk. There are all kinds of reasons people decide what they do in various situations. In many cases, why someone does what they do (or what their motives are) doesn't matter all that much as a practical issue. Whether I stop and wave you across because I am a nice guy or because I am afraid of getting a ticket does not practically matter: the action is the same either way, and you as the pedestrian are not likely to know the difference. But whether or not I *think* about what I am doing does matter, if for no other reason than whether I think about the situation is likely to impact what I do. That's why how I go about making my judgments correlates more closely with what judgments I make. Judgment, like throwing a baseball, is the culmination of a process; and the quality of the result will be affected by the quality of the process.

For this reason, Arendt spent a lot of time writing about the "how" of our judgments. Moral philosophers, she acknowledged, needed to think about not just what judgments people make but why they make them, as morality concerns motivations as well as consequences. But political thinkers like herself, she argued, need to focus on the ways people go about making judgments, for how—more than why or even what—is the most politically salient question.

You and I, for another example, might reach different judgments about legalizing marijuana; whatever our differences, the most politically salient issue is how we come to our respective judgments. Opposing legalization because it is a drug, plain and simple, entails a different way of making a political judgment than opposing legalization because it will lead to more crime. One approach is rooted in an attitude toward a category, the other in utilitarian calculus. Politically speaking, the person who opposes marijuana's legalization according to utilitarian calculus shares more with the person who, by the same reasoning, supports its legalization than with the person who says all drugs should be outlawed or strictly regulated because they are drugs. (This is but one way that politics makes for strange bedfellows.)

Are there ways of making political judgments that are superior to others? This is a crucial if fraught question, for no other reason than its answer is a political judgment of the first order. Arendt struggled with the question but clearly thought the answer yes. She argued that low-quality "judgments," if they can be called judgments at all, blindly follow the way of what she sometimes called prejudice, other times thoughtlessness, and still other times ideology. Ideology for Arendt entails the attempt to explain everything we encounter from one basic premise, principle, or idea; it therefore leaves us closed off to new experiences, new evidence, or new ideas.[9] Arendt described "thoughtlessness" as "the heedless recklessness or hopeless confusion or complacent repetition of 'truths' which have become trivial and empty."[10] Likewise, prejudice is content to go along with received "truths."[11] To be sure, we all possess prejudices. They play a necessary role in our everyday lives, as we can't think through every issue we encounter. Sometimes we have to just go with received truths. But prejudices should not be mistaken for judgments: they are at best, as the very word suggests, "prejudgments," the notions and assumptions on which we rely precisely when we are not actively seeking to judge something. The minute we set out on the road of genuine judgment is the minute we need to make even our prejudices subject to judgment. Otherwise, we engage in a kind of fraud, substituting prejudgments for judgment.[12] And this, Arendt concluded, is a recipe for disaster.[13]

Genuine judgment is *reflective*, consisting of a kind of "self-talk" where we work toward settling on a matter, even if for just a while.[14] Reflection is a process, but it is not reducible to a step-by-step recipe. Think about a time when you've reflected back on a mistake you've made. You probably mulled over the episode from a variety of vantage points, thinking about what you wish you would have done differently, and so on, such that you get to a point where you feel like you have a grip on the mistake, even if you still regret it. Of course, in a moment of hesitation, you might also reflect on your process of reflection (did I think it all through rightly?). Reflection can be smooth, or it can be bumpy. It can be conscious or semiconscious. It can be helpful or counterproductive. Regardless, it is something we all do all the time in making judgments about our actions.

Arendt argued that political judgment calls for reflection. Moreover, she suggested that we can get better at political judgment with practice, experience, and knowledge. Ultimately, she believed that because politics is itself a kind of art, quality political judgments are rooted in the same mental processes we use when making quality judgments about things like movies, art works, or craft foods.[15] Political judgment at its best is a form of connoisseurship, the independent and rigorous judgment of the *qualities* of things and events.[16]

How do you know if someone is a connoisseur? It is not a matter of their ultimate verdict. Various connoisseurs can disagree on the relative qualities of a film, painting, or a craft beer. Neither is connoisseurship a matter of laws and rules—there are no laws by which to judge the quality of a film, only examples of great films.[17] Nor is connoisseurship essentially a matter of motive or why people judge as they do. Of course, if a beer master judges the way she does because she is being secretly paid to do so, that matters. But at that point the beer master is not acting as a connoisseur but as a paid agent. Rather, connoisseurship is essentially a matter of *how* a person comes to make a judgment. The connoisseur approaches the film, painting, or beer from a variety of perspectives, considering the particular object's various qualities and dimensions, comparing it to other like objects, and even hearing what others have to say, so as to reach a particular judgment about a particular object.

Arendt suggested that high-quality political judgments are like this. They require, she wrote, "the ability to see the same thing from various standpoints in the human world"; the key to judgment is seeing an issue from its "many-sidedness."[18] Any political topic worthy of the name, like any quality work of art, is multifaceted. Its various sides make it a topic for political discussion and debate in the first place. To approach the issue from a single position reflecting only a singular standpoint is to refuse to take the topic itself seriously. It would be like judging Alex Haley's iconic television miniseries *Roots* by asking only if it was historically accurate. Anyone who has watched *Roots*, who has really paid attention to it, knows that there are many other good questions to ask about the production than its historical fidelity.

Even issues that are seemingly morally stark and singular—for example, slavery—appear in the political realm as multisided. The great political skill of nineteenth-century abolitionists was displayed in their talking about slavery as not only a moral issue—what scripture or reason morally prohibits—but to also draw public attention to slavery's economic and cultural dimensions. They argued that slavery, in addition to being morally wrong, had adverse economic consequences and sullied America's reputation in the world. "Thou shalt not" is not enough in politics (which is not the same thing as saying this phrase cannot be uttered at all in the political realm). Chattel slavery, to be sure, was a singular moral issue, but it was made a political issue only as its opponents and victims drew attention to its "many-sidedness."

Quality political judgment also requires that we approach each issue on its own terms, not just as an example of a type of issue—marijuana as "drug," for example, or flag burning as "anti-American." Because politics is about particular people in particular places doing and saying particular things, political judgments call for a sensitivity to particulars. It is true that marijuana is a drug, but that does little to help us toward a political judgment about the merits of legalizing it, as all sorts of drugs are legal or illegal. And it may be that a given flag-burning demonstration is anti-American, but that does not mean that all flag-burning demonstrations are so—for example, burning a flag in order to defend the first amendment of the US Constitution.

There are two ready objections to this approach to political judgment. Some argue that it is elitist, others that it is unrealistic. Arendt's work addresses these closely related objections, but her responses are noteworthy for the way in which they resist an answer from "above" and instead offer ones from the "below" of everyday political realities. If quality political judgment looks like connoisseurship, does that mean it is elitist, like wine tasting or art curation? Is high-quality political judgment reserved for a specially trained elite? There are, to be sure, easier ways of making judgments than reflecting on the many-sidedness of a particular issue. For instance, we could strictly follow rules already in place. We could judge according to what "feels right." We could follow our financial interests, and judge everything according to a cost/benefit analysis. Or we could adhere to a grand doctrine or set of teachings encapsulated in a "worldview," into which we "fit" all the events and happenings of an ever-changing world.[19] These are all, in fact, common ways of making judgments that don't depend on something like connoisseurship.

But Arendt held that these approaches are not wise forms of political judgment. Why? Because each rubs against the grain of political reality itself. Politics is not reducible to a rule, a feeling, an economic calculus, or a worldview, because it begins and ends from the fact that many different people inhabit the earth, not just one person or one type of person. The fact of "plurality" is the basis for Arendt's claim that taking a plurality of perspectives into account is part of the process of reaching a quality political judgment.

Skill in seeing things from a variety of standpoints is an essential political skill because political life is plural. For this reason, ancient teachers of wisdom from Solomon to the Sophists to Socrates, not to mention countless other cultures, have taught people to examine matters in their many-sidedness. As Arendt wrote of the tradition in ancient Greece teaching people how to argue all sides of a question:

> The crucial factor is not that one could now turn arguments around and stand propositions on their heads, but rather that one gained the ability to truly *see* topics from various sides—that is, politically—with the result that people understood how to assume the many possible perspectives provided by the real world, from which one and the same topic can be regarded and in which each topic, despite its oneness, appears in a great diversity of views.[20]

The reason we need to approach political judgment as connoisseurship is not to produce an elite class of political judges, but rather because politics must deal with our political reality as it is; and the most basic aspect of our political reality is the fact that many different people with many different perspectives live on Earth and share objects of common concern. To refuse to try to see things from the perspectives of different people is to refuse this reality. It is to try to escape the world as it is and create a virtual reality that feels better.

What about the second objection—the response that Arendt's approach to political judgment is too difficult and therefore not practical? Rather than regard this as a true objection, Arendt tended to consider it symptomatic of a genuine elitism, one that assumes people are not capable of considering the standpoints of others, or that they are too busy with their lives to care to do so. Such conditions, Arendt suggested, may accurately describe some people, but this is itself a political *problem*, not a hard-and-fast political reality. Indeed, such conditions are often produced by those in power as a means of fortifying their own power; people who are "incapable" of developing skills of political judgment, or just "too busy," are often people under domination of one kind or another. It is the political situation that we should condemn, not people or their capacities.

Forming Opinions, Making Judgments

How do we remedy a situation in which people are assumed to be either too ignorant or too busy to pursue skills in political judgment? Education is obviously key here. But it is not the sort of education to which we've grown accustomed in civics classes. We need education via civic architecture, opportunity, and even incentives. By creating spaces for everyday people to speak and act in public, and by encouraging and equipping people to do so, we can become political apprentices or autodidacts, depending on our situation, even as we speak and act as full-fledged citizens. This is why, historically speaking, republican societies have put such a premium on public squares, open forums, assemblies, and the free press. The basic conviction is that civic architecture and public media are means we have to educate ourselves in the art of political judgment. The more such spaces are open and freely used, the more practice we get with looking at topics from various sides. In such spaces, we form opinions and make judgments by, well, forming opinions and making judgments.[21]

"Opinions," it is important to clarify, are more than impressions. Impressions can merely be had, but opinions have to be *formed*. Again, the essential political question for Arendt is not, What is your opinion of the issue? but rather, How did you *form* your opinion of the issue? Opinions, that is, call for individual responsibility: because we form them and don't simply "have" them, we are accountable for them. We cannot outsource the responsibility for them to some higher authority like a teacher, preacher, or prophet. In order for our position to be genuine, we have to actively form it, even if we do so by turning in part to the teachings of someone we trust, respect, or fear. If our opinions echo those teachings, they are still *our* opinions as long as we have formed them and are responsible for them. Otherwise, they might as well be mere memes, reactions, or ideologies channeled through us from some other authority.

When our opinions result in decisions that have implications for others in our political community, we make political judgments. We are responsible for these judgments even more than our opinions. Political judgments, Arendt argued, come with a level of responsibility above that of opinions: the responsibility for others who are, or might as well be, strangers to us. Whereas with opinions we are responsible for actively forming them for ourselves—like a painting, poem, or pie we might make for ourselves—political judgments come with the additional responsibility of having to answer to others in some way, shape, or form for our judgments. It's the difference between making a pie for ourselves and making a pie to share with others. You have to answer for it, so to speak, while still having a responsibility to yourself.

For Arendt, political judgment, like making food to share, is therefore always a communal activity. There is no such thing as a solitary or private political judgment, for political judgments by their very nature concern other people, not just yourself, and make you responsible to others. Others, if given the opportunity, will want to know if you considered *their* standpoint, *their* perspective, *their* view of the matter. They will want to know if you considered how their lives might be affected by your judgment. Just as making a pie to share calls for you to consider the tastes and dietary needs of those for whom you are baking, so making a political judgment calls for us to consider the positions, perspectives, and existence of others who might end up having a share, for better or for worse, in the judgment.

This said, considering an issue from the standpoints of others is not simply to empathize with them. If I am making a pie to share with others, my goal should not be to somehow actually acquire their tastes and lose my own. Rather, my goal should be to keep my own tastes while considering the tastes and needs of others. Empathy in politics can too easily become a mode of feeling sorry for others, trying to momentarily acquire their "tastes" and identify with them. While the ability to feel with others is an important political skill, empathy can go only so far; as the rock artist Tom Petty sings, "You don't know how it feels to be me." That's why political judgments call for more than empathy; they call for the capacity to think for yourself as you work to see a matter how others see it.[22]

Let's briefly consider one controversial political issue as an example. "Stop and frisk" is the practice where a police officer who stops a person he or she deems suspicious will, prior to making an arrest (if an arrest is made at all), run his or her hands over the person's garments to check for concealed weapons or other potentially dangerous or illegal paraphernalia. If you look up the pros and cons of the practice online, you will find pros such as it's an effective form of "proactive community policing" or arguments that its intent is to "prevent a crime from taking place." The cons are typically put in constitutional terms: for example, that the US Constitution prohibits "unwarranted search and seizure" or that "stop and frisk" constitutes an invasion of privacy. You will also find some arguments that it is practiced in discriminatory manner, violating the equal-protection clause of the Constitution.[23]

These are all relevant issues, but note how the debate over "stop and frisk," so defined, is limited to two general perspectives: the effectiveness of the practice versus its legality as a police practice. This is, in fact, a quite restricted way of judging a practice that entails far more than questions of effectiveness or law—it also involves intimate issues of *fear* and *danger* for both police and the people they apprehend; of *trust* and *distrust* between police and people; of *systems* that regulate where police patrol and therefore are more likely to apprehend "suspicious" persons; of *statistics* about inequities with respect to black males in the US court and prison systems; and of, quite literally, *touch* between one person and another. To deem the issue of "stop and frisk" as only a matter of weighing "effectiveness" versus "legality" is to severely short-circuit our political judgment. It is to limit our intellect and imagination to the perspectives of engineers and lawyers, as if they are the only ones whose knowledge really counts.

The Poetry of Judgment

The Polish poet Adam Zagajewski has suggested that in making political judgments we learn to play with adjectives. In a short essay called "In Defense of Adjectives," Zagajewski, who grew up in authoritarian Poland, notes that what sets free people apart from those who live in totalitarian countries is, of all things, the freedom to use adjectives to describe events, objects, and issues. "Nouns and verbs are enough for soldiers and leaders of totalitarian countries," he writes. "The adjective," by contrast, "is the indispensable guarantor of the individuality of people and things."[24] For example, in a totalitarian country, people would only be allowed to say—at best—"The police stopped and frisked the suspect." In being able to say, "That practice is unconstitutional," we are in a far better place. Nevertheless, even in our free, liberal, and open society, the vocabulary of our political judgments remains remarkably restricted. Whether we are arguing about police practices, health care, immigration, abortion rights, or gun rights, we seem to have little else than the language of the engineer, lawyer, or moralist: it does or doesn't work, it is or isn't constitutional, it's good or bad. This, in fact, makes us quite vulnerable to adept demagogues, propagandists, and media personalities who come along with a focus group–tested vocabulary—*terrific! tremendous! evil! stupid! weak! dangerous!*—that nevertheless seems to be the stuff of the bold and the brave when compared to the language of engineers, lawyers, and moralists.

"What color is to painting, the adjective is to language," Zagajewski writes. In order to develop our capacity for political judgment, we need to learn to think about particular issues with adjectives that go beyond *effective/ineffective, legal/illegal,* or *good/bad*. Political judgment calls us to use our intellect and imagination to consider issues, events, and objects from a copious range of adjectives: *able, acrobatic, adept, admired, aggravating, agile, appropriate, awkward, babyish, bewitched, bleak, bold, bossy, bright, calculating, candid, cheap, clueless, colorless, colossal, damaged, dapper, dim, discrete, dopey, elementary, enchanting, ethical, exhausted, faint, feisty, filthy, flashy, foolhardy, frank, gleaming, glum, grandiose, grotesque, gullible, hasty, hefty, hospitable, hot, humiliating, icky, imaginative, impressionable, infatuated, insidious, jagged, jovial, juicy, jumpy, juvenile, kindhearted, klutzy, knowledgeable, knotty, kooky, legitimate, limp, linear, livid, loving, luminous, made-up, mediocre, meek, melodic, messy, mushy, naive, narrow, noxious, numb, nutty, oblong, orderly, original, overlooked, passionate, pesky, pessimistic, piercing, punctual, pushy, queasy, quirky, quixotic, quizzical, radiant, raw, realistic, rigid, robust, rotten, salty, scary, scornful, sentimental, serpentine, shabby, shallow, sturdy, sugary, tangible, teeming, tempting, thick, thorny, trifling, trusty, unkempt, unruly, unselfish, usable, useless, valid, velvety, virtuous, vivacious, vivid, warm, weary, wee, weepy, weighty, wobbly, wretched, yawning, youthful, yummy, zany, zealous, zesty*. In other words, to judge the matter politically calls us to try out a generous range of words so as to *think*—to think with others, and as much as possible to think the particular.

"Judgment," the eighteenth-century German philosopher Immanuel Kant wrote in a book on "aesthetic" or artistic judgment that Arendt frequently referred to, "is the faculty of thinking the particular as contained under the universal."[25] Thinking in and of itself, when done well, is an extraordinary act, drawing on learning as well as life experience, the opinions of others, imagination, feelings, and sentiments to frame issues, ask questions, pursue consequences, and fend off flights of fancy that might mislead or otherwise derail us. But thinking the particular, as Arendt argued, is even more extraordinary, as mathematicians and particle physicists now recognize. Given a mass of variously moving particles in a disorderly system, it is one thing to mathematically predict the path of most of the particles most of the time; this is what probability and statistics are all about. It is quite another thing to calculate what a particular particle will do at a precise time. Indeed, it may be impossible. But judgment puts this general kind of demand before us all the time: *thinking the particular*. We have occasion to so judge whenever we face particular problems or opportunities at particular times—a troublesome coworker, a budget deficit, a bad cop, a terror attack, a marriage proposal, weighing job offers, or choosing among candidates.

To think the particular, Kant noted, we often rely on adjectives and nouns in their "universal" capacity. *Beauty, goodness, fairness, justice, evil, equity, courage, right, wrong*—the list of universals is nearly as long as the list of adjectives above. This, however, does not mean that using universals in our judgments is not without troubles. Indeed, most of the universals we work with are difficult to rigorously define. "Beauty is in the eye of the beholder" is one way we admit this difficulty in our everyday talk with regard to the universal concept of beauty.

For some, the difficulty of rigorously defining universals leads them to doubt the validity of universals at all, such that "beauty is in the eye of the beholder" becomes "beauty is *only* in the eye of the beholder," and even to declare that "beauty" is a null and void concept, just another metaphysical fantasy. Except, we still regularly judge things beautiful or not beautiful, do we not? Except, we are clearly better off with beauty, are we not? Except, almost all of life's treasured concepts—happiness, peace, tranquility, fulfillment, victory, fame, glory, and so on—don't easily meet rigorous standards of philosophical analysis either, right? We know more about our life, our world, and what matters to us than we could ever defend with quasi-mathematical logical precision. Universals need not be reducible to precise formulas to be useful, meaningful, and powerful.

Still, if universals are inevitable in our everyday thinking, so is the inadequacy of any one universal to sum up our thoughts about most particular things. If any particular thing, event, person, or issue is in the least bit engaging, a single universal won't do. Rather, we need multiple categories to get our head around the matter, and we often do so in ways that leave us with some tensions: "That movie was way too violent, but the way it showed the horrors of war was so realistic"; "He's a good kid, even if all that extra energy gets him into trouble"; "The governor says she's tough on crime, but her policies only target poor minorities," and so on. Thinking the particular, or judgment, leaves us stitching together universals and particulars with *but, and, when, if,* and other means of qualifying, hedging, limiting, or even contradicting our judgments. Such stitching together, of course, can be a means of equivocating or deceiving, but it need not be. (And let's not forget that the difference between equivocation and an honest judgment is a matter of judgment too!) Indeed, stitching together universals and particulars is an essential part of the grammar of judging in a world loaded with complexities, contradictions, and fuzzy and wicked problems.

Arendt suggested that the most common way we go about stitching together universals and particulars is not by saying things like "stop and frisk" is unjust or just, but rather by *telling stories*.[26] Most of our judgments, whatever they are about, take place within and are part of stories we tell others about events, people, or predicaments. The retired men who gather at the coffee shop each morning to talk about the news and shoot the bull are in fact making daily, morning judgments in the form of stories they tell one another; so too with the college students who chitchat at the library about classes, classmates, and last weekend's happenings.

Judgments not only stitch together universals and particulars, they also do not follow strict procedures or methods of application. This, more than any other quality of political judgment, makes them qualitatively different from rigorous mathematical or logical reasoning, and it is why judgments are essentially *social*.[27] Mathematical and logical reasoning depend on laws and rules that can operate in isolation from people. The law of noncontradiction, for example, is valid for a person living in complete isolation, and it can operate in a machine as easily as in the mind of the solitary philosopher. The validity of political judgments is different. If I judge a policy "unjust" or a civic celebration "beautiful," the validity of my judgment will depend on the agreement of others, or, if not their agreement, at least their acknowledgement that the way in which I went about making my judgment is legitimate. If everyone I meet disagrees with my judgment or thinks I have no real grounds for making it—perhaps it is a policy I demonstrate that I don't understand, or an event about which I seem ignorant—then no law or formula can save my judgment from ill repute. This is because political judgments are first and foremost designed to evaluate and make sense of things with others in the world, rather than to conform to logical procedures. To fully appreciate the art of political judgment, we have to be able to appreciate *reasons without strict procedures,* which is to say that we have to believe it is possible for there to be good reasons that nevertheless can't be converted into a logical blueprint.[28]

The Problem with Procedures

Some four hundred years ago, at the dawn of the epoch we now call "modern," connoisseurship, judgment, and even wisdom were attacked as unreliable by an influential group of thinkers who became proponents of what they called the "new science" (*nova scientia*). This new science sometimes looked like physics, sometimes like mathematics, sometimes like philosophy, and sometimes like logic; in any case, it was premised on the idea that we need to get beyond dubious opinions, questionable personal judgments, and even everyday language to come up with strict rules and procedures that will lead to certain conclusions that can be deemed, like answers on a math quiz, either "correct" or "incorrect." As René Descartes, a major proponent for the new science, wrote in the 1620s in his influential *Rules for the Direction of the Mind*, knowers—true knowers—needed to "reject all such merely probable knowledge and make it a rule to trust only what is completely known and incapable of being doubted."[29] As such, Descartes suggested that the first task in knowing is purging the mind: true knowledge begins by wiping your mental hard drive of all former impressions, opinions, and judgments and replacing them with logically valid rules and procedures.[30]

Descartes, to his credit, understood that his "new science" would not in fact help us with many of life's questions: Is this person's accomplishment worth public celebration? Is this melody pleasing to my ears? Is this a compelling policy? Or, is this person fit for political office? All such questions—and a myriad of others—demand judgment calls, not rules-based, mathematical-like calculations. But Descartes wanted a world where the power of such "contingent" judgments are limited, for they can always be doubted, challenged, questioned, and indeed even regretted. As much as possible, he argued, we should try to approach as many of life's questions as we can as "rationally" as possible. He thought strict logical rules and methods could be used to order our disorderly world not so much by eliminating unique particulars—no culture or civilization could do that—but by regulating what gets to *count* as a valid statement about particulars.

This was far from a mere flight of fancy. The "new science" took hold, such that today we are quietly but powerfully told that for judgments to really "count" in public policy, they must be rational and quantifiable. On top of this, there is a whole school of influential modern philosophers (as well as a set of very powerful modern institutions) that says our judgments might be fine and good as "personal" judgments or "mere opinions," but they are not worth the serious attention of others until they are sufficiently methodical, rules-based, and rigorous—otherwise they do not merit paying much attention to.[31]

This position is sometimes called "proceduralism." Proceduralists insist that in order for our judgments to carry real public weight, the particular must be contained under the universal in a predictable, orderly manner. Otherwise, they say, our judgments might as well be mere expressions of "taste," as when I express my preference for chocolate over strawberry ice cream. Or, more seriously, our judgments may be seen as deeply held "convictions" that must be "respected" but not allowed to be authoritative, as when I, as a citizen, strongly oppose going to war against a particular nation on religious grounds.

Proceduralists tend to argue that because we as citizens cannot agree on a whole range of controversial issues—from abortion to drug policies to the death penalty to war—the only viable means of creating broad consensus in society is by agreeing on the rules of political decision making.[32] Proceduralism is therefore designed to construct a layer of consensus beneath the cacophony of opinions, attitudes, values, and judgments that exist in modern societies. It is aimed at legitimacy, making adjudicating institutions like the courts and elections credible when, supposedly, we just can't agree as a society on basic values. The notion is similar to the way we often think about rules in sports: the game is legitimate as long as the rules are followed, regardless of how people play the game.

Now, rules are indeed essential to politics; they provide shared standards of fairness and equity that underlie our sense of justice. But the problems with proceduralism as a full-blown political program (which is what it can aspire to be in modern liberalism) are significant. To begin with, we don't make everyday political judgments by looking to rules—the political game, so to speak, is far more open and fluid than football or basketball. Proceduralism therefore implicitly, and sometimes explicitly, undermines the everyday political judgments of people by rendering them insufficiently "rational." Moreover, there are all sorts of cases where proceduralism works to strip people of the power to do good to neighbors, fellow citizens, and the nonhuman world by putting up legal or quasi-legal barriers.

Proceduralism is tailor-made for what Arendt called the "rule of nobody": the impersonal bureaucratic structures that, among other things, substitute "behavior" for "action."[33] In a proceduralist frame, as long as we conform to a preset pattern of behavior—keep your place in line, check the correct box, or have the right tags on your car—you are no better, no worse, and no different than anybody else in the system. A proceduralist may argue that that's the point, and that it's a democratic point. The "rule of nobody" is a "rule of anybody," as anybody is allowed in the political game as long as they conform to the standards.

But to be "anybody," Arendt worried, carries two grave risks, both of which have come to roost anew in the twenty-first century. First, she argued that to be "anybody" is to approach being "nobody," and to be nobody is precisely the precondition necessary for the loss of our peculiar political identity as unique and individual actors in a common world. Politics, Arendt argued, is not for "anybody" who conforms to the standards or falls within the laws—it's for *everybody*. Second, she suggested that the "rule of anybody" is quite vulnerable to ethno-nationalism and racism. Since legitimacy would be premised on conformity to rules, those rules could quite easily get trumped by categories, types, or identities.[34] Indeed, this has historically been the case in US liberalism, which for well over a century nurtured legal categories that excluded minorities from full participation in political life based on race, and it is clearly at issue in new forms of ethno-nationalism and racism today.

Here let's consider again the police helicopter over that beach in Southern California. As the paddle boarders played on the water, ignorant of their predicament, the deputy hovered overhead waiting for formal authorization to do what anyone with good judgment could see was the most pressing and urgent thing to do: notify the paddle boarders immediately! The deputy implicitly approached the paddle boarders as "anybodies" rather than particular "somebodies," and he himself behaved like a "nobody," for anybody could have behaved just as he did, following protocol. While the abilities of the deputy to follow protocol in the midst of somebody else's life-threatening crisis might, from the vantage point of proceduralists and law enforcement officials, be seen as an excellent job of following procedure, I suspect from the perspective of many other people (myself included), it looks more like a systematic attempt to root out common sense from the very people officially charged with protecting human life in moments of danger. Moreover, there is the unsettling question that we have faced too often with law enforcement: What if the paddle boarders looked like they didn't "belong" on the beach? Would they even be "anybodies"?

Proceduralism not only risks being an exclusionary force, it is often used for the purposes of CYA (covering your ass), circumventing judgment at the point where it is most called for. It's true, judgment inevitably is a kind of wager: in making a judgment, we wager that it is justified as true or false, just or unjust, fitting or not fitting, popular or unpopular, or defensible or indefensible according to some criteria. There is always an implicit or explicit audience for our judgments, a jury of sorts (which could simply be ourselves) before whom we justify our judgments. Proceduralism is an attempt to minimize risk, with formulas taking the place of thinking the particular and rules taking the place of cooperation, trust, and other forms of social solidarity. What's wrong with that? Well, the world—above all, the political world—will not fully cooperate. We've never been able to live up to the dream of the "new science." Rational rules are integral to the legitimacy of certain modern institutions like science, law enforcement, or education; however, they do not characterize the way most people at most times go about making judgments about movies, kids, big purchases, laws, or policies.

Hence the crucial problem with proceduralism. Because it is rules-based, it can only approach people as "types" or within predetermined categories. This can lead to the exclusion of some of us from vital institutions, practices, and opportunities, as every predetermined category is a means of both inclusion and exclusion. If proceduralism functions as the be-all and end-all of political society, as it too often does in modern rules- and rights-based liberalism, it will end up functioning as a means of enforcing an inclusionary order that is inherently exclusionary. To be sure, political liberalism's great accomplishment has been to open the field of politics to more and more types, but this has been accomplished at a cost. This opening up comes with the condition that political actors, to be seen as legitimate at all, behave in such a way as to fit within the already established rules. They thus appear within the liberal order less as individual people and more as a type of person. Arendt wanted to push precisely against this typological and preset-rules approach in her insistence that politics was not for "anybody" but for everybody. The only "rule" is that you show up, speak, act, and judge with others, without forcing your way through. The only rule, that is, is that you act politically.

Judgments can be justifiable without being mathematizable. As Arendt wrote, "Judgments are not arrived at by either deduction or induction; in short, they have nothing in common with logical operations."[35] This is not to say the exact opposite, that procedures somehow invalidate judgments, that the only "true" or "authentic" judgments are those that cannot be articulated with rational rules. Again, there is a place for procedures, logic, and rules in some realms of judgment—especially in halls of justice like the courts, police departments, and parliaments. Nevertheless, these are particular realms of judgment and hardly constitute a template for all forms of political judgment, as some would have it. Proceduralism is an institutional logic more than a political one.

Political judgments tend to follow guidelines or "norms" without following strict procedures or rules. We *form* opinions to *make* judgments, and in making political judgments, we help make and remake the common world in which we live together. It was not just my "mere opinion" to stop at the crosswalk and let the pedestrian cross. And I did not do it because it was the law. Rather, it was my formed opinion that pedestrians should get the right of way because they are far more physically vulnerable than drivers, and it was my judgment to stop, and I acted accordingly. My judgment and action, though isolated and seemingly insignificant, was in fact a consequential judgment in the ongoing making of the community in which I live and work. (If I had judged otherwise—maybe honked my horn and raised my middle finger—that crosswalk might mean something different to that pedestrian for some time to come.) And so, in politics, we make judgments, and in making political judgments we participate in the ongoing work of making meaning and making our common world.

This chapter began with a story of a judgment call. Confronted with a potentially deadly situation, a deputy chose to take the time to follow protocol rather than break with procedure and act immediately. It's clear by now that I don't think it was a good judgment. Jurisdiction be damned! Get those paddle boarders out of the water! Nevertheless, with respect to the larger point of this chapter, the particular judgment that this particular deputy made matters far less to me than the fact that it was a judgment call and, even more, a political judgment, as it concerned how things were to go between people, and therefore what kind of "common world" they would inhabit together.

Political judgments tend to reverberate through society because we, each of us, are part of networks of relations with strangers that bear upon our common world.[36] In the instance of the deputy and the shark-surrounded paddle boarders, everything turned out all right; therefore, we might not even see the deputy's judgment as a political judgment. Yet, had the sharks behaved otherwise and the deputy waited too long, then surely we would be questioning the deputy's judgment, and probably the protocols of the sheriff's department. Or had the deputy ignored protocol and warned the paddle boarders only to be reprimanded and fined for doing so by his supervisors, at the very least the deputy and his family members would certainly become aware of his political relation to his superiors. So too a decision of a driver to not stop for a pedestrian crossing the street that results in an accident, or the judgment of the Supreme Court to count corporations as individuals and money as "free speech," or the directive from Starbucks to stop offering plastic straws—such judgments, big and small, become political, as they each entail common concerns that shape how things are to go among people, and reverberate to make and remake the common world we inhabit.

But even my judgment here about the actions of the deputy is political, for I do not know nor am I related to any of the persons involved. I am not thinking as an intimate but as a citizen. I approach the instance as a spectator who is, on the one hand, a stranger to the situation and, on the other, invested in it. What if that were *me* paddle boarding? What if *I* were the sheriff? Political judgment, Arendt has said, entails "the ability to see things not only from one's own point of view but in the perspective of all those who happen to be present."[37] It requires the "enlarged mentality" that is part of all sagacious spectating: seeing things from a variety of viewpoints and in different ways. The best way to go about such seeing, Arendt suggested, is by telling ourselves the story of a particular event, situation, or issue from a variety of perspectives.[38]

To be sure, some people are better than others at seeing political events and telling their stories from different viewpoints, just as some people are better than others at seeing all the ins and outs of a baseball game or a choir performance. Nevertheless, we can all learn to see things more fully by practicing. Judgment, Arendt reminds us, cannot be taught deductively; there is no "judgment for dummies" book out there that can make you a better judge of political events, baseball games, or choir performances. You can develop your capacity to judge only by judging; it is a practice, not a subject matter.

So, I invite you to start practicing. I am offering my judgment of the deputy's actions here to you. What do *you* think about his actions? Moreover, I am offering *my judgment* to you to judge. In certain situations, I want police to prioritize people over protocol. Now, I don't want law enforcement to make a habit of violating protocol. Rule of law and the separation of powers—both basic principles of republican democracy—depend on law enforcement officials following procedures and being predictable. Nevertheless, I think there should be exceptions to the rule, and the shark's tale is easily one such exception. If you are persuaded by my argument, you may join me in my judgment, and together—who knows?—we may someday realize some sort of modest change in police practices. But regardless of such "effects," you and I are now engaged together, through the remarkable medium of print, in political judgments.

FOUR

Lies, Damned Lies, and Politics

In 2018, news broke that a major political campaign had created various fake social media sites in order to mislead and divide supporters of the opposing candidate. The operation drew on research from the social sciences and military-grade information- and psychological-warfare tactics to spread misinformation, create scandal, and sow confusion among the electorate. It even got some special help from a major social media company. No, this was not the Trump campaign or its supporters, and the political operatives were not Russian-backed. Rather, this was the successful campaign of Doug Jones, the Democratic US Senate candidate who in 2017 faced off against Republican Roy Moore in a bitter special election in Alabama. Jones's campaign decided to test information-warfare tactics on Alabama's conservative citizens. In the words of one participant in the social media disinformation campaign, some felt that Democrats needed "to fight fire with fire."[1]

Any discussion of politics has to reckon with lying in politics. This much is certainly true: politicians have long lived tricky lives; they often are caught between their private positions and their public positions, what goes on behind the scenes and what happens on stage, what they believe and what they do. The lies of politicians are a major reason politics has such a bad name. Today, thanks to digital media, lies are being quite literally programmed into political campaigns. Lying in politics is becoming not only systemic, but quite literally automatic.

Hannah Arendt spent much of her career wrestling with the relationship between truth, lies, and politics. In an essay she wrote by the name of "Truth and Politics," she seemed to argue that truth is inconsequential for politics: truth is for philosophy and politics is about people's opinions, and never the two shall meet. But Arendt's position is in fact subtler than that, and it is this subtlety that I want to consider in this chapter as way of better understanding the place of truth and lies in politics in the twenty-first century. There has been much concern in recent years about fake news, disinformation, manipulation, manufactured realities, and the like, and for good reason. But for all the alarm, few have asked why and how lies matter in politics, and, more broadly, what the role of truth is in our political life.

The rise of fact-checking organizations at universities and news outlets has in some ways confused the situation further. Fact-checking groups will examine a politician's statements to check them for lies, mistruths, and half-truths. The *Washington Post*, for example, counts, classifies, and tabulates the lies of prominent politicians, resulting in a score they measure in "Pinocchios."[2] Other sites will give politicians an overall "grade" on truth-telling.

Fact-checking does us a public service by calling out politicians and members of the government when they mislead or outright lie. However, there are two big problems with these fact-checking efforts—problems that I hope will be apparent to you by this chapter's end. First, they tend to treat all lies as created equal. They operate in the spirit of the great Enlightenment philosopher Immanuel Kant, who insisted that *a lie is a lie is a lie*, plain and simple, and casted doubt on whether we should even allow ourselves to harbor the concept of the "white" or innocent lie.[3] Second, and more significant, they focus on the statements of individual politicians, ignoring the fact that the worst sorts of lying in politics come not from political personalities, but from organizations.

Indeed, if there is one big thing we can learn from Arendt about lying in politics, it is that not all lies are created equal; some are far more destructive than others. Therefore, we need to learn to distinguish a lie from a lie from a lie, to separate ordinary lies in politics from habitual ones and extraordinary, organized ones. Our tendency, Arendt noted, is to do the opposite: we want to lump together things that appear alike, even when they are very different. To the untrained eye, for example, most mushrooms look alike. But mushroom hunters know that not all mushrooms are created equal: some can nourish you while others can poison you. Arendt frequently stressed the importance of making distinctions among things that appear alike. Because politics takes place in the "space of appearances" rather than the hidden recesses of our souls, Arendt argued that we need to train our eyes to not only see politics where we may not expect to see it, but to discern the differences between different political phenomena that may initially look alike. Otherwise we will mistake the political actions that can nourish us for political phenomena that threaten to poison us. Even more dangerous, we might mistake political phenomena that poison us for those that nourish us.

The challenge of making distinctions in politics is magnified by the fact that political phenomena, unlike mushrooms, are capable of transforming in an instant from one thing to another, as when, for example, street protests degenerate into unrestrained violence, or police activities fall into acts of official bullying. How do we tell the difference between such shifty political things? Arendt would say that we need to learn to watch and think. Or better, as we saw in the last chapter, we need to learn the skill of political judgment and apply it not only to political issues, but to political actions and political discourse.

In this chapter I invite you to do some thinking about the different kinds of lying in politics. Like the rest of this book, I am going to be asking you to think qualitatively rather than quantitatively or in terms of strict categories. I will argue that in one sense, lying in politics is really no different than lying in everyday life. The truth, as uncomfortable as it may be, is that we are all frequently less than fully forthcoming with the truth, and we all recognize that some lies are qualitatively different from others. Yet, I will go on to argue that in another sense politicians are unlike the rest of us deceivers, in that the context and consequence of their lies are different. I therefore distinguish between three basic kinds of lying in politics: what I call "ordinary lies," "habitual lies," and, following Arendt, "organized lying." I argue that while each are forms of deception, they are *structurally* different from one another, and that it is critical—indeed, crucial—that we see the differences. Otherwise, we run the grave risk of mistaking lies meant to destroy us for those simply meant to deceive us.[4] The gist of the chapter, therefore, is that not all lies are created equal—a lie is not always a lie, plain and simple.

It's True, Everybody Is Untrue

Around one hundred years ago, one of the most famous scholars of his era, the German social theorist Max Weber, gave a lecture in Munich called "Politics as a Vocation," his own defense of politics. In the lecture, he argued that there were big differences among the "occasional" politician, the "civil servant," and the "professional" politician. We are all, he claimed, occasional politicians, inasmuch as we all may vote, circulate a pamphlet or petition, or engage in a political conversation with our friends. Civil servants are government officials whose job it is to execute the policies of elected officials. And professional politicians are what we think of simply as "politicians." Weber described professional politicians as a different breed than the occasional politician and civil servant: for the professional, politics is a calling, a *vocation*, and with this comes certain burdens and responsibilities—above all, the burden of power and the responsibility to lead. These burdens and responsibilities, Weber further argued, necessarily force the professional politician into some awkward spots, especially when dealing with the truth. He said that professional politicians, unlike the rest of us, are responsible not only for their actions but for the "foreseeable results" of those actions.[5] This means always calculating what you say and do in terms of the effects. Hence, he concluded, people of "high moral standing" who focus only on whether or not they do the "right" thing, like always telling the truth, will be poor politicians.[6] To be a responsible politician, in other words, is to *not* be directly responsible to the *truth*, or so Weber suggested.[7]

It does not take a great intellectual like Weber to conclude that politicians have a convoluted relationship with the truth. Yet, we *all* do, don't we? Whether we're talking to our intimate friends or casual acquaintances, even the most honest among us are not always forthcoming with the truth. Think about all the ways we steer around the truth in our everyday interactions: One rainy morning as I start my car I realize that I am almost out of gas; I get halfway to the gas station and realize that I left my wallet behind, so I have to turn around; on the way back to the gas station my engine dies, and I have to trudge down the street in the rain with a gas can to rescue myself. When I get to the counter at the gas station and the clerk asks me how my morning is going, I simply say, "Fine." The answer, of course, is a plain untruth—some would even say an outright lie. And yet I do not feel any guilt about my answer. The clerk's question is kind, but it is a formality; it is best just to say "fine" and move on. It's true, I am not forthcoming about how my morning is going. I am just trying to manage the situation and move on.

We sometimes lie or mislead because we are communal creatures. For better and for worse, part of our social nature is that we engage in what the sociologist Erving Goffman has called "face work."[8] We are aware not only of ourselves, but of the fact that others see us and make judgments about us. They form an "image" of us. Depending on the situation, Goffman observed, we wear different "faces": my face before the store clerk is different than my face before my daughter as I help her do her homework; the clerk's face before me is different than her face with her daughter; and our daughters' faces vary, depending on if they are at school, with friends, with their siblings, or with their grandparents. If someone wore the same "face" all the time, irrespective of the situation, we would think they are socially inept!

A big part of "face work" is how we navigate what we disclose about ourselves. This includes, strictly speaking, forms of deception. When I tell the store clerk that my morning is going fine, I am deceiving her. Why do I deceive her? For a variety of reasons. I act deceptively to save myself from slight embarrassment, but also to save her from the awkwardness of having to respond to an honest answer like "horrible." I also do it for the sake of social efficiency: there is a line behind me and no one in the store likely wants to hear my morning saga. And my answer is, in part, just automatic: store clerks ritualistically ask how things are going and I, as a matter of unthinking habit, typically respond with "fine."

David Nyberg argues in his book *The Varnished Truth* that if there is one basic truth about our everyday lives, it is that "even under ordinary circumstances, when the chance of getting caught is not great, almost all of us are willing to deceive others or deceive ourselves, with untormented conscience."[9] Indeed, the oath we take in a court of law to "tell the truth, the whole truth, and nothing but the truth" is a formal acknowledgement of the fact that for us to tell the truth, the whole truth, and nothing but the truth is the extraordinary exception rather than the rule of our everyday lives. Those who say otherwise are deceiving themselves.

In fact, as Nyberg suggests, a social existence in which everyone always told the truth, the whole truth, and nothing but the truth would be intolerable. There are all kinds of daily interactions we have with friends, family, coworkers, and strangers where the truth and nothing but the truth could be told but isn't, for the simple reason that telling the unvarnished truth would be to miss the point of the interaction altogether. To be sure, we could pat ourselves on the back for being straight-shooting truth tellers, but everyone else would be trying to figure out how to avoid us.

Like a flu shot, in small doses lying makes us, collectively, more immune to certain kinds of social stressors. Lying is a way in which we inoculate ourselves against the demands and responsibilities of truth telling. Truth telling calls for vulnerability, recollection, the right words, and sufficient time. It is not always easy, and sometimes can be quite disruptive and difficult. While not a matter of strict cost/benefit analysis, we do have to count the costs of telling the truth, and there are more than a few situations where we might conclude it is just not worth it.

Politics is no exception to this social rule. The fact is, while we say that we want politicians and government officials to be straight-shooting truth tellers, we often don't, and often for good reason. Most of us are not, for example, all that interested in hearing about the complicated negotiations a political representative is having with various persons and parties about a piece of legislation; we just want to know where she stands on the matter and hear her promise to get the job done. Likewise, at the local school board meeting, few of us would be interested in hearing the superintendent take time at the meeting to frankly tell us about the ways that his digestion problems at one point got in the way of his work; we just want him to get his work done, and if he's behind, we'd rather be spared the details and just be assured that he'll catch up. So we may say that we want our political leaders to be nothing but forthcoming truth tellers, but we all recognize that politicians and government officials, like the rest of us, have to manage "face"—frequently by navigating around the truth, the whole truth, and nothing but the truth. If they didn't, we'd likely deem them not only socially inept but also politically ineffective.

In this most basic way, then, politicians are no different from the rest of us. Max Weber was wrong to suggest that they are, that "professional politicians," unlike the rest of us, have a special calling to untruth in the name of "responsibility." Weber said this because he assumed that politics is ultimately a means by which people in power rule over others through an admixture of law and violence; he just added "deception" to the brew.[10] But if politics is not a form of, or front for, violence, and instead is a human phenomenon in which people freely interact with fellow citizens about matters of common concern, then we should resist creating extraordinary exceptions for politicians, or for ourselves. We should recognize that all social phenomena require "face work."

Being Truthful

At the very same time, we need to recognize that that untruths, half-truths, and lies often tempt us as an easy way out of uncomfortable or otherwise sticky situations. A student cheats because he's too hung over to get his work done; he then lies to his professor about it when he is caught; and then lies again to his parents when they find out about it. At each descending step, the student follows what he takes to be the path of least resistance, only to find that he's made his life significantly harder for himself. Clearly politicians all too often do the same thing: their lies can be a matter of "convenience" rather than social cooperation. And they often dig a deeper hole for themselves, making the matter worse, not better.

Moreover, every time we lie or deceive, no matter the reason, we risk losing credibility and undermining trust. This is true even with the "white lie." Parents experience this all the time with children who fudge: How, they will ask their child, can I trust you the next time if you are lying to me now? But children experience this just as much with their parents. When parents are caught in forms of deception—be it about Santa Claus or a dark family secret—it is natural for children to wonder how they can trust adults. So too, every time a politician is caught in an act of deception, they risk losing some authority. Deception, duplicity, and lying may be common in our social lives, but we still value the qualities of honesty and integrity because we know that unregulated, unprincipled, willy-nilly deception is a recipe for undependability and uncertainty. Those whom we trust as honest and dependable are not so much straight-shooting truth tellers as they are thoughtful people, mindful of the social situation, the needs of others, and the stakes of their speech. They are, in a word, trustworthy.

Here it is helpful to draw a distinction between "telling the truth" and "being truthful." Imagine with me being in an extremely awful situation: You are a German in Nazi Germany. You are strongly opposed the Nazis, so you join the underground resistance. You and a group of others members of the resistance conspire to assassinate Hitler, but your plot fails and you are apprehended, arrested, and thrown in prison, where day after day you are questioned by interrogators about the resistance. They want names, places, and dates. Instead, you give them the names of people you know are dead, lead them to places that are empty, and make up dates. That is, each day you are interrogated, you lie extravagantly. Are you telling the truth? No. Are you being *truthful* to the cause of the resistance and to the millions of victims of Nazi violence? Clearly, yes.

Just such a thing happened to Dietrich Bonhoeffer, a pastor and well-known theologian in Germany in the 1930s and '40s. Bonhoeffer was opposed to the Nazis from the get-go, and soon joined the resistance movement. He ended up participating in a plot to assassinate Hitler. The plot failed and Bonhoeffer was imprisoned. In prison, he was regularly interrogated, and he regularly lied to his interrogators in order to protect other members of the resistance. From prison Bonhoeffer wrote about the matter. He noted that he had been told for years that "telling the truth" was the utmost responsibility of any truly ethical person, and yet here he was lying daily and elaborately.[11]

Bonhoeffer wrote that, though lying, he was nevertheless "being truthful"—for being truthful, he argued, entails seeing one's words in light of the whole situation: "The truthful word is not in itself constant; it is as much alive as life itself."[12] If we detach the truth from its implications for others, if we tell the truth without considering to whom we are speaking and in what context, then "this truth has only the appearance of truth, but lacks its essential character."[13] In other words, it is possible for someone to say what is true without being truthful. It is obvious that if Bonhoeffer told the truth, the whole truth, and nothing but the truth to his interrogators, he would have betrayed his friends and done horrible harm to unknown others. For him, lying was a way of being truthful, and of being trustworthy.

Trust, fidelity, solidarity, care—these are the reasons we should tell, or not tell, the truth. Lying becomes a plague in our lives not because it violates the truth, but because it violates others. Indeed, great harm can be done by lying. It can foster profound relational dysfunction and woeful forms of self-deception and self-destruction. Abusive family systems are built on more than physical violence—they can be built on the violence of lies. Self-deception can lead to self-harm. Trauma, psychological disorders, and even physical illness can result from lies. Careers can be lost; marriages can fail; friendships can be ended. For all the ways in which we are untrue in our daily interactions, lying is no casual matter.

The difference between lies we can defend as being consistent with being truthful and lies that do damage is clearly not a matter of quantity. It is not about how *frequently* we lie. Rather, it is a *qualitative* difference. Lying and truth telling are both like physical touch between two people: it is the quality of the touch that matters. Was it casual? forced? desired? welcome? unwelcome? unexpected? perfunctory? violent? Quantitatively speaking, a relatively healthy family might tabulate more lies in a given week than an unhealthy one. In fact, an abusive family system may put a great premium on telling the truth, the whole truth, and nothing but the truth, all toward the end of reinforcing the one big lie of the patriarch's infallible power.

So it is with lying in politics. We have to learn to see this issue qualitatively, not quantitatively. In this one respect, Weber was right: there is something qualitatively different about the lives of professional politicians. They typically work in very complex social situations involving a wide range and large number of different people with different interests, perspectives, and experiences. Therefore, the pressure on their "face work" is magnified. Moreover, they tend to work in public, or at least in semipublic; given that they act on the public stage, so to speak, the opportunities for deception are amplified. Finally, professional politicians wield more power than a lot of us. Therefore, the consequences of their duplicity can be great. Nevertheless, allowing for these differences, the gap between lying in our everyday lives and lying in the professional political arena is not as great as we often make it out to be. In both contexts we can be more or less truthful; in both contexts lies can be isolated or become systemic; and in both contexts the crucial issues are context, quality, and a trustworthiness, not sheer quantity, as the professional fact checkers too often imply.

Why Do Politicians Lie?

Why do politicians mislead us? Let's start by considering three valid, and even good, reasons. First, politicians can be loose with the whole truth because they have to speak to different constituencies with different interests. As such, they will say different things to different people. In my congressional district, for example, my representative may tell farmers that agriculture is his top priority, law enforcement officers that law enforcement is his top priority, working parents that health care is his top priority, and university administrators that education is his top priority. It is tempting to immediately object that all these things can't be true. He can only have one "top priority," right? Yet, I could imagine him responding that when agricultural legislation is on the floor, it is his top priority, and when health care legislation is on the floor, *that's* his top priority. To be sure, he would probably not go out of his way to tell each of his constituencies that he has other top priorities. "People don't want to hear that," he might say. "They just want to know that I have their concerns as a priority, and my job is to make clear that I do." Of course, my representative could well find himself someday in legislative negotiations where he has to choose between two or more of these "top priorities," in which case he may have some explaining to do, and may even be made to pay electorally. Regardless, one obvious reason that politicians can be less than straight shooters is that their job is to speak to various constituencies with different interests and expectations.

Another reason that politicians work around the truth is to keep the wheels of the political process greased. For example, consider the politician who, in order to get the pulse on an issue, tells her constituency she is "open minded" about an issue when she is really not. Or imagine a situation where she "plays nice" in public with another politician she despises, or where her staff writes letters in her name to her constituency. These are each examples of duplicity, yet none of them pains the conscience of the politician. Nor should they—it is all part of the work of keeping the political process running. At the same time, each of these examples of public deception could come back to bite the politician: some voters, for example, could really resent her "open-mindedness"; she could look like a fraud if news broke about just how much she despises the politician she glad-handed; and the office staff could make a big mistake in a ghostwritten letter. Here again we can see why politicians deceive and the risks they run as they do.

A third reason politicians lie is the one you might expect: to hide the truth. Politicians engage in "spin" and other forms of deception because they know that *the truth can hurt*. In some cases, deceiving or otherwise working around the truth can be readily justified, as when the lives or livelihoods of others would be risked or ruined by the truth. Politicians are frequently in positions of power where they have access to information that could damage others if it were made public; clearly, as Weber suggested, they may have a responsibility to lie in such situations. Still, politicians lie not only to protect others, but to save their own political hides. This is the sort of lying in politics that can justifiably earn our ire. Yet, Arendt might caution us about being too quick to judge, especially in cases where it is the private lives of politicians that are at issue.

There is no hard-and-fast line between the private and the public, but there is a line—for if nothing is to be kept private, nothing is really public either. The line between the public and the private, wherever it is placed, has a vital public function: it protects the integrity of the "public" by asserting that some things are *not* public. Paradoxically, to make all things public is no different than making all things private. For example, take the story of the 1990s dot-com millionaire Josh Harris. Having made his fortune in early webcasting, Harris decided to go much further and livestream his own life nonstop, 24/7, over the internet. He rigged his apartment with thirty cameras and sixty microphones, had his girlfriend move in with him, and locked the door for six months. Nothing was hidden from public view—not even his bum on his toilet or his girlfriend's pimples. The "experiment," Harris announced, was in making all things public. But it might as well have been referred to as an experiment in making all things private, for the point was to destroy the dividing line between the private and the public—to make both concepts equally meaningless.

What happened? Harris's lovely relationship with his girlfriend turned lethargic and then violent. She eventually left him. Harris grew depressed. People stopped watching, stopped chatting, and stopped caring, and Harris found himself all alone online. To be sure, retroactively, Harris's self-imposed saga became a kind of living parable for the fraught nature of privacy and publicness in the age of the internet. But the living parable was entirely unnecessary.

Even the barons of Silicon Valley need their privacy. So do politicians; therefore, they lie to protect their privacy. Do you blame them? Is every vice fit to be seen by all?[14] Is every foible worthy of broadcast? If the problem doesn't have any direct bearing upon us, do we have any business demanding the truth? Might its disclosure risk transforming our common public life into the stuff of tabloid exposé, leading to all sorts of confusion about who is worthy of the public's trust by invading, and potentially destroying, the private lives of the very people who would want to earn our trust? If a politician lies to hide a matter he wants to keep private that has no direct bearing on the public trust—for example, that he was abused as a child—it is not only understandable but a political good for him to lie. The lie protects his own person as well as the integrity of the public, by preserving the privacy of the public person.

That said, there are a host of not-so-good reasons politicians lie: illicit office affairs, under-the-table deals, substance abuse, the unwarranted influence of donors and lobbyists, bribes, slander, manipulating facts to make the record seem better than it is, and so on. These scandals are stumbling blocks not only for the politician, but for the people they serve, as they have a direct bearing on public trust. While we do not need politicians to always tell the truth, we do need them to be basically trustworthy. If they lie about matters that have a bearing upon us, they break trust.

Nevertheless, there is a saving grace even here in these trust-breaking lies. For in lying to hide or obscure a truth that will hurt him, the politician is in fact showing a strange respect for the truth by implicitly acknowledging that the truth is powerful, that *the truth matters* to a watching public. He does not want to tell the truth, because the truth could hurt him. Indeed, this homage to the truth in the lie often goes even further, as the politician tries as much as he can to make it *seem* like he is telling the truth. For example, when news broke that President Bill Clinton had had an affair with a White House intern (a matter with clear bearing upon the public trust inasmuch as the affair was with an employee and took place in the Oval Office) Clinton infamously got on national television, pointed his finger at the camera, and definitively declared, "I did not have sexual relations with that woman." It was a bald-faced lie, but in making it Clinton acknowledged, even if only indirectly, that the truth about the matter was so powerful that he deemed it had to be hidden. He respected—one might better say *feared*—the truth that much. And so, he tried to make his lie appear true.

This may seem like a very odd way for politicians to respect the truth, and it is. But politics is full of such strange homages to the truth precisely because in politics the truth can be so very powerful. Revelations about scandals can be "explosive" in politics because facts can matter so much in politics. In "professional" politics, more so than our everyday lives, facts about who did what with whom and where have the potential to shift the political winds in an instant. Therefore, so long as politicians lie to hide uncomfortable or reputation-damaging truths from us, we can draw comfort—cold comfort though it may be—from the fact that in their lies they are paying odd tribute to the truth, and that their lies, though perhaps worth sharply criticizing, are often not in themselves a direct threat to the place and power of the truth in politics. "In this sense," Arendt wrote, "truth, even if it does not prevail in public, possesses an ineradicable primacy over all falsehoods."[15] In other words, ordinary political lies are always built on the edifice of the truth.

Things grow progressively more ominous, however, with another kind of lying in politics: habitual lying. Here a particular politician shows *no regard for the truth at all* by habitually, regularly lying. We have a problem here, and a significant one, for if a habitual liar holds political office, we are entrusting our governance to someone who cares little for the truth. The difficulty is not just a matter of their trustworthiness and integrity, although that's a big part of it. It's that habitual liars are not *responsive* to the truth, which means that they will not likely be readily *accountable* to the truth, which means they are not likely to be responsible politicians in the least.

The lies and mistruths of the habitual liar are therefore qualitatively different than lies told to navigate constituencies, keep the political process running, or save face—each of which represents a form of lying that can be highly cognizant of the truth. Rather, the lies of the habitual liar emanate from an ingrained disregard for the truth, a disregard that is consistent with a certain kind of narcissistic quest for power. The difference between the ordinary liar and the habitual liar is, in essence, the difference between lies that are tactical and lies that speak volumes about one's ambition and attitude.

Under ordinary circumstances, as we have seen, politicians may lie because they know the political stakes of speaking the truth. For such politicians, public scandal is always a felt risk; the truth can hurt. Yet, as he would have his lies appear *as truth,* the politician who tells the lie pays that strange homage to the truth. He may lie repeatedly, but he does so under the sign of the truth. However, the second sort of lying politician—the habitual liar—lacks sensitivity to the truth altogether. Here the politician operates with ample consciousness of the stakes of his words, but with little consciousness of their stakes in relationship to the truth. Rather, words are measured in relationship to power, and nothing more. So, the big difference between the ordinary political lie and the habitual liar in the political realm is that the former implicitly respects the truth whereas the latter does not. One says, even in the lie, *the truth is powerful,* whereas the other—the habitual liar—says, *Truth? What is truth?*

Still, habitual lying is not the most dangerous form of political lying. For that we have to turn to "organized lying," a phenomenon that Arendt probed with extraordinary acuity in her studies of official government lying. Organized lying is like habitual lying in that the liars have little to no regard for the truth. But organized lying is different in that it entails a planned, concerted, and distributed organizational effort to deceive. Like a disease gone viral, organized lying destroys by means of the power of systems. More than the mere cause-and-effect mechanism—turn the knob and out pops the puppet from the box—systems, like the electrical grid, allow for innumerable points of impact, feedback mechanisms for making ongoing adjustments, and the capacity to scale up or scale down. Because the most destructive forms of lying are systemic, Arendt discussed lying in politics more in terms of institutions and social structures than in terms of strict moral categories.

Arendt argued the historical roots of modern-day organized lying are less in government and more in the commercial industry, particularly with the advent of public relations.[16] Edward Bernays (1891–1995), the founder of public relations and, not incidentally, the nephew of Sigmund Freud, instructed corporate clients to stop trying to give consumers explicit reasons to buy their products and instead to associate their products with an image, identity, or feeling. Politicians learned from Bernays that politics can become a form of salesmanship, and that there are powerful but subtle ways to "influence" or "condition" people to buy in to certain programs, platforms, policies, or ideologies without having to persuade them with good reasons. For some government ministers and many intelligence officials, Bernays gave them a new box of tricks.[17]

But it was a Pandora's box, out of which came new techniques for what Arendt called organized lying—techniques of propaganda, disinformation, doublespeak, spectacle, scapegoating, and gaslighting. These techniques are aimed not at changing people's minds, but at manipulating their attitudes, emotions, affections, and allegiances toward ends that will serve the narrow interests of the organized liars. Whereas a corrupt government may be made up of a bunch of habitual liars who are in it for themselves, organized lying produces more than corrupt politicians—it is reflective of corrupt and dangerous forms of antipolitical organization. Habitual liars ignore the truth but do not directly attack it. Organized lying represents a direct attack and assault not only on the truth, but on politics itself, as it works to manufacture "alternative facts" and false "truths" that ultimately undermine the very conditions for establishing the truth in political discourse. Organized lying can leave us, like victims of abuse, unable to tell which way is up and which is down. Indeed, Arendt argued that the ultimate danger organized lying poses is not that it leaves us confused about what is true but about what is *real*, for reality itself is the battlefield that organized lying seeks to dominate.

As Arendt explored at length in *The Origins of Totalitarianism*, organized lying was the operational logic of Nazi Germany and the former Soviet Union. She argued that both states made deception a matter of organization. The goal here, she pointed out, was not steering around facts or ignoring the truth, but the creation of new "facts" and "truths." Totalitarianism is built on an organized maze of deceptions that makes fidelity to a truth that is not already of the totalitarian system a feat of extraordinary heroism. This is because the goal of totalitarianism is to deceive by making the totalitarian system itself identical with the truth. The Big Lie, in other words, was a means of producing a Total Truth—totalitarian truth.

Not all organized lying is so total. Arendt also explored in her book *Crises of the Republic* the ways that democratic states—above all, the United States—have participated in murderous forms of organized lying, trying to fabricate "truths" about, for example, the war in Vietnam. Organized lying has been a modus operandi of the US government in and around wars, various covert paramilitary operations, and nuclear weapons testing. And organized lying is upon us again in the twenty-first century with a new vengeance.

With each new election or major public controversy, it seems, teams of programmers and propagandists are launching various organized-lying operations using social media. The goal of such operations can be specific: to elect a certain candidate or defeat a certain referendum. But for the more sophisticated ones, the goal has not simply been to steer around the truth in order to achieve an electoral victory; these are not mere "spin" operations. Rather, the goal has been to construct virtual realities, alternate political universes, and new "truths" to foster suspicion among citizens about facts, reality, the reliability of institutions, and ultimately each other—such that confidence in democracy itself is severely undermined. Given the early "successes" of these operations in the second decade of the twenty-first century, they no doubt will be imitated and expanded in the decades to come. Be aware: a new age of organized lying is just beginning.

Organized lying needs to be met with an organized defense. Constitutions, institutions, and indeed bureaucracies are the surest defense against organized lying. This is why, for all the ways that Arendt insisted that politics spontaneously "happens," and for the particular way in which her approach to politics was "anarchic" (see chapter 2), she was republican in orientation, holding that government has a legitimate and important role in our political lives. Republicanism (particularly federal republicanism, a layered and differentiated system of republican governing structures), represents for her a political system capable of checking other systems—be they technological, economic, military, or administrative—that would otherwise, if left to their own devices, seek to dominate the world in which we live and even attempt to eradicate politics from the Earth.[18]

Still, before we will be ready to organize our defenses against organized lying, there is something more basic that we need to do: *recognize that not all lies in politics are created equal*. A part of the reason organized lying in politics is gaining ground is because so many of us have become so cynical about politics, and in this cynicism have become lumpers: we throw all lies, no matter what their intent or nature, into the pile of politics, destined for the dustbin. We badly need instead to become sorters, putting different lies into different bins. If the twentieth-century lie detector had only two registers—truth or lie—the twenty-first century lie detector needs multiple registers, organized according to a scale of severity. We need to stop treating all lies as equal.

Here we can return to the ordinary politician and her ordinary lies. The ordinary politician, so thoroughly conditioned to the tensions and pivots of public life, can be a bundle of contradictions and ripe for scandal by virtue of the gap between her public persona and her private one. Yet, the habitual liar is even worse: he would be immune to scandal because he creates for himself a world where the facts just don't matter that much at all. Arendt thought both types of liars were problematic, but the latter more so than the former. Moreover, she thought both types of liars were bound to unravel: "Under normal circumstances the liar is defeated by reality, for which there is no substitute; no matter how large the tissue of falsehood that an experienced liar has to offer, it will never be large enough . . . to cover the immensity of factuality."[19] In democratic politics, Arendt confidently concluded, facts tend to win!

But not all the time. Organized lying, Arendt noted, *does* successfully cover (for a time, at least), the "immensity of factuality," especially when coupled with fear and resentment. There can come a point

> when the audience to which the lies are addressed is *forced* to disregard altogether the distinguishing line between truth and falsehood in order to be able to survive. Truth or falsehood—it does not matter which any more, if your life depends on your acting as though you trusted; truth that can be relied on disappears entirely from public life, and with it the chief stabilizing factor in the ever-changing affairs of men.[20]

Totalitarian organizations, Arendt argued, are just that: *organizations*. Less top-down than they are center-periphery, totalitarian organizations depend on numerous subgroups—secret police, the party hierarchy, party members, professional societies, and front organizations—to do more than enforce obedience.[21] Totalitarian organizations want to dominate the very meaning of "reality" and thus the lives of people—their truths and facts, their thoughts and attitudes, their speech and actions. This "total" agenda is why totalitarianism inevitably resorts to something more than organized, planned, and coordinated deception; its ultimate ambitions also require guns, battalions, tanks, police, and concentration camps.

"Truthfulness," Arendt wrote, "has never been counted among the political virtues, and lies have always been regarded as justifiable tools in political dealings."[22] To be sure, it is precisely because truthfulness has enjoyed relatively little esteem in politics that many of us don't like politics. We think it shady from start to finish. Again, I am not going to try to convince you that politics is in the business of the truth, the whole truth, and nothing but the truth—or that it should be. The Enlightenment model of truth telling is not only unrealistic, it is inadequate for dealing with reality. The political world is too precious and precarious to heed Immanuel Kant's austere maxim that telling the truth is "a sacred and unconditionally commanding law of reason that admits of no expediency whatsoever."[23] Kant's mistake is in denying that there are qualitative differences among lies. An ordinary lie can be told in the name of being truthful and trustworthy, or for the purpose of hiding corruption and scandal. A habitual liar lies for purposes of pure power and expediency; for her the truth does not even register. Organized lying is not so much oblivious to the truth as it is determined to manufacture "truths" and indeed "reality" to suit a will to power or profit.

Clearly, therefore, not all lies are alike. If we assume that they are, like mushroom hunters who assume all mushrooms are alike, we are gluttons for poison. But most of us are not like this. Most of us recognize intuitively and even explicitly that not all lies are created equal. Our struggle is in telling the difference between kinds of lying, and determining which is which. And this, no less than the rest of politics, comes down to the quality of our political judgment.

FIVE

Why We Need Rhetoric

In what may be the most well-known piece of political fiction ever written, Plato's "Allegory of the Cave," we hear of a group of people shackled in a cave where, for their entire lives, day and night, they look at a wall upon which shadows are being cast by hidden puppeteers standing behind them. For all intents and purposes, the people think the shadows are real, until a prisoner is freed from his chains and dragged into the great wide world to see, for the first time, what reality *really* is. Feeling liberated, the newly enlightened man returns to the cave to tell his former cell mates what the real world is like. "There's a bright world out there!" he exclaims. His fellow cave dwellers are at first a bit bemused, only to grow outraged. "You are delusional," they decry, ridiculing the man. "How dare you talk to us like that?" they protest. And so, as Plato writes, they cry out to have the newly liberated man killed.

For Plato, the "Allegory of the Cave" was personal. In 399 BCE his beloved teacher, Socrates, was put to death by the citizens of Athens for "corrupting the youth." The execution of Socrates is one of the most infamous examples of democratic excess in history. The meaning of Plato's story is not hard to decode: the cave is the democratic political community (the *polis*); the freed prisoner represents those who, like Socrates, have been freed of the shadow casting and show business of the *polis* to see what is true; and the remaining prisoners are the obstinate, ignorant, and violent people (the *demos*) of the democracy who would rather listen to entertaining rhetoric than enlightened experts.[1]

Can you relate? Have you ever been distressed by the ignorance of people? Have you ever been dumfounded by our willingness to believe what we hear? Have you ever felt like democracy might not be such a good idea because we can be so gullible and ill informed? There is a lot out there to

Imprisonment/Enlightenment

leave us wondering if democracy is practical, and even more to leave us cynical. Anyone who has watched hysterical talking heads go at it on cable news, been subjected to an onslaught of bogus political advertisements, or seen obviously made-up "news" go viral should feel a bit repulsed not only by what they see, but by the fact that millions of people seem to find such puppet shows compelling. As the *Washington Post* announces on their masthead, in an allusion to Plato's allegory, "Democracy dies in darkness."[2]

Hannah Arendt was certainly sympathetic to such criticisms of democracy. She saw in democracy a potential for dangerous deception, demagoguery, and even totalitarianism. The dystopia of Plato's "Allegory of the Cave" anticipated in her era the propaganda and public-relations campaigns of the twentieth century, which could, and at times did, result in the total domination of human life by powerful, self-interested image- and message-makers. The apathy, ignorance, and anger of the people was part of Arendt's explanation of the rise of totalitarianism in her *Origins of Totalitarianism*. Indeed, it is important to remember that Hitler led a democracy—in name, at least.

Nevertheless, Arendt did not draw from these disasters the same lesson that Plato drew from the unjust death of Socrates. For Plato, the remedy for democracy's delusions is enlightened escape artists, a class of experts who are empowered to guide—or as the case might be, "nudge"—others in the right direction, as a teacher leads her pupils or a parent nudges his children.[3] Plato would heartily approve of the tagline of the *Washington Post*'s "Fact Checker" site: we need to turn to experts capable of seeing "the truth behind the rhetoric."[4] For Arendt, on the contrary, the rule of experts is as great a danger as the ignorance of the people. Even more, the rule of experts combined with the ignorance or apathy of the people is among the gravest political dangers, for it could turn "the people" into the puppets of experts. For Arendt, the antidote to democratic disasters is not more experts but a better democracy—a democracy in which we do not try to free ourselves from what she called the "space of appearances" but rather learn to discriminate among appearances; and a democracy in which we do not get behind rhetoric to the truth, but give authentic rhetoric room to thrive.

"Authentic rhetoric?" you ask.[5] Isn't rhetoric a bad thing, a problem rather than a solution? For generations now, enlightened experts have told us that "rhetoric" is nothing but chicanery, blowing smoke, or, in the words of the Enlightenment philosopher John Locke, a "perfect cheat."[6] Indeed, as far as we know, Plato himself invented the word *rhetoric* (*rhêtorikê*) as a term of insult: derived from the Greek word *rhema*, which simply means "word," Plato coined *rhetoric* to designate the ways in which politicians and salesmen play deviously with words to cast dark shadows upon the people.[7] And verbal trickery is usually what we think of when we think of rhetoric today. What good, therefore, can come from rhetoric? Understood in the way Plato understood rhetoric, not a lot. But understood differently, a great deal of good indeed.

For this other way of understanding rhetoric, we can look to what Arendt taught about the vital role of persuasion in political life and to what Aristotle taught about the role of rhetoric in a democracy. Aristotle challenged his teacher Plato on the subject of rhetoric. He argued that rhetoric was not shadow casting but rather a crucial citizenly art of persuasion; he went so far as to claim that rhetoric was the *"ethical* branch of politics."[8] For him, rhetoric was at the very heart of the art of citizenship, for it has to do with *how* we go about speaking to one another *as citizens*. The qualifier "as citizens" is critical. In rhetoric, Aristotle suggested, we speak to one another not as teachers speak to pupils, parents to children, doctors to patients, ministers to congregants, or know-it-alls to imbeciles, but as citizens speak to citizens. We speak, that is, as *equals*.

Rhetoric can be abused. It can be a form of shadow casting. Yet, as the ancient maxim goes, abuse does not negate good use. Aristotle and Arendt argued that we need rhetoric for the very same reason that we need politics: given all the other demands and pressures on our lives, we need to talk to each other in freedom and as equals. We do this by using what Arendt typically called "the arts of persuading and arguing," or what Aristotle called "rhetoric."[9] If I want you to drive less and walk more, there are at least three distinct ways I can try to get you do so. I can *coerce* you, in the manner of a heavy-handed legislator, by getting the law on my side. Alternatively, I can *manipulate* you, in the manner of much advertising, through false promises and guilt trips. Or I can *persuade* you, using examples, arguments, and even emotional appeals to try to bring you to a point where you too deem that walking more and driving less is a good thing. Authentic rhetoric, Aristotle taught, is what we do when we seek to persuade rather than coerce or manipulate.

Arendt suggested that the disasters of democracy almost always stem from coercion or manipulation rather than persuasion. The reason the prisoners in Plato's cave turned against the enlightened man, the citizens of Athens turned against Socrates, and we turn against one another is not fundamentally because we lack expert knowledge, as Plato argued. Rather, it is because we develop habits of talking with one another that are manipulative and hostile. We resort to force, be it in the form of "law and order" or by manipulating emotions of fear, paranoia, hatred, and resentment. More knowledge will not remedy this. Indeed, more knowledge can make the situation worse, because experts can be tempted to resort to force, frustrated as they become by the slow work of persuasion. Clearly, Plato felt that the only reliable way to get the people of a democracy to see the light was to force them along, even with "noble lies."[10] Otherwise, they'd rest contently in their chains.

In this chapter, I make a case for rhetoric. In the previous two chapters, we have been looking at the pivotal role of judgment in sorting through with others what is true, false, good, bad, right, crooked, trustworthy, or unreliable. In chapter 3, we looked at political judgment as kind of connoisseurship, a skill of looking at a topic from multiple standpoints so as to reach a judgment. Such connoisseurship happens mostly inside our heads; we have to let our "imagination go visiting," Arendt said.[11] In chapter 4, we put political judgment to work by distinguishing between different kinds of lying in politics. In this chapter, we are going to look at how judgment also depends on what happens outside our heads, for in reaching quality political judgments, we have to hear the arguments of others—we have to listen, then judge. We may also need to make our own arguments, asking others to listen to us and judge what we have to say and how we say it. The art of speaking, listening, and judging is what Aristotle called rhetoric. If politics is the one art by which we freely shape and reshape our common world with others, rhetoric is the one art by which we try to bring others along in this common venture, and indeed allow ourselves to be brought along.

Knowledge Is Not Power

For Arendt, Plato's "Allegory of the Cave" is a pivotal political tale not for its Platonic lesson about the pigheadedness of the people and the virtues of philosophy, but rather for the way in which it articulates an enduring and powerful critique of politics made by elites and experts: *people don't know what we know.*[12] What do scientific experts on global warming say? "We know what causes global warming. We know what damage it will do. We know how to slow or stop the process. We know how to mitigate its effects." What do experts on marriage and family say? "The data clearly shows that two-parent households are economically better off than single-parent households. The science demonstrates the psychological benefits of couples staying together. Study after study proves that the children of empathetic parents have higher measures of well-being than the children of aloof parents." What do experts in macroeconomics say? "It is demonstrably true that regulation hampers market efficiencies. It is a proven fact that capital accumulation spurs innovation in the long run. We know that labor unions increase wages but reduce corporate profits and therefore stifle innovation." Given all that these experts *know*, it is no wonder that they are surprised and frustrated when others don't seem to listen. Their frustration is a magnified version of what we all feel when people won't listen to us even though we know what we're talking about.

Expertise is good and necessary, in its place.[13] We of course would not want an amateur pilot to fly the commercial plane we board, or a surgeon with mere "hunches" about how to operate. Still, expertise in democratic politics is not unequivocally a good thing, and we should be especially cautious when it is presented as though it is. Any expert—be they a scientist, doctor, preacher, economist, engineer, professor, or military general—in claiming mastery over a subject matter does more than make a claim about their knowledge; they also make a claim about their *authority*. And, indeed, their authority is "rightful." They've earned it. They know more than the rest of us; they've done their homework and paid their dues. We rightly heed experts in the medical office, the classroom, the laboratory, or the pulpit if they know more than we do about a matter within their range of expertise. If their knowledge is genuine, experts have real authority on their side.

However, here is the problem with expertise in politics: political authority does not come by way of degrees and diplomas. Political authority is never essentially a matter of knowledge—it is not built on the edifice of knowledge, but on the formal and informal political mechanisms of law and custom that grant a person legitimacy to exercise authority in the political sphere. It may be problematic to elect a know-nothing to the presidency, but it is not illegitimate. Ignorance about medicine should automatically disqualify a person from practicing surgery; however, ignorance about policy does not, and should not, disqualify a person from exercising political authority. Political authority is, well, politically derived. Even more important, *political power* cannot be directly derived from expert knowledge, but only from the interpersonal political skills of building trust, exercising judgment, and showing proficiency in cooperation, compromise, debate, and dialogue.

In short, while expert authority is earned and accredited, political authority is granted and constituted; and while the power of experts resides within their knowledge, political power is built among people as they work together. The danger of experts in politics is not that they will tell us what to do, but that they will replace political authority and power with the authority and power of knowledge. "Knowledge is power" is true for engineering, not politics.[14] When "experts" appear in the political realm, authoritarian dangers are always present—Arendt went so far as to call them "totalitarian" dangers.[15]

Think about an imperfect but helpful example. Let's say you live in a college dormitory and you and your floormates are tired of the limited food selection in the dining hall. You and some others go to the director of food services and ask for a wider variety of food choices. At that point, the food services director has a choice to make: he could approach the problem by engaging in a dialogue or even debate with you, leaving the "solution" to the outcome of your discussions; or he could claim outright "expertise" about the matter, say that he knows what he is doing, and say you simply need to learn to get on board. If he took the latter approach, you would not be wrong to feel like it was "authoritarian," for it was. In fact, anytime anyone enters the political sphere from a position of expert knowledge, they risk becoming authoritarian.

Arendt saw in expertise a "totalitarian" potential that goes even further than authoritarianism. Her concern was that experts would want more than for people to get on board; in the political realm, they might have incentive to propagate lies and falsify facts to maintain their authority, especially if they hold powerful positions in government. Experts, Arendt noted, pride themselves not just on a mastery of the facts, but on the power of their theories. Given tension or even contradiction between particular facts and an expert's theory, the expert may be tempted to ignore the inconvenient facts or, even worse, try to force them to fit the theory by engaging in lies and deception.[16] Experts in positions of political authority will be particularly tempted to do this if they feel their position depends on the power of their theory. When a political regime rests its legitimacy on knowledge, science, or theory, it may go to great lengths to hide, destroy, or manipulate any facts that challenge their foundation. As Arendt explored at length in *The Origins of Totalitarianism*, both the Nazi and Bolshevik political regimes claimed a dubious if definite "scientific" basis for their legitimacy, the former racial science and the latter historical and economic science. That both regimes were relentlessly propagandistic, she argues, was a consequence of their appeal to science, not a mere supplement.[17]

During the Cold War, foreign policy experts in the United States had a theory about communist expansion: the "domino theory." It taught that if communism were to gain ground even in a relatively remote corner of the world, it could set off a process wherein the rest of the world would rapidly fall, like dominoes, into the ideology's grip. The domino theory drove a wide range of American foreign policy adventures in the Cold War—above all the Vietnam War, about which the United States government lied to the American people repeatedly and systematically. In her essay "Lying in Politics," Arendt argued that one driving force behind these organized lies was a commitment among US foreign policy experts to the "domino theory," even before facts that flew in its face.[18] Rather than revise their hallowed expert theory, the Pentagon and the White House lied over and over about the facts. More than two hundred thousand American soldiers died in Vietnam beneath the dark cloud of their lies.

As you can see, the problem of experts in politics is not fundamentally a matter of knowledge. The problem is not that they know more and we less. Rather, it is a problem with *what people do* with knowledge and expertise, and *how people speak* or do not speak to other members of their political community. If I claim expertise about a matter, telling you I know what I am doing and that you simply need to learn to cooperate, then I am speaking to you in an authoritarian manner. If I lie and deceive in order to make inconvenient facts fit my expert theory, then I am attempting to manipulate not just you, but the world in which we live. More ordinarily, if I know considerably more about a given topic than you, or at least pretend to know more, I am going to be less inclined to speak to you as my equal—if I speak to you at all—when we are talking about that topic. I may instruct you, exhort you, or command you, but I am not likely to talk with you as though we were equals in the conversation. Needless to say, debating and discussing matters *as equals* is precisely what politics calls for, especially democratic politics.

Talking as Equals

The most influential philosophical defenders of human equality in the last several hundred years have argued that we are equal "by nature." Thomas Hobbes got this line of thinking going by arguing in the 1600s that all are equal in a "state of nature." How so? He argued that though each person may have different aptitudes and capacities, they are all equal by virtue of the fact that they are all equally capable of killing one another.[19] That's quite a theory of equality! John Locke, in the generation after Hobbes, also argued that in a state of nature men are all equal ("men" being a crucial proviso). However, Locke focused not on the capacity to kill one another, but on equal "natural rights" to life, liberty, and property.[20] The writers of the Declaration of Independence followed Locke, famously writing, "We hold these truths to be self-evident, that all men are created equal, that they are endowed by their Creator with certain unalienable Rights, that among these are Life, Liberty and the pursuit of Happiness." In all these declarations, the consensus position, expressed in the 1700s by Jean-Jacques Rousseau, is that humans are born equal only to become unequal through social norms, customs, and structures.[21] Any inequalities we experience in life must be the product of social or political forces. Equality is *natural*, inequality *artificial*.

Arendt never tired of pointing out how patently inaccurate this is.

Humans are definitely not naturally equal, not even if we take Hobbes's approach and say we are all "equally" capable of killing each other (which we are not!).[22] We may, as Locke asserts, "share in the same common nature, faculties, and power," but to be strictly equal by nature we would have to be identical in nature.[23] Atoms of isotopes are by nature equal because they are by nature identical. Each human, by contrast, is born individual and unique. We are by nature unequal in all sorts of ways because each of us is nonidentical to every other human on Earth, even if we share the same type of skin color, language, or genitals. Our nonidentities are at the heart of what Arendt celebrated as the "plurality" of the human condition—we are plural, not singular; persons, not atoms.

What, then, of equality? Is it a useless idea? Far from it, Arendt argued; equality is, along with freedom, the most decisive and important of our political concepts, for it is in political community, and political community alone, that we become equal. Equality, that is, is a *political achievement*.[24] That is why people have marched, petitioned, sat at lunch counters, sacrificed, and constituted and reconstituted democratic political communities. In a democracy, many individuals—each unequal to every other individual "by nature"—become equal. Even rulers become equal to the ruled under law.

As Arendt noted, the ancient Greeks therefore did not speak of "natural equality." It seemed obvious to them that nature did not make humans equal. Rather, the Greeks spoke of *isonomy*, a word derived from the Greek *isotês*, "equal," and *nomos*, "law." *Isonomy* means, in Arendt's words, "equality within the range of the law," or, as we might say, "equality before the law."[25] As she explained, "Isonomy guaranteed *isotês*, equality, but not because all men were born or created equal, but, on the contrary, because men were by nature (*physei*) not equal, and needed an artificial institution, the *polis*, which by virtue of its *nomos* would make them equal."[26] Just as in joining together to build houses and other forms of shelter we make for ourselves an artificial refuge from the harsh conditions of nature, so by joining together in democratic political association we make ourselves equal, and therefore fabricate for ourselves a refuge from some of the negative ways that bare nature would leave us exposed and unequal.

That equality before the law is an "artificial" phenomenon should no more alarm us than should the fact that architecture, agriculture, and education are all matters of art. Human life is "artificial" in a myriad of ways. We are fabricators: we make all kinds of things, from lemonade, to laws, to lavish expressions of love. Rather than leading us to take our existence less seriously, this fact should lead us to take it more seriously. We have to ask, What kind of culture do we want to cultivate? What kind of world do we want to help make? By what powers do we want to be ruled? Who do we want to count as equals, and by what criteria? These are critical political questions, none of which "nature" automatically solves for us.[27]

Democratic constitutions *make* us equals. That they do this artificially is no slight on their power or significance, though we frequently assume anything artificial must be inferior to that which is natural. A lot of stratospheric claims about the future of artificial intelligence, cyborgs, and the posthuman would be brought back down to Earth if we remembered that human life has, as far as we can know, always been artificial life. From the get-go we lit fires, made tools, and used symbols. The essential questions presented by new technologies and various medical means of artificial enhancement bring us back to a quintessentially political and constitutional question: How do we want to craft the contours of our coexistence?

But, as we saw in chapter 1, politics is more than constitutions; it is a three-dimensional art that includes arts of governance and citizenship. The art of rhetoric is useful for both of these, since speech is an essential means by which humans negotiate relationships with one another. Different types of speech can be correlated with different types of human relationships. A command correlates with a human relationship among people having unequal authority. A lecture correlates with human relationships where there is unequal knowledge about a topic. And an advertisement correlates with human relationships where some are buyers and others sellers. Aristotle presented rhetoric as a form of speech correlated with relationships among political equals. The art of rhetoric, he suggested, teaches us to talk to one another as equals.

Therefore, he argued, we can practice rhetoric in better and worse fashions, more democratically or less so. The difference for him was mainly a matter of ethics rather than immediate effects.[28] Results matter, but the results that really matter need to be measured in the long run as well as in the moment. This is readily seen if we take the vantage point of the listener, to whom Aristotle gave a primary (but certainly not the only) place in the rhetorical encounter because, he argued, it is as listeners that we ultimately judge. As a listener, I can ask myself three basic questions. I can ask, Was this persuasive? I can additionally ask, Who showed themselves to be trustworthy—who would I listen to again? And I can ask, Does this person seem to respect me as an equal? If I find one speaker more persuasive than the others, I may want to heed her advice. But if I don't think she is trustworthy, I may be reluctant to do so. And if I suspect that the speaker sees me as an inferior, I may be even more reluctant. Rhetoric in a democracy works well only if we see it as a trust-building art and learn to talk as equals.[29]

Rhetoric Rules

The first rule of rhetoric, so to speak, is that we need to *approach others as both equals and as different*—for in a democracy we are political equals even as we are each unique and different from everyone else.[30] In the second part of his book on rhetoric, Aristotle described at length different types of people: older, younger, wealthier, poorer, frustrated, happy.[31] He assumed that each and every member of the political community is unique due to both nature and circumstance. We play different parts in society and perform different roles; we should not speak to everyone in exactly the same way (even though this is what some say the principle of political equality calls for). We have to adjust, adapt, or otherwise adopt different "means of persuasion" that are suited to the particular concerns and capacities of different audiences. And yet, we remain equal in two critical ways: we are all equally *worthy* of participating in the conversation (even if we are not all identically capable), and we are all equally *free* to judge.

The second rule of rhetoric, therefore, is to *persuade*. As we have seen, a commitment to politics means a commitment to action. But action without explanation and persuasion can be tyrannical. A commitment to democracy, therefore, means a commitment to rhetoric, and a commitment to rhetoric entails a commitment to persuading others of the opinions, judgments, reasons, and positions we hold, even those we hold dearly. Persuasion is neither a means of commanding nor teaching (though teaching can be more or less rhetorical); and it is certainly not a means of manipulative shadow casting. Rather, persuasion is a form of speech in which we give reasons, stir emotions, and appeal to images and the imagination in ways that might bring others to see things how we see them or want others to see them.

We persuade by three basic means: our public character (*ethos*), our public reasoning (*logos*), and our capacity to carefully engage people's feelings and emotions in public (*pathos*). Depending on the situation—rhetoric is essentially situational—the rhetorical art may mean prioritizing one of these means over the other, or balancing all three. Regardless, our aim is to win over our listeners, as well as to cultivate trust and maintain respect. To do rhetoric well, Aristotle suggested, we have to learn not only to persuade but to be persuaded, to let ourselves be brought along by others—for if we are not open to persuasion, we are not likely to know what it means to persuade others well.

The third rule of rhetoric is, wherever possible, to *rule rhetorically*. As a means of persuasion, rhetoric is also a potential means of political rule, a vital part of both citizenship and governance. As a contemporary defender of rhetoric, Bryan Garsten, writes, "In trying to bring an audience . . . to thoughts or intentions they might not otherwise have adopted, rhetoric intends to wield influence over them. In this sense rhetoric is a form of rule."[32] Rhetoric rules by starting from where people are at—their knowledge, experience, opinions, and feelings—to make a case for a policy, platform, or solution that listeners are in turn free to judge. That the speaker has a desired goal in mind when addressing others does not necessarily mean that she is manipulating or coercing her audience. As long as she leaves them free to judge, no matter how impassioned her speech, she is talking to them as equals and seeking to rule rhetorically.

The other major form of rule in a democracy is, of course, the rule of law. Rhetoric and law rule differently. Law rules as opinions and judgments are converted into coercive force by means of legislation and law enforcement, whereas rhetoric rules by building shared opinions and judgments.[33] Of course, in order for laws to gain consent and legitimacy in a democracy, lawmakers themselves need rhetoric: they need to bring the rest of us to a point where we agree that the coercive force of the law is warranted. When we start to doubt this—as, for example, with drug laws or health care policies in the United States—laws are weakened and can begin to seem unfair. People may then start to feel that the coercive force of the law is unwarranted and even illegitimate.

Here we come back to questions of expertise and authority. Even when there are disparities in expertise and authority due to knowledge, position, wealth, fame, or any other number of factors, democracies need the art of rhetoric in order to avoid moving toward authoritarian modes of governance—an ever-present risk in societies where laws and institutions are powerful. If we are doing politics rather than commanding, teaching, parenting, or simply trying to maximize short-term profits, we need to talk as equals—as uncomfortably "artificial" as this may feel at times.

As an example, let's consider debates about "political correctness." A 2018 survey stated that 80 percent of Americans view political correctness negatively.[34] What's wrong with political correctness? One 28-year-old woman quoted in the survey states, "I have liberal views but I think political correctness has gone too far, absolutely. We have gotten to a point where everybody is offended by the smallest thing."[35] Another person, a 43-year old conservative, is quoted as saying of political correctness, "I define it as lying. Not saying what you really think. It really hurts everybody."[36] Others, of course, will defend political correctness (though probably not calling it that), arguing that people do not have the right to describe others in ways that those being described find offensive or dehumanizing.

As we look at this debate, it is difficult to find anyone, no matter their side, asking questions about a means of "bringing people along" in ways that maintain and even build trust and respect. Instead, many are saying, in essence, "I am tired of having to accommodate others," be it the intolerant and racist language of others, or the "oversensitivity" of others, or the demands from others that I censor my language. Some people may be saying something even more damaging: "I am tired of having to work at talking in public. I am tired of having to speak 'artificially' to other citizens. I just want to be authentic. I just want to be true to myself or to my cause."[37] People on either side of the debate may even be saying, "To hell with those people! They're sick and stupid. Screw 'em." That, in fact, is a sentiment all too common, and it is a sentiment that is quite well suited to authoritarianism.

The Humble Art of Rhetoric

Rhetoric is humbling. It is humbling because it can feel artificial, like we have to work at something that we wish were just natural or automatic. The exasperated question "Why don't these people get it?" needs to be humbly converted to asking "How can I best talk to others about the things I care about?" Debates about controversial issues need to ask not only how to win the case, but also how to speak to others to win trust.[38] Rhetoric calls for political humility: over and over, when we are met with the many differences that characterize the plurality of the human condition, we have to ask ourselves, How can I talk to this person as an equal while still accommodating our differences? This is difficult. It is an art as well as an ethic.

Rhetoric also calls for a humble approach to questions of knowledge, competence, and expertise, for rhetoric always starts and ends with the assumption that, whatever is true about ourselves, others, and the topics we discuss, the minute we begin talking to fellow citizens *as* fellow citizens, our knowledge appears as "opinion," or at least as a "claim" that needs to be attested to by some and recognized by others. Arendt emphasized that opinions and claims are the everyday stuff of democratic politics.[39] In a democratic political community, every assertion by every citizen automatically has the status of a claim if only because no assertion in a democracy is permitted to shut all others up. You can swear, "This is the truth!" but that does not mean that others have to receive it as the truth. You can say, "I know the facts!" but that does not mean others have to acknowledge your facts. To assume so can be the essence of naivete and gullibility as well as a recipe for authoritarianism. It turns us into receptacles rather than judges of political speech. And it therefore makes us vulnerable to all sorts of manipulation, deception, and power plays.

Stressing the role of opinions and claims in a democracy raises concerns for some about the dangers of relativism and subjectivism. Opinions seem to be a foundation of sand; they can leave us wanting to flee from politics to more certain ground. And, indeed, more certain ground is exactly what some engineers, preachers, imams, economists, and politicians offer us as alternatives to politics: a means of authoritative decision making founded on certainties rather than opinions. The foundation that rhetoric offers, admittedly, is not so certain.[40]

But it is surer in the long run, for two big reasons. First, by prioritizing the art of persuasion, rhetoric works to keep us free and equal. Compared to the seemingly rock-solid certainty of indoctrination, such democratic freedom and equality may feel squishy, but it is a squishiness that makes for soft political landings rather than hard, violent ones. Second, by converting all statements to the status of an opinion or a claim, democratic rhetoric leaves open the possibility that that the truths we hold and the decisions we make can be revisited and revised. As such, we keep ourselves from dangerous temptations to ignore new voices and as-yet-unknown facts in the name of our comfortably kept certainties. Together, these two features of democratic rhetoric make for means of change while conserving trust.

To see how rhetoric does not consign us to the quicksand of relativism and subjectivism, consider its relation to *facts*. Arendt stressed the paradoxical fact that facts, which seem so self-evident to us, in reality require witnesses in order to appear and become meaningful to us. George Washington was born on February 22, 1732. This fact is a fact *for us* only because it has been attested to, and credibly so. Unlike 2 + 2 = 4, Arendt writes, "factual truths are never compellingly true."[41] There is nothing logically necessary about the date of George Washington's birth. He could have been born on a different day. Instead, "facts need testimony to be remembered and trustworthy witnesses to be established in order to find a secure dwelling place in the domain of human affairs."[42] Rhetoric's job, among other things, is to take the events and happenings of any given day and to convert them, when needed, into meaningful facts.

Rhetoric also works to transform "mere opinions" into credible opinions, persuasive positions, and, ultimately, effective judgments. Rhetoric helps us take our opinions and make them positions we *form* as we work to persuade others of their validity or credibility (or as others work to persuade us). The culmination of this rhetorical process is nothing but the beating heart of politics we've been looking at: judgment. It is by rhetoric that we come to make judgments in a democracy, and those judgments in turn become the new facts we attest through rhetoric.

But doesn't throwing ourselves into the confusing, messy world of rhetoric leave us subject to a new kind of tyranny, be it the tyranny of the majority, the tyranny of the spinmasters, or the tyranny of collective ideologies and illusions? If democratic politics cannot give a foundational place to truth and certainty, aren't we all, as Plato argued, stuck in the cave of "mere opinions"? Indeed, that's exactly where we would be if there were no place at all for truth in politics. But that is not what I am arguing here—and it is not what I take Arendt to be arguing. Instead, I am arguing that truth in a democracy does not have the place we might think it has. Politics, in fact, always operates under the "sign" of the truth: the truth is always *there*, it is just never there *directly*, in an unmediated fashion. To see what this could mean, let's consider further the place of opinions in politics.

The Truth about Opinions

Aristotle argued that persuasion begins with opinions. Arendt went further to argue that in the political realm, in a certain sense, *all we have are opinions*. Strictly speaking, truth appears *as* opinion in rhetoric and politics not because it is no longer true, but because citizens have no other way by which to distinguish truth from falsehood other than to treat every claim as though it were an opinion that needs to be attested to, discussed, arbitrated, and judged.[43] This includes facts. It is practically impossible for things to be otherwise, and the danger of pretending otherwise—of insisting that a truth must be accepted by citizens as the truth and nothing but the truth, with few or no questions asked—is that the truth tellers, frustrated by the people's stubbornness before their truth, will resort to coercive force, via the violence-backed power of the law, indoctrination, or some other means of hammering home the truth.[44]

Far from being a remote possibility, resorting to the violence-backed power of the law has been basic to modern liberal (individual, Lockean "rights-based") societies, so much so that a liberal thinker like Max Weber could state unabashedly that "the decisive means for politics is violence" and, as a corollary, that the state is nothing but the human institution that monopolizes the "legitimate use of physical force within a given territory."[45] In such a view of "politics" (all too common on both the political left and right today), legitimate electoral processes become but the means for capturing state power so as to enforce one's truth, will, or agenda on the population, where efforts at a more general campaign of persuasion are not even tried—for, really, people ask, what kind of idiot needs to be persuaded of what is right and true?

Arendt never argued that there is no truth, or that the truth is not worth pursuing, be it about a moral matter or a scientific one. Rather, she respected the power of the truth a great deal, and that is why she thought its power needed to be checked in the political realm. It is a commonplace, dating back centuries, to represent math-like logic as a closed fist and rhetoric as an open hand. Indeed, because the truth is so powerful, it bears antipolitical temptations: "Speak the truth, let the people be damned!" This is the stuff of cults, not political communities. Moreover, because some forms of truth, especially what Arendt would call "rational truth," are logically *necessary*— 2 + 2 = 4—the truth can have a coercive force in the context of the political realm.[46] It does not matter in the least whether you, me, your neighbors, or people living in remote villages think 2 + 2 = 4; it is true, people's odd contrary opinions be damned. However, to seek to *rule* from the position of such rational truth, Arendt argued, would be nothing but a disaster, for such truths coerce and compel us like a closed fist.

Consider the story of Mike Hughes, a flat-Earther. In 2017 he built a homemade rocket that he hoped would carry him some 1,800 feet into the air so that he could snap of photograph to prove that Earth is flat, contrary to "fake" NASA photographs of a spherical Earth. A scientist would call this crazy—any geographer, astronomer, or physicist can demonstrate conclusively that the world is not flat, and do so quite apart from NASA photographs. But a political thinker like Arendt would take some solace in Mike Hughes's adventures, for they reveal that in the political realm even scientific findings are but opinions. Why? Not because of the nature of scientific findings themselves, or the quality of their proofs. This has nothing to do with it. Rather, it is because to enter into politics is to enter into a world where people are free to differ. The alternative—to say people are *not* free to differ on the question of the shape of the Earth—would entail *forcing* people to hold a demonstratively true position. And forcing people to hold positions is inimical to political freedom. Opinions are the essence of politics because freedom, not force, is the starting point for politics, with speech, not violence, its decisive means.[47]

Therefore, Arendt stated that every assertion within the political realm has the status of opinion, not because the claim cannot be strongly supported or even conclusively proven in a logical, scientific, or empirical sense, but because in the political realm any assertion must remain open to being contested or challenged. This is true for even very grave moral matters, like the meaning of the word *murder*. While to claim Charles Manson was a murderer is not "just" an opinion, the claim is nevertheless a matter of judgment, not only about Charles Manson's actions, but also about the nature and meaning of murder. That the meaning of the word *murder* itself is, in our common political life, a matter of judgment, and therefore incorporates opinions and common beliefs, is evident in areas where its meaning is more contested—for example, with respect to killing in war or in self-defense, or abortion.[48]

For Arendt, insisting that within the political realm every claim has the status of an opinion is another way of saying that all speech within politics is "free speech," in the sense not only of being open to expression but also being open to refutation, qualification, or other forms of challenging. Within the world of politics, to insist that one's position is truth, such that it needs no justification or persuasion and cannot be legitimately challenged, is to assume the position of the authoritarian leader, whose only means of operating with others is by coercion. Indeed, the most basic reason authoritarian and totalitarian societies repress free speech is not because such speech would directly challenge the regime but because to tolerate free speech—the right of people to publicly express their opinions—would be to admit on a more basic level that all public speech has the status of opinion and judgment, not plain truth. The authoritarian dictator cannot long survive where public speech cannot masquerade as irrefutable truth enforceable by violence.

So, let's say, hypothetically, that Mike Hughes gets frustrated after his adventures fail to persuade others that Earth is flat. But Mike has options other than building rockets. He's charismatic, and rich! Through the power of his personality and the riches in his coffers, he launches a successful bid for governor of California, which turns into a successful bid for president of the United States. Before you know it, he's sitting in the White House. Telling people "Elections have consequences!" and that he has a "mandate," he announces that the flat-Earth theory is no longer theory but truth. Why? Because he and his team of experts (fellow flat-Earthers) say so! Airplane flight paths will have to be redesigned, weather predictions revised, and GPS coordinates reconfigured. Moreover, all dissenters in the federal government who object or otherwise resist will be fired. "Elections have consequences," the White House declares, "and we will not tolerate federal employees who resist the will of the people." This would be an authoritarian condition.

Yet, as the purging takes course and the new policies are put in place, airplane accidents suddenly spike, national weather predictions are woefully off, and GPS navigators start taking people to places they've never heard of, let alone meant to go to. What happened? *Reality* resisted the authoritarian pronouncements of the president; *facts* challenged the authoritarian machine. For Arendt, as for a writer like George Orwell in his *1984*, it is at this point that either authoritarianism can begin to crumble, or it can transform into an even more terrifying totalitarian condition, where not only truth but what people are able to learn, hear, and believe is ruthlessly enforced.[49]

A Republic of Facts and Acts

Arendt's world, therefore, is the inverse of the world outside Plato's famous cave. Whereas Plato saw humans as trapped in a dark world of fleeting shadows, desperately needing to escape into the timeless rational light of truth, Arendt pictured the ascent out of the cave as an ascent *into* the world of contingent facts and acts. Unlike the Platonic sense of reality, Arendt insisted, "facts and events—the invariable outcome of men living and acting together—constitute the very texture of the political realm."[50] And whereas Plato, even when writing about politics, began from a metaphysical reality that is timeless, unchanging, and permanent, Arendt began thinking about politics by beginning with *political* reality. In this everyday reality,

> facts and events are infinitely more fragile things than axioms, discoveries, theories—even the most wildly speculative ones—produced by the human mind; they occur in the field of the ever-changing affairs of men, in whose flux there is nothing more permanent than the admittedly relative permanence of the human mind's structure. Once they are lost, no rational effort will ever bring them back.[51]

Facts, acts, and opinions are equally "contingent," equally particular, and can be equally powerful or powerless.[52] This contributes to why facts and opinions get mixed up with each other. "Factual truth is no more self-evident than opinion," Arendt wrote, "and this may be among the reasons that opinion-holders find it relatively easy to discredit factual truth as just another opinion."[53]

But Arendt noted one big difference between facts and opinions: opinions are far more flexible, changeable, and manipulable than facts. This is not to say, of course, that the latter are not manipulable at all. Certainly, they can be interpreted in a variety of ways, and the factuality of acts can be disputed: Did Mike Hughes actually fly that rocket? Did I actually brake for a person crossing the road? Did the politician actually say that? These acts are the sort of thing we can dispute as facts. But they are also acts we can potentially establish beyond reasonable doubt . . . *if* the governing power structures allow for it.

This *if* is absolutely critical, and is at the heart of Arendt's case for republicanism as a form of government. Arendt's republicanism tended to seep through her writings rather than focus her attention. Nevertheless, all the basic themes of her writings resonate with republicanism; it represents for Arendt a relatively stable and reliable means of navigating the circuitous and often messy world of truth, opinion, judgment, rhetoric, and reality that is the world of politics. Republicanism, we might say, institutes (or institutionalizes) two phenomena that Arendt held are necessary for a healthy political life: publicity and plurality.[54]

Publicity shares with *republic* the root word *publicus*, a Latin adjective meaning "of the people," where the people are seen as constituting the body politic. Publicity as such entails making things public both in the sense of "visible to the people" and "belonging to the people." Publicity, in the way republicans conceive of it, entails making facts, acts, and opinions public as though they "belong" to the people as a whole and are thus subject to the people's evaluation and judgment. Republicans have long held that the only way to reliably sort through the contingent, changeable political world is to subject it as much as possible to the judgments of the people. Here "the people" become the one constant in the ever-changing political world, and publicity becomes the constant means by which the people encounter their ever-changing political world.

The case for publicity is, more than anything else, a negative case. The fragility of facts—that they can be lost, forgotten, missed, and manipulated—means that they are vulnerable to power, be it in the form of the police, public relations, or propaganda. As Arendt wrote, "The chances of factual truth surviving the onslaught of power are very slim indeed; it is always in danger of being maneuvered out of the world not only for a time but, potentially, forever."[55] And what is lost when we lose the possibility of factual truth taking hold in our political community? The very possibility of our political freedom—for our freedom, politically conceived, is nothing but the possibility of acting without compulsion in the world so as to change, in some small or big way, the course of events in the world we share together. If no fact matters, if no fact counts, other than the "facts" projected by those in power, then freedom is nothing but power and power becomes the be-all and end-all of "politics."

There is a political contradiction here: political power, if unleashed in an authoritarian manner, would want to dominate the world of facts, eviscerating the very meaning of "fact." This is because facts, much more than mathematical axioms or philosophical truth, shape our sense of the meaning and significance in our everyday political lives, as well as determine the course of contingent events. Yet, political power is itself factual: while philosophers and pundits might want to argue for who *should* be in charge, who *should* have a voice, who *should* be able to see, who *should* get to judge, answers to who *is* in charge, who *has* a voice, who *is able* to see, and who *gets* to judge are *facts*. Hence, the paradox: in attacking "facts," the powers that be undermine the very factual nature of their own power, which not only is a fact, but can operate only by means of facts and acts that "might have been otherwise."[56] Even in the face of the grossest expressions of totalitarianism, this fact—the fact of political power—is a kind of political solace for Arendt.

As we have seen, Arendt returned over and over to *plurality* as a foundation of political reality: "Politics is based on the fact of human plurality."[57] And: "Men, not Man, live on earth and inhabit the world"; this fact, more than any other, is "*the* condition . . . of all political life."[58] As we have also seen, the fact of plurality has profound implications for politics. Arendt stressed especially its implications for "action." When I, as an individual, act in the world, I lose some control of the effects and interpretations of my act. My act is given over to a plurality of people with "innumerable, conflicting wills and intentions" for them to respond to, or, as the case may be, not respond to.[59] Plurality also has implications for political judgment, as Arendt argued that any truly "representative" judgment will attempt to consider a variety of perspectives and positions found among people. Finally, plurality has institutional implications. The fact that everybody—not anybody or any one body—is the condition of political life will be either reflected in or resisted by political power structures. Put concisely, republican democracies attempt to mirror the fact of our plurality; authoritarian states to resist it; and totalitarian states to obliterate it.

Arendt's defense of politics is premised on a fundamental opposition between force and freedom that she saw in ancient Greek culture. "To be political," she wrote, "to live in a polis, meant that everything was decided through *words* and *persuasion* and not through force and violence. In Greek self-understanding, to force people by violence, to command rather than persuade, were prepolitical ways to deal with people characteristic of life outside the polis."[60] As she understood it, the difference between force and freedom can be conceived of as the difference among forms of speech: to command rather than to practice rhetoric is to operate according to the logic of force rather than freedom.

For the Greeks, persuasion was represented by the goddess Peitho. In Hesiod's *Works and Days*, composed around 700 BCE, Peitho is the attendant to Aphrodite, the goddess of love and seduction.[61] Persuasion, we might surmise, was imagined as having the power of erotic love. The ancient Greek teacher Gorgias, a contemporary of Socrates, argued as much, explicitly comparing the power of speech (*logos*) to erotic love. But he went step further, comparing the power of speech also to drugs, violence, and tyranny. "Speech," he stated, "is a powerful lord."[62] Here speech appears as something other than persuasion. It appears rather as a form of force, which means that there is nothing particularly special about speech, or erotic love, in this instance. Drugs, guns, or threats can do the same job.

Indeed, the Greeks were well aware of the fact that not all love is free love, and not all speech is free speech. Take another ancient Greek allegory, one found painted on a vase dated to 410 BCE, the time of Gorgias. On it we see Peitho and Aphrodite flanking a bride. Aphrodite touches her on the shoulder, joining her body to the bride's, an indication not only of the love goddess's intoxicating power, but also a gesture that anticipates the consummation of the marriage. Peitho, by contrast, sits at some distance from the bride, using speech to persuade her to wed. Thus, as one deity lights upon the bride at her back, the other makes the case to her face in word and gesture.

Peitho flees.

Let's imagine this further in its allegorical form. Two ancient Greek lovers find themselves in the hands of *eros*. They are lovestruck. But the consummation of their love, if it is to be anything but fleeting, requires marriage, and marriage depends on the agreement of the fathers, who for all intents and purposes are overlords of their respective households (recall the discussion of *kýrios* in chapter 1). How does the marriage agreement come about? Not through the power of *eros*—the fathers, we can presume, have no strong sexual desire for their families to be tied together. Here Aphrodite is helpless. Rather, it is Peitho who does the work of persuasion by means of word and gesture as the fathers, spurred on no doubt by their lovelorn children, negotiate the terms of the marriage.

Were such meetings between households the beginnings of the Greek discovery of politics? Aristotle suggested they may have been.[63] Erotic power was the occasion of the fathers' meeting; nevertheless, the fathers meet in relative freedom and were dependent on the powers of speech and judgment to reach a satisfactory agreement. The space between the fathers is the space of Peitho, the space of persuasion. No one forces their way through. This is as it should be not only in politics, but also in love.

There is another Greek vase from the late fifth century depicting Aphrodite and Peitho together. Here they are at stark odds. The image shows the rape of the daughters of Leucippus by the twins Castor and Pollux. In the scene, which takes place in the sanctuary of Aphrodite, Aphrodite stands serenely on a pedestal, overseeing the erotic cruelty which she has blessed with a cool indifference, while Peitho turns and flees in horror. Persuasion, whose divine works were celebrated in the public spaces of democratic Athens, is not only averse to violence, she flees from it.

Here's the thing: as water depends on oxygen, so persuasion depends on the free air between persons, parties, perspectives, or positions. This is why persuasion and freedom are so intricately entwined. The space of freedom is the space of persuasion, or the space that persuasion gives so as not to be violent or otherwise forceful. A sure way to kill political freedom is to quash the conditions for persuasion to thrive. Long live persuasion!

SIX

The Political Imagination (or, Freedom!)

Freedom! There is no word that better declares the political ambitions and efforts of so many people. Freedom is the theme of Beethoven, the anthem of America, and the stuff of rock 'n' roll. Bumper stickers boast of it. Movements struggle for it. Commercials sell it. People die for it. And millions daily long for it. Wherever you are on the political spectrum, *freedom* is the watchword. Conservatives fight to protect it; liberals want to expand it; and ethnonationalists assert their freedom over that of others. The vast impersonal forces that vie for power in our lives—technology, economy, history, government, and society—each claim to be paths to freedom, be it in the form of "liberating technologies," "free economies," "the historical growth of freedom," "free governments," or "free societies."

Given its preeminent role in our vocabulary, it is not surprising that we fight not just *for* freedom, but *about* freedom. What *is* freedom? Must we all be free? What are the limits on freedom? How are they drawn? Does your freedom violate my freedom? Indeed, the word *freedom* most often appears in our ordinary speech as either an interrogative or a declarative, a perplexed or probing question, or a confident and assertive answer. The meaning of freedom is not just a philosophical question; it is also a practical, everyday one: at best, freedom is what distinguishes our life from all the other ways which we are forced to do things; but at worst, freedom itself becomes a force, be it in the form of coercive "free market" forces that compel us to relocate for a job, "freedom" militias that use fists or guns to enforce their way, or credit card slogans ultimately meant to indenture us. We therefore struggle not only *about* freedom; we struggle *with* freedom.

For Hannah Arendt too, there was no single more important word in the political vocabulary than *freedom*. "What distinguishes the communal life of people in the polis from all other forms of human communal life," she wrote, "is freedom."[1] Nevertheless, as insistent as she was on the central place of freedom in politics, she warned against getting too exclusively focused on it. Freedom, Arendt cautioned, is *not* "the end purpose of politics."[2] If it were, then politics would be only a *means* to our freedom, a vehicle to transport us to the higher life of freedom, and—who knows?—there might be a better, more direct vehicle to the destination. Plenty of people seem to think there is. The gurus of Silicon Valley tell us that their digital machines can get us the equivalent of a direct flight to personal freedom; advertisers tell us that the scent of a new lotion can make us feel free; politicians tell us that their economic policies will grant us greater freedom; generals assure us they can "win" freedom; and prophets of the "posthuman" have told us that science will get us there (as have totalitarian leaders).

Indeed, the world is full of powerful people who promise, in one way or another, to engineer or enforce our freedom. This fact worried Arendt a great deal, for politics, she argued, is not a simple "means" to freedom; rather, she held that "politics and freedom are *identical*."[3] Human freedom in human community is always *political* freedom: "Freedom exists *only* in the unique intermediary space of politics."[4] At the heart of "the very *existence* of politics" is "the cause of freedom versus tyranny."[5] For Arendt, any dream of freedom apart from a dream of politics is a recipe for tyranny of one kind or another, be it the tyranny of technology, of markets, of history, of states, of selves, or of the sciences. Human freedom can be realized only politically, and ultimately democratically, as we related to one another as equals apart from force or violence. Freedom therefore depends on politics, and politics on our understanding, and indeed our imagination, of freedom.[6]

In the last chapter of this book, in order to stimulate our political imaginations (and therefore our imagination of freedom), I look at two of the most imaginative political writers ever to live at the same time in the same place, Thomas Hobbes (1588–1679) and John Milton (1608–1674). You probably know of Milton's *Paradise Lost*, and you've probably heard of Hobbes's book *Leviathan* (or, at least, of the comic strip *Calvin and Hobbes*, a subtle allusion to John Calvin and Thomas Hobbes). Hobbes and Milton were on opposing sides of an epic civil war in the 1640s between the English king and Parliament. Hobbes was a pro-king royalist, Milton a pro-Parliament republican. For both of them, *freedom* was the watchword. But as we will see, their conceptions of freedom were at odds. The differences came down to the way they imagined *freedom*. Their stories, in turn, give us an opportunity to think about our own political imaginations and our imagination of freedom.

What Is the Political Imagination?

Arendt gave a starring role to the imagination in politics. Politics, she argued, is among other things an art of new and renewed beginnings.[7] Every time we speak and act in public, we have the potential to start something anew, and even to introduce something altogether new into the world. But to act anew, Arendt noted, we have to be able to "mentally remove ourselves from where we are physically located and *imagine* that things might as well be different from what they actually are."[8] Our imagination, she continued, allows us to see that "we are *free* to change the world and to start something new in it."[9] "Imagination alone," she wrote elsewhere,

> enables us to see things in their proper perspective, to be strong enough to put that which is too close at a certain distance so that we can see and understand it without bias and prejudice, to be generous enough to bridge abysses of remoteness until we can see and understand everything that is too far away from us as though it were our own affair.[10]

This is the essence of the political imagination. It takes effort, practice, and persistence. For this reason, imagination for Arendt is intimately tied to thinking. If, as Arendt argued, so many of the horrific humanitarian crimes of the twentieth century depended on the cooperation of thoughtless people like Adolf Eichmann, their thoughtlessness, she argued, came down to a "lack of imagination." They refused to make the effort look beyond the screens of the murderous machines of which they were a part to consider their victims.[11] Lacking a political imagination is more than lacking interest in partisan politics (something that can be excused, for sure). It is a basic and sometimes catastrophic failure to think creatively about what it means to be human on Earth with others.

Such imaginative thinking requires no special qualifications and is not out of our everyday reach. Consider the liveliness of our imagination in other areas of life. For example, many of us have moments where we imagine a gadget that can fix problems. My car breaks down on the side of the road. Couldn't they, I wonder, just make a small, battery-powered reserve motor, built in to the car, that would give me just enough power to get to the nearest mechanic? Or what about using body heat to keep our smartphones charged? Or—a favorite of an old science teacher of mine who thought a lot about radioactive waste—why not seal toxic stuff in a fortified container and shoot it into deep space? Some of our ideas are practical, others fantastical; in any case, they tap into a *technological* imagination, one that is nurtured in our lives in hundreds of little ways throughout the week, from movies to commercials to our everyday use of all sorts of gadgets. Few of us have difficulty thinking about how technology might be able to make our lives better.

Our economic imagination is no less developed. Profit making, competitive individualism, property rights, and the laws of supply and demand are widely understood and broadly embraced. The "market"—that most mysterious of global forces—is taken for granted by many millions, if not billions, as a real thing that powerfully if elusively regulates our job prospects, the price we pay for milk, our opportunities for a mate, and our rent. We have no problem imagining the market as a living thing; we hear all the time about the market "wanting," "thinking," "checking," "reacting," "wishing," and a myriad of other things that people used to think only persons could do. And so, it is clear that we have a lively imagination for the economy.

So too, let's be frank, with violence. For many people, war does not need to be imagined at all. It is a living reality, in memory or in everyday life. But for many others, it is a far-off reality that is nevertheless very active in the imagination. We have movies, books, Netflix shows, video games, and newspaper accounts that constantly feed our imagination of war. And it's not just war that occupies our imagination of violence—we live with images of not only war heroes, but superheroes; not only battle scenes, but street fights; not only massacres, but rape and domestic violence. As the ubiquity of America's gun culture, the popularity of American football, and the billions made on prize fights all attest, we have no problem imagining violence. We can see what it means to use force to get what we want, or to have it used against us.

But most of us are not nearly so imaginative when it comes to politics. We are slower—much slower—to come up with practical or fantastical political approaches to various problems. Relative to technology, the economy, or violence, most of us struggle to think creatively and dynamically about politics. We lack an active political imagination. There is both a good and a bad reason for this lack. The good reason is that we sense, if subconsciously, that politics is uncertain. All of us, like Arendt, are children of the twentieth century, even those of us born in the twenty-first century; and the wars, revolutions, genocides, and dictatorships of the recent past have shown just how horribly awful—indeed evil—the rulers of the world can be. Understandably, then, people reacted to these horrors by looking for non- or suprapolitical solutions to the world's problems. We started looking beyond politics to improve our lot and to better our world.

Is a world beyond politics possible?[12] If so, would it be a better world? Is there really a technological, economic, or violent fast track to freedom? Is there a gadget to heal the wounds of historical hatred that entrap us? Can the markets restore broken trust among people? Will more force and violence make our world more livable? When we look to engineering or markets or force to solve the problems of living together, we ask more of them than they can ever offer. The same, you might object, can be said of politics: Can politics fix all our problems? Clearly, no. But politics, as we have seen, can improve the quality of our lives in ways that technology, the economy, and violence cannot—for authentic politics is possible only under conditions of freedom, and freedom possible only within political relations. This, I think, is what Arendt meant by saying that politics and freedom are identical. All political problems are in one way or another problems of and about freedom.

But Arendt also declared, "Men *are* free—as distinguished from their possessing the gift for freedom—as long as they act, neither before nor after; for to *be* free and to act are the same."[13] Arendt seemed to think that not only are politics and freedom identical, but so are freedom and action. Politics, freedom, action: these are the three central characters in Arendt's political imagination. They interanimate one another and are for her so interdependent as to be virtually indistinguishable.

Here Arendt was clearly taking sides in a historic debate between those who see freedom as a state or condition of being—especially of a self in isolation—and those who see it as a quality or way of being with other people.[14] Hobbes and Milton articulated what would become two great imaginative currents of the modern age: the imagination of freedom as action (Milton), and the imagination of freedom as movement within borders (Hobbes). Part of the great energy of their dispute came from the fact that they were directly involved in a major conflict over freedom, the English Civil Wars. The English Civil Wars were off-and-on bloody battles between King Charles I, Parliament, and their respective armies. The clashes lasted nearly a decade and culminated in one of the most momentous acts in English history, the beheading of Charles I in 1649. The English Civil Wars are thought by some to be the first modern political revolution, laying the groundwork for later revolutions in places like America, France, and Haiti.[15] They were certainly the first great civil war to be fought explicitly over the cause of "freedom."

The English Civil Wars also stirred extraordinary political ambitions and anxieties. Milton articulated the ambition: he wanted a republic where people were free to act, speak, write, and judge. Hobbes, by contrast, articulated the anxieties: he wanted a stable political order, a nation where people were "free" so long as they stayed in their place. As a consequence, though

Hobbes is considered a great political philosopher, he was in fact quite fed up with politics and ready for a new regime, a regime of social engineering. Hobbes's imagination was better suited to the physics laboratory (or, as I will point out, the pool hall) than the sometimes-topsy-turvy world of politics. Milton, by contrast—despite the fact that he is considered a literary figure rather than a political theorist—was possessed by a lively political imagination that infused even his most famous literary works like *Paradise Lost*. This meant that Milton could imagine freedom *politically*, whereas his fellow citizen Hobbes could only imagine it *physically*.

Hobbes and the State of Freedom

Thomas Hobbes might be the most important philosopher of freedom in the last five hundred years. He was also a careful student of billiards (a favorite pastime of the French monarch Louis XIV, at whose court Hobbes spent time during a period of political exile). For Hobbes, freedom, like a billiard ball in motion, was a physical condition or state. "Liberty, or freedom," Hobbes wrote at the beginning of the twenty-first chapter of his famous book *Leviathan*, "signifieth properly the absence of opposition." By "opposition," he clarified, "I mean external impediments of motion." He continued: "A FREE-MAN, is he, that in those things, which by his strength and wit he is able to do, is not hindered to do what he has a will to."[16] It is this conception of freedom as that which belongs to an isolated physical body that Hobbes wished to forward. "Free-men" are free by virtue of the absence of opposition to their power to move, as are free particles or free billiard balls. For Hobbes there are two sorts of bodies in the world: they are not the animate and inanimate, or the rational and nonrational, or the human and the nonhuman, but rather those bodies that are free to move in a given space and those that are not. Accordingly, freedom or liberty—Hobbes used the words interchangeably—is but matter in motion.

This definition of freedom was in Hobbes's time rather novel. Nevertheless, it would become extraordinarily persuasive. Indeed, most of us think today that to be "free" is essentially to be free *of* or free *from* something (for example, free of meetings, free of the intrusions of the government, or free from nagging children). This view of freedom is sometimes called "negative freedom" because it sees freedom as a *not*—not being bound, hindered, or obligated. Negative freedom is at the heart of the rights- and rules-based form of political liberalism associated with the works of John Locke and his interpreters. But its first great architect was the absolutist Hobbes.

One of the most influential liberal philosophers of the twentieth century, the Oxford scholar Isaiah Berlin, wrote that negative freedom is "the degree to which no man or body of men interferes with my activity"; it is "simply the area within which a man can act unobstructed by others."[17] This sounds just like Hobbes, for whom freedom is essentially a *physical* phenomenon. As Hobbes went on to explain, the words *freedom* and *liberty* therefore "may be applied no less to irrational and inanimate creatures than to rational."[18] That is, you don't have to be a human to be free; you don't even have to be an animal. Water will do:

> For whatever is so tied, or surrounded, as it cannot move but within a certain space . . . has not [the] "liberty" to go further. And so [we say] of all living creatures, while they are imprisoned, or restrained with walls or chains [that they have no "liberty" to go further]; *and of the water* while it is kept in by banks or vessels, that otherwise would spread itself into a larger space.[19]

Therefore, the caged-up prisoner and water caught in a pool both lack liberty, or freedom. For Hobbes there is no significant definitional or qualitative distinction to be made between humans and water with respect to the concept of freedom. Both are equally unfree if they face external impediments of motion.

Or perhaps I should say they are both equally "free," for this now commonsense conception of freedom sees it as a state, a bounded condition. For Hobbes the organizing metaphor for freedom is always the movement of concrete bodies within a bounded space. This is a conception that would seem suited more to a physics laboratory (or a billiard table) than a political society, except that this is exactly the conception Hobbes is advocating for a political society. By its logic, the prisoner walking within the prison yard is indeed free—at least, within the bounds of the yard—just as a retired person walking the sidewalks of a suburban community is free within the bounds of the public sidewalks. With respect to freedom, therefore, the difference between the prisoner and the retired person is quantitive but not qualitative. The retired person simply has more room to roam. That's it. But neither the prisoner nor the retiree has unlimited room to move. Both are thus simultaneously both bound and free.

Note also that both the prisoner and the retiree may possess certain rights within these bounded spaces. It is quite possible, in other words, to reconcile the protection of certain rights with imprisonment. Hobbes was a philosopher of politics by wall and border, through and through. As such, he set a low bar for freedom. It requires only space to roam. Within that space you are free, and may even be endowed with certain rights. The political challenge for Hobbes is determining *who* is free to roam *where*. Not coincidently, this question has been a preoccupation of modern law as well as modern law enforcement. Property law is in fact at the origin of modern rights-based political liberalism. As Locke argued in the generation immediately after Hobbes, our first and most fundamental right is the right to "own" ourselves; everything else can be said to follow. Therefore, law comes down to drawing and defending boundaries that create a space for our individual "freedom" over and against that of others.[20]

When we talk about freedom today in a political context it is hard for us to resist the territorial metaphors Hobbes gave us: walling, guarding, enclosing, fencing, restraining, defending, protecting, and so on. If freedom is the absence of opposition, then to protect my freedom I paradoxically need to build oppositional barriers to opposition. This includes opposing other people—for in this way of imagining freedom, *people* represent a primary, and not a mere secondary, hindrance to my freedom (especially people who I don't know, who are strange to me, or who seem powerful or threatening to me). For this reason, when Hobbes imagines a lawless "state of nature"—a condition where there are no formal, legal barriers in place to protect my freedom—all he can envision is a great body of people knocking into each other like a great mass of billiard balls, where each encounters the others as impediments to freedom. These people, stuck in a state of nature, will do what in Hobbes's view is natural and logical, and what moderns have done millions of times since: they kill each other. The result is Hobbes infamous "war of every man, against every man."[21]

Sovereign States and Sovereign Selves

Given such an imagined catastrophe, Hobbes envisioned a politics of freedom by borders. For him, though, a politics of freedom by borders comes with a hitch: it is also a politics of freedom by domination. The ironic conclusion of Hobbes's reduction of freedom to the freedom to move within boundaries is that, in his view, every polity absolutely depends on a "sovereign"—a person or institution with unlimited freedom to set boundaries. If politics is essentially a boundary project aimed at determining who can go where and in what ways, then by this logic someone has to stand outside and above the system to operate it. For Hobbes, this is the sovereign.

Sovereignty is as important a concept in modern politics as freedom is, and not coincidentally. The word itself comes from the fusion of two older words meaning "super-reign." A cluster of historical, philosophical, and theological factors lay behind the modern concept, but at its core it entails the power and authority to do whatever one wills in an absolute way. Hobbes argued that freedom apart from such sovereign power inevitably results in war and chaos. Therefore, sovereign power is the deus ex machina of Hobbes's political fantasy and the one great exception to his political logic. Sovereign power must itself, by Hobbes's rendering, be boundless—for how, he asked, could that which is bounded effectively set boundaries for all others? Such checked power could never be "sovereign" power. Sovereign power must be absolutely free, or simply absolute.

Arendt saw in this identification of sovereignty with freedom a notion that was "most pernicious and dangerous" to politics; it set up an equation where "the freedom of one man, or a group, or a body politic can be purchased only at the price of the freedom, i.e., the sovereignty, of all others."[22] Indeed, though Hobbes sought to overcome the supposed "war of all against all," he did not actually overcome war so much as reorganize and redirect war into the freedom of an absolute sovereign against the freedom of all the others. For Hobbes, we will always be at war.[23] The Hobbesian question comes down to: Who is fighting against whom, and in what ways? This is what "politics" was all about, he thought.

Nearly three centuries after Hobbes published *Leviathan*, the German political philosopher Carl Schmitt, a contemporary of Arendt, published a little book called *The Leviathan in the State Theory of Thomas Hobbes* (1938). Schmitt, unlike Arendt, was a very sympathetic reader of Hobbes. He advocated for strong sovereigns and strong sovereign states, so much so that Schmitt embraced the cause of the Nazis, seeing it as, among other things, a necessary antidote to what he considered the weak governments of Europe. Schmitt thought that Hobbes's project had been tragically cut short. Whereas Hobbes set out to establish sovereign states with strong sovereign rulers, Schmitt argued "sovereign selves" had instead won out under the guise of "liberalism." In an explicitly anti-Semitic argument, Schmitt blamed this "weakness" of European political society on Jews scheming to protect their religious beliefs from the authority of the state.[24] The result, he argued, was a Western world of strong selves but weak states incapable of rousing their people—for example, the people of Germany—to act on behalf of state interests against the enemies of the state.

As uncomfortable as it may be, Schmitt articulated many of our own assumptions about politics, and this is in part because for all his criticisms of liberalism, Schmitt was working within the same Hobbesian outlines as political liberals. In this liberal vision, the crucial questions of politics come down to the question of sovereignty: Who is in charge? Who has power? Who has the freedom to decide?[25] The answer to this question for many of us has the form of an equation: *political power = the right to choose + the power to enforce that choice*. Political power, that is, is sovereign power. By this logic, the essence of political power is the freedom to use force to enforce one's decisions, for without force, we cannot *en*force our decisions. This thinking is basic to modern states, liberal and authoritarian alike, such that Max Weber, a political liberal, could define the state as "a human community that (successfully) claims the *monopoly of the legitimate use of physical force* within a given territory."[26] What, then, is politics in Weber's rendering? It is "any kind of *independent* leadership in action"; *modern* politics is "the [independent] leadership . . . of a *state*."[27] Weber argued that the essence of modern politics is the sovereign state with its sovereign ruler.

But let's take this down to a more personal level. If I, as a member of a political community, feel as though I have strong political standing as an individual, or that the group of which I am a member has strong standing, it is most likely because I feel my or my group's decisions, choices, or will is both *reflected in* and *enforced by* the state (or government). I "see" my or my group's interests reflected in the sovereign power of the state. If, on the other hand, I feel powerless, unrepresented, or disenfranchised, it is likely because I neither "see myself" in the sovereign nor feel like I can appeal to the state to enforce my will. What the enfranchised and disenfranchised alike share here is a sense of the state as a means of enforcing and protecting interests. "Politics" becomes but a means of furthering one's will in the world, an instrument of power; it also becomes inextricably bound to the sovereign power as the only means of enforcing our sense of political representation or enfranchisement. We are thus all subjects of the sovereign, just as Hobbes insisted.

And this is why Arendt, who did not share these ideas, thought that sovereignty was such a pernicious threat to politics. It reduces politics to the logic of enforcing will and makes power the be-all and end-all of politics. It makes politics a "means" only, a virtual feat of engineering or policing, rather than a means *and* an end of human community. Even more, Arendt suggested that sovereignty is a threat to the very peace that Hobbes claimed he sought, because sovereignty is possessed by an insidious circular logic that creates conditions where violence makes more, rather than less, sense.[28] Think about it: sovereignty—be it a sovereign state or a sovereign self— entails the fantasy of total freedom to do what you will.[29] This is clearly incompatible with living peaceably with others who also consider themselves sovereign, be they states or selves; for if two or more "sovereigns" each ascribe to a fantasy of total freedom, what happens when these "sovereigns" find each other blocking their freedom? True, if they are especially reasonable and possess great foresight, they may choose to compromise or qualify their freedom in the name of getting along. But if sovereignty is ultimately freedom, how long are they likely to tolerate such a compromised state? So, sovereignty creates, rather than mitigates against, conditions for a violent clash of sovereign wills.[30]

Schmitt was fully aware of this violent conclusion, and he embraced it. "The political," he said, comes down to the existential distinction "between friend and enemy."[31] Individuals who see themselves as sovereign will find in those who confront, challenge, or otherwise make difficult their exercise of sovereignty not just rivals but downright *enemies*. So too with states committed to their uncompromised sovereignty. Hence, politics really is for Schmitt, as with Hobbes, war by other means; politics has its logical end, Schmitt said quite explicitly, in "physical killing."[32]

But why ennoble the concept of combat with the dignity of politics? Why do Hobbes and Schmitt bother with "politics" at all, given their conclusions that there is really no escaping the condition of war, only the nature and extent of it? It seems that both Hobbes and Schmitt wanted to preserve a place for "politics" in a world of war not because the force of their reasoning but because common sense told them that there is little sense, or at least little self-dignity, in championing a world of war and nothing but war. Such militarism would undermine the conceptions of politics in which they claimed to be philosophically interested. Perhaps Hobbes and Schmitt too, at this point, stopped ever so briefly to *think*?

Arendt asks us all to stop and think about the concept of sovereignty. The Hobbesian concept of sovereignty emerged as a solution to the problem of war and conflict, but it was just a quick fix. Sovereignty has in fact done nothing to end the conflicts Hobbes hoped it would. In fact, it has made the peace he sought difficult to achieve because it leads to the absolute logic of rights, power, and will, leaving us in one state of war or another. This logic lives on in contemporary political cultures in a myriad of ways. It keeps us bound to the state as an instrument of force, and constantly wary of others as potential combatants. Yet we, like Schmitt, continue to talk of "politics." Perhaps we too want to find a better way. If so, Arendt would suggest that we should interrogate more the meaning of *freedom*.

The Quality of Freedom

As a rule, Arendt was not interested in the precise technical meanings of words as she was in the phenomena and experiences that we try to describe when we use words: "Each new appearance among men stands in need of a new word, whether a new word is coined to cover a new experience or an old word is used and given an entirely new meaning. This is doubly true for the political sphere of life, where speech rules supreme."[33] Yet, understanding the word *freedom*, she admitted, "seems to be a hopeless enterprise."[34] Science, she suggested, tells us that we are not nearly as free as we might think: "Under the concerted assault of the modern debunking 'sciences,' psychology and sociology, nothing indeed has seemed to be more safely buried than the concept of freedom."[35] This is because psychology, sociology, and now certain expressions of neuroscience and the cognitive sciences, tell us that we are never really free, that our environment, our genes, or our neural pathways strongly condition, if not determine, our lives. At the very same time we have seen the word *freedom* used and abused both to justify the grossest forms of domination and violence and to sell the most trivial of consumer goods. Still, how could we not try to understand freedom, given that freedom is so central not only to our political vocabulary, but to our inner sense of self as "free and hence responsible"?[36]

Arendt argued it is politics that holds the clue to the meaning of freedom, for in politics we experience freedom "as a worldly tangible reality" rather than a scientific, ideological, or even philosophical concept.[37] In an essay called "What Is Freedom?," Arendt argued that if we want to solve the riddle of our freedom we have to return to the fact of our political existence. In politics, unlike philosophy, science, ideology, or even our ever-changing sense of self, we find humans who are either free or not free inasmuch as they are able to freely *act*. Without assuming that freedom exists, we could never conceive of ourselves as acting in the world with others, as opposed to simply moving along with the currents of culture, history, or biology.

As an analogy, think of what it feels like to be carried along in a large crowd down a tunnel after a sporting event or concert. Here we feel ourselves simply moving, literally pushed along by the mass of people, just as much as a ball or a wheel would be. We do not act, we simply move; so too, we are not free—we are compelled by the force of the bodies around us. Now imagine yourself shouting out, "Stay calm! Everybody move along together!" Unlike the movements of your body in the tunnel, your words here are not compelled. They are freely chosen. Thus, you *act* through your speech, even as you are moved along. Politics for Arendt is the point in our existence when we choose to "shout out" or otherwise act with others so as to address the myriad of social and historical situations around us that seem to be out of our control, and *freedom* is the word that we use to try to account for the experience we have of being able to so speak or act.

It is not a coincidence that in classical Greek and Latin, as well as in West

Germanic dialects, Old Norse, Old French, and Middle English, words associated with freedom have tended to range from denoting a state to a status to, finally, a *quality*. In a lengthy discussion of the word *free* in his book *Studies in Words*, C. S. Lewis argues that words for freedom often begin as words denoting someone's status—typically a legal or social status, as with "free men" versus slaves—but then move over time to take on what Lewis calls a "secondary, social-ethical sense" describing the *quality* of a person, action, or even thing.[38] And so, for example, in Greek, *eleutheros* means "free" as in "not a slave."[39] It can also refer to a *polis* or some other bounded area that is autonomous or free of any bondage to another state. In his *Politics*, Aristotle contrasts the "free square" (or free agora) from the commercial space; the former is free by virtue of being full of men having the status of "free" who are engaged in leisurely activities; the latter is unfree because it is devoted to commercial activities, or matters of necessity, many of them carried out by slaves and servants.[40]

But within ancient Greek cultures, *eleutheros* could also mean a *quality* of being, the *character* of a person or thing, which is associated with the sorts of qualities a free person has, or ought to have. For example, a fragment of Menander can say, "Live in slavery with the spirit of a freeman (*eleutherôs*) and you will be no slave."[41] In Latin, *liber* is used to describe both a free person, rather than a slave, and a free thing, as when Ovid (in a passage that no doubt would later please Hobbes) describes the water of the sea as *liberioris* than the water of rivers, as the latter is comparatively open and unconfined.[42] But *liber* in Latin also refers to a quality of mind, of character, or of an action: Cicero speaks of the generous people who ransom prisoners of war as *liberalis*.[43] Indeed, until the end of the eighteenth century, the English and the French *liberal* (both descending from the Latin *liber*) appeared overwhelmingly as adjectives indicating the quality of a person or act.[44]

The same basic tendency is seen in old Northern European languages and dialects. For example, the word *frank* began as a name for a people, the Franks. But the Franks were conquerors: in the sixth century they conquered Gaul, taking control of a bunch of Roman villas. Hence the free persons, the Franks, became *frank*; whereas the inhabitants of the Roman villas became servants and slaves, or *villains*. Over time, of course, well after the end of the Franks, *frank* came to strictly mean a quality of speech: open, honest, and direct; and villains were, well, villainous.[45]

So goes the story of these words: in each case we see them range from a state of being, a status (typically a legal status), to a quality or attribute (most often an "ethical" quality or attribute). In each case, that is, we see their meanings move in significance from a state or status to describe a *quality* of a person or a thing. In each case, that is, except for one: the English word *free* itself, which never takes on a strongly ethical or qualitative meaning that all those other words did.[46] Indeed, today, my *New Oxford English Dictionary* has eight entries for *free*, none of which have an ethical denotation, and in seven of the eight entries *free* is defined negatively, centered on "not" or "without," whether "not physically restrained," or "without charge."

Admittedly, these relatively narrow etymologies and sample dictionary definitions do not in themselves tell us nearly everything we would need to know about the history of the idea, concept, or even language of freedom. But the evidence here, limited as it is, gels with Arendt's claim that significant pressures have been put on the concept and ideal of freedom in the modern world. In keeping with Hobbes, "freedom" has become a state and no more. We so-called "freedom lovers" seem only to know how to be free like billiard balls, within borders and against oppositional forces. We only know how to be free within "states" where we have a certain "status." We are free, but in the way that the prisoner in the prison yard is free.

Therefore, with Arendt, we need to get imaginative and start to push on our ideas of freedom. In the remainder of this chapter, I am going to turn to John Milton, a major poetic figure (and in his own day an active political figure), to stimulate our political imagination. Milton was on the opposite side of Hobbes in the English Civil Wars and the various debates and contests that surrounded them. Whereas Hobbes was allied with the monarchy, Milton was allied with Parliament in its ongoing struggles with the king. As we will see, though, Milton challenged acts of Parliament too, willing to stand up to them on the matter of censorship. He was nothing if not a republican, committed to the power of the people, especially their power to speak and act about matters of common concern. Milton brought "free" and "freedom" into a political-ethical semantic domain that Arendt would have recognized.[47] Like Arendt, he rendered it a *quality of action*.[48]

Political Paradise

Milton's *Paradise Lost* is among the most famous poems ever written. More than a poem, it is an epic allegorical commentary on both the human condition and the condition of the people of England in Milton's own day. It is nothing if not a political myth, a tale of rulers and rebels, laws and lawbreakers, sovereigns and subjects, order and disorder. It is also a tale about freedom and its opposites. Given the title, one way to read *Paradise Lost* is as a tale of political paradise at war with political hell—which, for more than a few in Milton's day, was the essence of the contest in the English Civil Wars.

What does political paradise look like? For Milton, this is a poetic and theological question as much as it was a political one. It is also, in some sense, the hidden question lurking behind Hobbes's hellish "war of all against all," the question Hobbes and so many of his liberal successors dare not ask for fear of fueling into flames an incendiary, "utopian" political imagination. But it is for Milton an essential question in that it provides people on Earth—where neither heaven nor hell are fully realized—a guidepost around which to organize their political efforts, and a motive, other than Hobbes's fear, from which to act.

In *Paradise Lost*, paradise is a place of freedom, or what Arendt would call "public freedom."[49] This, of course, resonates not only with Arendt, but with our own political desires, yes? And "freedom" here is the freedom to *choose*. This too is our desire, yes? Milton is no fatalist or determinist; no political thinker is, nor can they be. To leave the future to the fates, or to historical, market, technological, or social forces, is to be an antipolitical thinker. Every political thinker, on the other hand, is a humanist by default, committed to the power persons have to change the course of events. Therefore the will—indeed, "free will"—is a critical concept in Milton's work, as it was in Arendt's.[50] More than a notion, the will is for Milton a power—*the* power, we might think—by which we assert our self as a self into the world, by which we take our stand, stake our ground, make our declaration of independence. The exercise of free will: here we come very near to our political paradise.

But not to Milton's. Not yet. For Milton the will is not enough; choice is not sovereign. The will is "mutable," subject to outside influence, including the influence of "discourse" or speech. The will may be free but it is not self-sufficient, and can never be so. The lone will, like a lost and isolated human, is naked, vulnerable, and exposed. It needs others. It needs a kind of governance, its own little political society, a house of parliament composed of speech and wisdom.[51] This, then, is the political republic at the heart of Milton's political paradise: the separate but equal powers of will, speech, and wisdom.

It is within this republic that Milton offered a poetic picture of a political paradise in *Paradise Lost* of what he called "Rational Libertie." The phrase, when contrasted with *freedom*, sounds not only antiquated but severe; in seventeenth-century England, though, *rational* did not carry the austere denotations of later-day Enlightenment Europe. It did not suggest "removed." Rather, it would have suggested a well-ordered freedom. To put it another way, the "rational" for Milton is not the seat of abstract computer-like calculating, but of wisdom, or even better at this point, prudence—the capacity to judge what is most fitting among various priorities, policies, and possibilities, especially with respect to judgments about the future.[52] Therefore, in Milton's political paradise, humanity is God's vice regent, presiding in and over creation by virtue of judging *what is fitting*. Could there be anything more political? No. For as we saw earlier, judging is not only a primary political act but also the most ubiquitous of political acts. All political acts, big and small, from revolutions to voting on resolutions, begin and end in judgments.[53]

Judging is a theme probed at some depth in another book that was written when Milton was a child: Hugo Grotius's 1625 *Rights of War and Peace* (*De Jure Belli ac Pacis*). It was an enormously influential book, not the least for Milton.[54] One of the distinct contributions of *Rights of War and Peace* is its argument for *attributive* justice. Attributive justice, for Grotius (modifying Aristotle's notion of "distributive" justice), consists not in granting to each his or her due—or what a person is *owed*—but in offering what is *fitting* or *apt*. To illustrate it, Grotius retold the story, recorded first by the Greek historian Xenophon, of the Persian king Cyrus the Great, who, when giving two coats to two boys, determines to give the small coat to the small boy and the big coat to the big boy for the reason that they are suitable or fitting (quite literally). But for this decision, Cyrus, according to Xenophon, is blamed by his teacher for not asking who rightfully owned each tunic, regardless of whether it fitted. Was one tunic *due* or *owed* to one of the boys?[55]

Grotius suggested that Cyrus's teacher overreacted, and argued further that while there are very important instances where "What is owed?" is the right question, there are a whole range of other questions that are more like judging, "What fits?" That is, there are a whole range of political issues where the central question is not what is owed or due—What *rights* are at stake? we often ask—but rather what is fitting or appropriate. It is not that attributive justice replaces compensatory justice; it compensates for the latter's limits. For example, in considering the justice of war, Grotius argued that while a king may claim a due "right" to wage war on another king as a strict means of retribution for a prior injustice, this is a thin basis on which to judge whether to wage war or not. "There are many arguments whereby we may be dissuaded from exacting punishments," not the least the "welfare" of others.[56] The particular situation should determine the course of action, Grotius argues, rather than the mere right.

Milton's paradise is a place where this sort of attributive justice is arbitrated, these sorts of judgments enacted. Note that for Grotius and Milton alike the paradigm for this kind of attributive justice is not the commercial marketplace—the exchange of this for that according to that which is owed or due, as John Locke would have it. Rather, it is *discourse*, or even better *rhetoric* (see chapter 5), in which the speaker seeks a fitting reply to a situation or statement, rather than looking for an outside or "sovereign" rule or standard for a response.[57] For example, Grotius described "prudence" as "persuading" or "dissuading" decision makers, rather than commanding or dictating to them a right course of action.[58] So too, for Milton the highest human faculty, reason, is intimately tied to rhetoric, such that Raphael, the great angel of *Paradise Lost*, presents reason as "discursive" and manifest in "discourse."[59]

In tying free will to wisdom and speech—and ultimately to situated, prudential acts of judgment—Milton gives us a picture of freedom that is not delimited by boundaries but is realized in action. Anyone can be politically free by acting in word or deed, for, as Ariella Azoulay summarizes Arendt's thinking on the matter, "it is never possible to know where action will end."[60] There is a strange kind of free power in action: anything can result.[61]

So much for Milton's political paradise. What, then, of his political hell? In Milton's hell, which is Satan's hell, freedom is understood exclusively in terms of a state or a status. Much as Carl Schmitt would later insist that "the political" rests on the distinction between friend and enemy, Satan in *Paradise Lost* can approach his own political being only in terms of an absolute distinction between sovereignty and servitude: "Better to reign in Hell, than to serve in Heaven."[62] The angel Raphael, in rehearsing the story of Satan's great rebellion to Adam, quotes Satan as saying:

> Will ye submit your necks, and chuse to bend
> The supple knee? ye will not, if I trust
> To know ye right, or if ye know your selves
> Natives and Sons of Heav'n possest before
> By none, and if not equal all, yet free,
> Equally free.[63]

Freedom is here nonsubmission—no more, no less.[64] Liberty is thus "hard," as Mammon puts it amid the company of rebel angels, but hard liberty is preferable to what Mammon renders as "servile Pomp."[65] Freedom is but freedom *from*. Freedom is but a state.

So, in Milton's *Paradise Lost* there are two concepts of freedom coinciding with the two poles of the historical meanings of liberty, frankness, and so on—status and quality—as well as with two political realms in Milton's epic imagination, hell and paradise. Hell is a state—and here let us imagine with Milton a "state" as both a state of being and a political state—hell is a state where freedom is nothing but a state, or a status. It is akin to Hobbes's pool of water, "free" within its bounds. In paradise, on the contrary, freedom is realized in a distinct quality of thought, action, and speech; and in speech it is actualized rather than bounded. Milton thus characterizes true liberty as "inward," in the sense of that which is potential and waiting to be realized in particular situations.[66] Milton's "inward freedom" is neither a natural state granted to some humans over others (as political freedom was for Aristotle[67]), or a product of fortune (as freedom was for the Machiavellians in Milton's day). Freedom is "inward" for Milton because it is rooted in a general human *capacity* that is realized in a quality of action that entails the cooperation of will, reason, and speech—or, to put it otherwise, the political trinity of the power of choice, the governance of prudential wisdom, and the exercise of rhetoric. In Adam's fall in *Paradise Lost*, it is this order that goes awry, and consequently human discord erupts.[68] From this vantage point, servitude itself is transfigured into ethical terms. Abdiel, Milton's noble angel, thus declares: "This is servitude, to serve the unwise."[69]

Rhetorical Freedom

But what else can we say about the quality of freedom other than this cooperation of will, reason, and speech, or choice, wisdom, and discourse? In Milton's earlier work, *Areopagitica* (1644), freedom also entails a *corporate* quality of the commonwealth that looks a lot like Arendt's "public freedom." *Areopagitica* is often taught as the first great defense of "free speech," but it is more profound than that: it is a defense of *freely and faithfully speaking*. Milton penned this work as protest against Parliament's Licensing Order of 1643, which required all writings in England to first be approved by a censorship board before being published. Crucially, Milton published the tract without license, in defiance of Parliament's orders; indeed, he explicitly presents his tract in its opening pages as a rebuke of Parliament. But this was an act of rebuke and defiance, Milton claimed, done not only "freely," but in an act of fidelity to Parliament: "For he who freely magnifies what hath been nobly done, and fears not to declare as freely what might be done better, gives ye the best *covenant* of his fidelity."[70] Irrespective of whatever conciliatory aims Milton may have had, the political logic of the statement is especially poignant in 1640s England, a decade of broken "covenants." The measure of political fidelity is not, Milton suggested, the keeping of the letter of the covenant, but the quality of your political action in the public sphere.

It is difficult to overstate just how significant the matter of keeping and breaking covenants was amid the English Civil Wars. It was not only a constant matter of debate, it was *the* issue on which the future of England was debated by king, Parliament, and Parliament's army alike.[71] For a sense of just how central covenant keeping and breaking was to the political crises of England, consider the words of Henry Ireton at the Putney Debates (or "Army Debates") of 1647, much of which were preoccupied with the question of whether one could ever have any sort of social or political order apart from the foundational role of the covenant or constitution: "And for my part I account that the great foundation of justice, [that we should keep *covenant* one with another]; without which I know nothing of [justice] betwixt man and man. . . . There is no other foundation of right I know . . . that we should keep covenant with one another. *Covenants* freely made, freely entered into, must be kept one with another. Take away that, I do not know what ground there is of anything you can call any man's right."[72] Ireton wanted a state where law was king—an admirable idea, to say the least. But for him this seems to mean that even very bad laws need to be obeyed as though they too were king. Milton claimed to the contrary, that political fidelity is best expressed in speaking freely—freely declaring "what might be done better"—even if this means disobedience to the letter of the law. As such, Milton suggested that political order really could be rooted in freedom and in something like Grotius's attributive justice. Freely speaking what is *fitting* is, for Milton, not only the best mark of political fidelity but also the surest foundation for political order.

Indeed, like *Paradise Lost*, Milton's *Areopagitica* was motivated by a basic concern with the relationship between speaking freely and political order. It is not an anarchist tract; it is not even a libertarian one. Rather, like *Paradise Lost*, it is an argument for order over disorder, and more specifically for an order based on prudential acts of judgment done in public. Though *Areopagitica* is famous for being the first great defense of "free speech" against state censorship, its argument is not rooted in the language of rights, but rather in the idea that a people, especially under the guidance of virtuous leadership, need in each case to prudentially judge what the fitting response is to a given text, rather than render speech subject to a before-the-fact censorship. Therefore, *Areopagitica* is concerned with the quality of freedom, and by extension the quality of a commonwealth, more than a "right" to say whatever you want.

In an essay on civil disobedience written later in life, Arendt made a similar point: "There is all the difference in the world between the criminal's avoiding the public eye and the civil disobedient's taking the law into his own hands in open defiance."[73] One person breaks the law to get away with something, the other to do something for others and indeed to defend the integrity of law by challenging it when it is unjust. "The civil disobedient, though he is usually dissenting from a majority, acts in the name and for the sake of a group," Arendt wrote.[74] In this regard he acts in public as a representative, just as an official political representative does. An example of such a civil disobedient in Arendt's day was Diane Nash, who in the 1960s joined other Freedom Riders in refusing to abide by segregation laws in the Deep South on the basis of the gross unjustness of those laws, and who said in her disobedience that she too was not only free to speak and act, but to participate in the political community on behalf of others. That Nash did this in the full view of public light, as Milton did in his defiant act publishing *Areopagitica*, is the furthest thing from criminality. It is, as Milton argued and Arendt affirmed, a form of political fidelity.

"Liberty, or freedom, signify properly the absence of opposition," Hobbes wrote in the opening lines of the twenty-first chapter of *Leviathan*. Liberty or freedom, therefore, are terms that may equally be applied to "irrational and inanimate" creatures as to "rational" ones: "For whatsoever is so tied, or bounded, as it cannot move but within a certain space, which space is determined by the opposition of some external body, we say it has not liberty to go further." Therefore, as we saw, the caged-up prisoner and water caught in a pool both have liberty to a point, a boundary beyond which they lack freedom altogether.[75]

To conclude this chapter, I want to reflect a bit more on Hobbes's physics-like rendering of liberty and freedom as the absence of physical opposition. His thinking here is a lot like popular accounts of freedom today, which in one way or another define it in terms of force. I am "free," the thinking goes, if I can get my way, if my will wins, or if the powers that be enforce my interests or rights. But Hobbes's approach is also a lot like scientific accounts of human behavior today that want to explain everything through neuroscience, "brain matter," or mechanisms of material causality. In both cases, the physics of freedom, so to speak, leaves us in a position where force has the last word. Such a world, Hobbes no less than others realized, makes "politics" nothing but another regime of force.

Arendt, like Milton, was not an anarchist, opposed to laws of any kind. Nor was she a pacifist, believing that violence and force are categorically wrong. Neither did she disavow national borders; to the contrary, she saw them as crucial elements in the constitution of political rights. Arendt was, however, deeply skeptical of the seemingly overwhelming modern habit—and she saw it as a distinctly *modern* habit—to default to force in order to regulate, and even account for, the full range of human experience, including political experience. Her skepticism was rooted in common sense: though we sometimes profess and often believe that everything comes down to force, most of us simply don't live that way. Above all, this is true in the political realm. There, more than anywhere, "we hold human freedom as a self-evident truth."[76] Rather than try to explain away our allegiance to freedom as a delusion or as ideology, Arendt took our common sense seriously as a clue to what, until we can definitively prove it otherwise, is real about our human existence. Freedom is not, in Arendt's rendering, only a word, idea, or slogan; it is a *fact*—above all, a political fact.[77] Freedom, in other words, happens.

Indeed, Arendt saw Hobbes as the ideologue. In arguing for a physics-like conception of "freedom" and for a sovereign state premised on force, Hobbes had to completely eliminate the possibility of freedom being a *quality* of action and make it strictly something that can be quantified in terms of a bounded space. For Hobbes, a man who sits comfortably at home watching his slaves work for him, barking orders here and there, would be fully free within the boundaries of his plantation. For Arendt, he would hardly be free at all. He would be, to be sure, liberated from bodily want and need, but as a slave master he would have little to no experience of freedom because he would have no political, or free, relations with his fellows on the plantation. Freedom, as Margaret Canovan summarizes Arendt's case, is always a quality of "action carried on in the company of one's fellows" rather than a mere license to move around your private confines as you wish, or to boss other people around.[78]

To return to the example used earlier of the crowd departing the stadium, if you exit a sporting event with a mass of people through a tunnel, your movements can hardly be seen as *qualitatively* free; you are more or less bound to go along with the flow of the crowd. However, as we saw, if you shout out, "Stay calm! Everybody move along together!" this can be seen as a qualitatively free act on your part. If, in a different scenario, someone in the crowd puts a pistol to your back and commands you to shout, "Stay calm! Everybody move along together," in obeying you clearly are *not* qualitatively free. Therefore, we have an identical script but a qualitative difference. The sense of freedom that Arendt, Milton, and others have urged is, above all, a quality of human action, where the script is secondary. To be sure, it requires definite conditions—say, a space for speaking, fellow humans with whom to speak, the absence of compulsion—but freedom cannot be formulaically reduced to such outward conditions, as if it were merely a matter of bodies and bounded space. This is why Arendt claimed that politics, freedom, and action are so interdependent as to be virtually identical.

A good analogy for this approach to freedom is found in the world of improvisational theater. In improv, all the various actors on the stage work together to build a common story. Each is free to act in whatever way, yet each feels a strong sense of responsibility to act in such a way as to contribute the unfolding story. The conditions necessary for a successful improv performance are analogous to the conditions necessary for authentic political freedom: a stage or setting, the outlines of a common story, skilled actors or citizens, and, above all, freedom to act—the freedom to say or do what you will, and then leave it up to the others to respond as they will in the ongoing performance without anyone demanding their own way, let alone turning to violence to enforce that way. Now, an improv stage without actors is not a performance at all. A stage with mute or irresponsive actors is not a performance either. As such, improvisational theater is a qualitative phenomenon more than a simple recipe of material ingredients. It is realized in the outward performance itself, not in its setting or conception.

So too with political freedom: it comes in the form of the quality of acts and interactions.[79] Arendt held that such freedom was a positive political possibility in our age, a capacity that could be cultivated widely within our political culture. Hobbes and many of his successors, liberal and illiberal alike, implicitly or explicitly have denied the possibility of such freedom by arguing or simply assuming that freedom is nothing but a state of affairs, a relation among bodies, a status, a force, or a combination of forces. Therefore, the ultimate question before us is whether we believe, as Hobbes argued, that politics is ultimately war by other means—in which case we are no more or less free than the extent of our force in the world—or agree with Arendt that "politics and freedom are identical."[80] This is a question to which the answer demands more than academic analysis; it demands our imagination, our political imagination.

CONCLUSION

Politics Reborn

Several years ago, while working on another book, I had the opportunity to visit a massive manmade mountain cave in the southwestern United States. It was built at the cost of millions of dollars in the 1950s by the federal government and consisted of a maze of tunnels and an array of big and small rooms. It was constructed to house the president and other high-level government officials in a nuclear war. More than an underground hideout, it was an underground city designed for security, survival, sustenance, and plenty of sleep. (One of the rooms was called the "Eisenhower bedroom.")

For all its mid-twentieth-century engineering sophistication, the facility is no longer used, other than for storage and certain forms of weapons testing by the military. Indeed, even in its own time there was something elementary about the complex. To be sure, living in the mountain amid a nuclear holocaust would have presumably been better than living out in the open, but this sheltered existence would have been dim, drab, and depressing. Like prison life, it would have entailed, at best, a simple Hobbesian freedom to move within a confined space. Life there would have been more like that of the prisoners of Plato's cave: as delusional as it was dark. Does the fact that United States built this and other facilities like it in the name of fighting for "freedom" suggest, perhaps, just how mistaken we have been about freedom? If this is freedom, what then, exactly, is bondage?

What is freedom? That is the essential question on which Hannah Arendt's defense of politics turned. Freedom, she keenly argued, is the fundamental reason for politics, its *raison d'être*.[1] Apart from freedom, politics makes little sense—for machines and markets are more efficient, and force is more immediately effective. If we just want to be satisfied with "stuff," we might as well build for ourselves little gated communities, pay our association fees, install our screens, plant our flag, and call it "patriotism." And if people near or far start to threaten "our way of life," we can use guns and missiles to fend them off and hope it works. What freedom! This is precisely the sort of "freedom" that leads to literal and metaphorical caves, be they military bunkers or isolating surround-sound "man caves."

Arendt wanted us to come out of our caves and give political freedom a fighting chance, not by fighting, but by politicking—that is, by speaking and acting with one another as equals. For Arendt, as I have argued, freedom, action, and politics are identical. She wrote,

> The field where freedom has always been known . . . as a fact of everyday life is the political realm. And even today, whether we know it or not, the question of politics and the fact that man is a being endowed with the gift of action must always be present to our mind when we speak of the problem of freedom; for action and politics, among all the capabilities and potentialities of human life, are the only things of which we could not even conceive without at least assuming that freedom exists, and we can hardly touch a single political issue without, implicitly or explicitly, touching upon an issue of man's liberty.[2]

That is, to talk politics is to talk freedom for no other reason than politics is the one means we have of freely acting and interacting with everybody. As we have seen, there are numerous other ways to coordinate human behavior, to enforce order, and to exercise power and authority, but none of these other ways—not machines, not markets, not machine guns, not missiles—leave everybody free. To be sure, *a few* may be relatively free—the company of engineers, economists, generals, or presidents; but this only means that they get to live politically and we don't—and they won't be living politically in the wide world but only in the narrow confines of their secured facilities.

Politics is the art of freedom in the wide world. That's the first big takeaway of Arendt's life's work.

Since politics concerns you, me, others, and the common world we share, politics is the never-ending art of making judgment calls about what kind of world we are going to live in. The nature and scope of political power and authority comes down to the range of people who get to make such judgments. In monarchies, tyrannies, and dictatorships, authority is limited to one. In oligarchies, aristocracies, and plutocracies, it is extended to an elite few. In democracies and republics, it depends on the people. One way to think about these different types of governments is to think about them as an answer to the basic question, Who gets to live politically? (which as we now know, is virtually identical to the question, Who gets to live freely?).

But another way to think about these different types of governments is as an answer to the question, Who is responsible for making judgments? Living politically, that is, is to live freely *and* with responsibilities—responsibilities for your words, actions, and judgments.

Of course, to live with responsibilities is not the same as living responsibly. This is true across the whole of human life. There are plenty of people in all sorts of sectors who have responsibilities but do not handle them responsibly: parents who neglect children, teachers who neglect students, doctors who neglect patients, and so on. The political realm is no different in this regard from the rest of human life. Nevertheless, when citizens, politicians, or government officials act irresponsibly, we tend to jump to condemning politics as such—even though we don't attack families as such when parents are negligent, education as such when teachers are irresponsible, or medicine as such when doctors are reckless. Why is politics so vulnerable to criticism? Why are we so quick to judge politics?

As we saw in chapter 1, politics gets in our crosshairs because it is so easily twisted into something other than, more than, or less than politics: entertainment, palace intrigue, partisan maneuvering, and war by other means. And as we saw in chapter 2, politics is vulnerable because we have been told over and over again that there are better ways of ordering and organizing society than politics: markets, machines, the forces of history, or social forces like identity and ideology. But the biggest reason may be the very nature of political responsibility itself. Think about it: when markets go south, we have all sorts of ways of shifting responsibility away from ourselves to the impersonal mechanisms of the market—we say, for example, "The market is undergoing a correction," as if it were programmed with autocorrect. Likewise, when technology runs awry (which it frequently does), we turn to the language of "error," as if the designers and operators of our machines were no more responsible for their mishaps than a kid in math class. And, of course, if it's History or Society at fault, there can be no real finger-pointing.

With politics, on the other hand, when something goes awry, there are always people at which to point a finger. This is because politics begins and ends with people. It is a human art. There's no hiding the people in politics. And this is its great asset! In politics we are met with the fundamental truth of our collective existence: people are responsible. Indeed, this is true even when it comes to those supposedly "impersonal" powers like technology, the economy, history, and society: people are responsible. This is why even these supposed "alternatives" to politics have political cores. Bankers are *politically* responsible; engineers are *politically* responsible; *we the people* are politically responsible.

The great thing about politics is that responsibility is not inconsistent with freedom. Indeed, responsibility is the key to freedom: to be responsible for something means that you did whatever you did, or said whatever you said, not by force or machine-like cause and effect, but because you were *free to act*. To be sure, not everyone is equally free; there are degrees of freedom that depend on external circumstances and internal, bodily dynamics. Nevertheless, inasmuch as we can be held responsible for something, we can say that we were free in doing it. Responsibility may at times feel like a burden, but to be responsible should also feel liberating, for it means you are free to act in the situation at hand.

Policies supporting things like widespread education, health, access to opportunity, and living wages can extend the scope of responsibility and freedom. From the perspective of republican democracy, these policies are crucial, despite the fact that they are sometimes criticized as too costly. Critics of public services sometimes underappreciate the ways in which being free to act is constrained by bodily and mental well-being, and that for the human animal, like all animals, bodily and mental well-being depend in part on environmental, social, and economic factors. Still, policymakers who push for better public education, stronger health care, and basic income can be as prone as their conservative critics to forget the democratic end goal of such efforts: widespread freedom of action among the citizenry. By neglecting this manifestly political end, they default to turning us into nothing more than the subjects of social engineers.[3]

Politics is an end as well as a means. This is the second major takeaway from Arendt's work.

The basic question before us is not how to get rid of or otherwise get around politics, but how to do politics better. Some will tell us that the way to do politics better is to just let the leaders do it. Others will tell us that the way to do it better is to just let the experts do the political decision making, navigating, and nudging. And yet others will tell us that *we* need to do politics better, but the way to do this is think rationally, act civilly, and play by the official rules. Each of these approaches has a grain of truth. Faults in leadership, expertise, or officially sanctioned rules can have grave consequences for our political lives; therefore, it's certainly true that they could help as well. However, leadership, expertise, and officially sanctioned rules are not sufficient political remedies—and moreover, because each has authoritarian potential, they can exacerbate our political crises, and indeed sometimes have.

Given that politics is more a matter of quality than quantity or category, we need a renewed commitment to the politics of virtue.[4] The word *virtue* sounds old, stodgy, priggish, and for some too gendered. However, in the history of political thought dating all the way back to the ancient Greeks, it is a word with a range of meanings that goes well beyond stuffy morality. The Greeks saw virtue (*aretê*) as both a moral and a performative quality. To be virtuous was to have certain character traits like patience, friendliness, generosity, courage, and self-control. Amid the ever-changing winds of politics, virtues formed an underlying basis of stability, reliability, and trustworthiness. You may not agree with your fellow citizens, but at least you can count on their good intentions. But virtue meant more than moral qualities. It meant an ability to perform, or what we today call "virtuosity." According to Greek and Roman political ideals, it was not enough to be virtuous; one also had to be an everyday virtuoso of sorts, possessing cardinal political skills in speaking, judging, and cooperating.[5]

There is nothing inherently democratic about virtue or virtuosity. At the same time, there is nothing inherently antidemocratic about them. Indeed, it is hard to conceive of a functioning democracy apart from a quorum of citizens possessing basic moral virtues and everyday virtuosity. And there is no reason they cannot be had by every citizen: unlike charisma, expertise, or the possession of a political office, virtue and virtuosity are not embedded within an exclusive hierarchy. As with a jazz ensemble, one person's virtuosity does not detract from another person's—there is plenty to go around.

But we may need something more than virtue and virtuosity amid the political crises of the twenty-first century, such as what Machiavelli (1469–1527), the unduly infamous Renaissance political thinker, called *virtù* in Italian. *Virtù*, like virtuosity, is for Machiavelli a performative or active quality. However, unlike the political virtuoso who demonstrates skill in self-contained arts like speaking, judging, or cooperating, the person who has *virtù* is skilled at responding to uncertainties.

Indeed, if there is one characteristic of our day, it's that little seems assured. Neighborhoods are changing, technology developing, markets shifting, ideas moving, values transforming. Who knows where we will be in a decade, let alone a century? Who knows if human civilization as we know it will exist at all? If it does, it will depend on *virtù*, skill in navigating the uncertain winds of change. Such *virtù* is not determined by where you were born or how much money you have, but on the skills we have been looking at in this book: judgment, rhetoric, imagination, and action.[6]

For Machiavelli, *virtù* is the political skill of navigating winds of change so as to create new, relatively stable political orders.[7] This will be a major political challenge in the coming years of the twenty-first century. The crises that confront us now—climate change; massive wealth and income inequalities; debt crises; the capture of communication networks by powerful interests; the automation of industry and thus the displacement of workers; refugee crises; nuclear and chemical weapons; growing surveillance powers—these will not magically dissolve. There are no simple market solutions available, no technological fixes, and no automatic historical destiny on which to rely. There is only you, me, a bunch of other people, and our capacity for judgment, rhetoric, imagination, and action. We need to renew our commitment to our own political power and do something new.

Politics is an art of renewal and of doing new things. This is the third and final big takeaway from Arendt's work.

As Arendt looked at the horrors of the twentieth century, she saw just how difficult it would be for us to devote ourselves to renewal and doing new things. Our collective past—too often violent or otherwise unfair and exploitative—hangs over us like a trap waiting to be dropped on us, ensnaring us in feelings of resentment and hopelessness. Therefore, Arendt argued for the especial importance of a political capacity that I have not discussed in this book: the capacity to forgive.[8] Forgiveness, she stated, is a quintessential political activity if for no other reason than it represents the possibility of

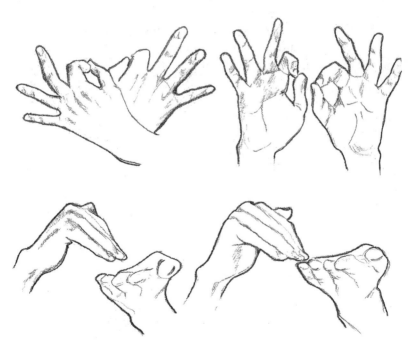

Free, forgive.

a new beginning among people. Here, Arendt suggested, Jesus of Nazareth is our best political teacher. "The freedom contained in Jesus' teachings of forgiveness is the freedom from vengeance, which incloses [sic] both doer and sufferer in the relentless automatism of the [retaliation] action process, which by itself need never come to an end."[9] Indeed, there is no end to the cycle of getting back at people who have done us harm—for once we get back at them, they want to get back at us, and so on. And we have all, in one way or another, participated in the doing of harm, have we not? Who can throw the first stone?

Faced with histories of harm, Arendt suggested, we have two ways to try to start anew with others: punishment or forgiveness. Punishment can stop a chain of public wrongs by removing the wrongdoers from the public realm. But if all wrongs are to be remedied by punishment, we might all have to be removed from the public realm.

Forgiveness, by contrast, stops the perpetuation of wrongs by acting in the public realm itself. According to Arendt, it attempts "the seemingly impossible, to undo what has been done." It does this not by literally reversing what we've done, but rather by dismissing what we've done from the court of public life and therefore "making a new beginning where beginnings seemed to have become no longer possible."[10] The act of forgiveness is our true escape art, and the means of our political rebirth. For what we ultimately need in the twenty-first century is not political revolution, but political rebirth, apart from which no revolution will liberate.

ACKNOWLEDGMENTS

For a number of different reasons, this was an especially difficult book for me to write. It would not have been possible without the community of people that gathered around it at one time or another and made it, to use Arendt's phrase, an object of common concern. My sister, Eileen O'Gorman, read through an early draft of the manuscript and offered numerous bits and pieces of advice, encouragement, and criticism—as did my friend and pastor, Tim Bossenbroek. I am grateful to you both for your time, energy, and intellect. The folks at the *Hedgehog Review* were crucial in the eventual formation of this book as they gave me a platform in which to try out some of these ideas. Thanks to the *Hedgehog*'s Jay Tolson, Leann Davis Alspaugh, B. D. McClay, and Jane Little, as well as to the journal's sponsor, the Institute for Advanced Studies in Culture at the University of Virginia. Chad Wellmon, Kevin Hamilton, Dave Tell, Christa Noel Robbins, Jennifer Geddes, Luke Herche, and Cheri Bowling have also provided crucial and much needed support and encouragement along the way. Terri Weissman relayed a message to me from afar that the world needed a populist Arendt: the encouragement stuck with me.

Some of the material in chapter 6 was published in *Advances in the History of Rhetoric*. I thank Susan Jarratt and Art Walzer for their efforts in shepherding that work. I also want to thank Leif Weatherby at New York University for the invitation to give a talk there on some of my work on Arendt. The Department of Communication at the University of Illinois has continued to be a wonderful scholarly home for me, full of great colleagues and students. Department head John Caughlin has advocated for me and my work, and my departmental colleagues in rhetorical studies—David Cisneros, Cara Finnegan, and John Murphy—have, together with the delightful group of other faculty in other research areas in the department, made working at

Illinois a pleasure. I would name you all, except that I am afraid I will forget somebody! My super-capable research assistant (and formidable scholar in her own right) Katie Bruner has been especially helpful in bringing this book to press. Thank you, Katie!

Much of this book was written at a local coffee shop, where I make new friends regularly. Lou Turner has been a particularly wonderful new friend: a man with a mind-blowing mind and an extremely high tolerance for espresso. My wife, Linda, read portions of the manuscript as I wrote it and gave me regular encouragement to keep at it. Thank you, Linda, for being with me and letting me be with you in all of this.

My kids have been with me in this too. This book is dedicated to my oldest, Graham, who is getting ready to head off to college. As I wrote, I frequently imagined what it would be like for him and his college classmates and buddies to read it. Thanks, Graham, for keeping me focused. Thank you also to Will, my other son, who is all head and all heart all at once, and to Mariclare, whose combination of tenacity, compassion, and intelligence continues to floor me.

Part of the "laboratory" for the writing of this book has been my students at the University of Illinois. I love teaching them. They are a diverse, smart, and fun group, and they let me digress as needed. I hope that many of them will take the public mission of the public university seriously and continue to grow as active and honest public citizens. The other part of the laboratory is an old group of friends with whom I stay in regular touch online and in occasional face-to-face gatherings. They have provoked me, frustrated me, encouraged me, and humbled me. I am grateful especially for the humbling. Thank you.

The two anonymous outside readers for the University of Chicago Press gave me encouragement and criticism. I hope they think this book improved over what they read when reviewing the initial draft manuscript. Johanna Rosenbohm copyedited this book, but she did more than that—she made it substantively better by asking hard questions that, in the end, most definitely made the book better. I am grateful. Finally, I want to thank my new editor at the press, Kyle Wagner, who has been a delight to work with. Doug Mitchell, however, brought this book to the press, only to retire and then tragically pass away as it was in production. Doug was one of the most important figures in my professional life. He was a remarkable person and an outstanding editor. Doug's editorial enthusiasm will be profoundly missed, as will his presence with us.

ARTIST STATEMENT

My personal work seeks to capture the intricacies of African American history and culture, past and present, by depicting people of color in acts of radical self-love and emotional preservation. I enjoy exposing the flaws of the imperialist, white supremacist, and capitalist patriarchal culture through my subjects engaging in the simple revolutionary act of existing as a minority in our society. In my eyes almost everything can be deemed in a political or radical light, even through qualities as simple as the facial features and hair textures of my subjects. The love, pain, trauma, softness, and healing of my subjects are what inspire me to use my creative energy to represent people of color in a realistic and honest way. Addressing these issues in my artwork based on personal research and my understanding of the life experiences of those similar to me is my method of answering the constant subconscious question running through the minds of the tragically ignored: Do I matter? My artwork attempts to alter the perspective of those navigating life without a secure knowledge of self, and the world around them, through representation and in actuality.

Sekani Kenyatta Reed

NOTES

PREFACE

1. For a still-valuable philosophical discussion of liberalism and libertarianism, see Barry, *On Classical Liberalism and Libertarianism*. One of the things Barry stresses is that liberalism has been justified on "utilitarian" grounds (i.e., "it works!") and on ethical bases (e.g., the sanctity of the individual), but that these two different strategies for defending liberalism (and libertarianism) cannot always be neatly reconciled. In this book, drawing on Arendt, I will be implicitly challenging both claims: I don't think liberalism has "worked" in a utilitarian sense all that well, and I think its ethical foundations are incomplete.
2. For more on the relationship between liberalism and republicanism, see Deudney, "Publius before Kant," 317; and Pettit, *On the People's Terms*, 10–11.
3. See Adams, *Works*, 10: 378. In the important 1984 book *Strong Democracy*, the political philosopher Benjamin Barber argues for a view of politics similar to what I present this book, but completely shuns the label "republican," suggesting that it is somehow hopelessly nostalgic and elitist. "Democracy" is enough for him, without the "republican" qualifier. I cannot provide an adequate response to Barber's (and likeminded thinkers') concerns about republicanism here. I will simply say two things: (1) I think he still borrows heavily from republicanism despite repudiating it, and (2) I think he does not offer an adequately complex concept of political *power*, and therefore underestimates the importance of the systems-oriented approach to institutional political power that republicanism offers.
4. Browne, "Arendt, Eichmann, and the Politics of Remembrance," 47.
5. When quoting from Arendt's essays compiled in various collections, I cite book titles in which the essays are found rather than essay titles to keep those notes shorter and more general.
6. For those looking for a succinct and timely introduction to Arendt, I recommend Bernstein, *Why Read Hannah Arendt Now?*.
7. Numerous scholars have influenced my approach to Arendt, some of whom are not cited in the bibliography for the simple reason that I am trying to keep the book essayistic as much as I can. This said, I want to acknowledge the work of Linda Zerilli and Richard King as particularly important to what follows. This is not to say that I

rehash their work, or that they are in anyway responsible for what I explore in this book; these arguments are mine, and I accept full responsibility for them. Rather, it is to say that here I have not only dug deep into the writings of Hannah Arendt, but also of these particularly insightful interpreters of her work theoretically (Zerilli) and historically (King).

INTRODUCTION

1. The parable of the prodigal son can be found in Luke 15:11–32.
2. Arendt's use of the word *authentic* may raise some questions for more critical readers. Here I would draw attention to the rich complexion of the term, which is etymologically related to words like *authority* and *authorize*. It can connote, and even denote, validity, trustworthiness, and credibility. It seems to me to function in Arendt's accounts of politics in the way that it might function in accounts about, for example, letters penned by Abraham Lincoln—some of which are authentic, others that are inauthentic or forged, and therefore lack historical and normative authority. When Arendt used the phrase "authentic politics," she implied that some forms of politics bear more historical and normative authority than others.
3. *Filter bubble* is a term coined by Eli Pariser in his book of the same name. On "affective polarization," see Iyengar et al., "Affect, Not Ideology." On "expressive partisanship," see Huddy et al., "Expressive Partisanship."
4. The Pew study is titled *A Wider Ideological Gap between More and Less Educated Adults*. Other research has confirmed this conclusion; see Henry and Napier, "Education Is Related to Prejudice."
5. For example, a 2017 study from the Pew Research Center found that the most ideologically polarized subgroups are also the most politically engaged; see Pew Research Center, *Political Typology Reveals Deep Fissures on the Right and Left*. Political scientists have also noted that politically active social media users curate their own social media feeds in order to reduce exposure to content from alternative political perspectives; see Spohr, "Fake News and Ideological Polarization."
6. Jeremy W. Peters, "As Critics Assail Trump, His Supporters Dig In Deeper," *New York Times*, June 23, 2018, https://www.nytimes.com/2018/06/23/us/politics/republican-voters-trump.html.
7. The definitive biography of Arendt remains *Hannah Arendt: For the Love the World*, by Elisabeth Young-Bruehl. See also Richard H. King's outstanding *Arendt and America*.
8. Arendt, *Eichmann in Jerusalem*, 252.
9. For a succinct, compelling discussion of Arendt's worries about "not thinking," see Young-Bruehl, *Why Arendt Matters*, 1–6.
10. Arendt, "Thinking and Moral Consideration," 445.
11. Arendt, "Thinking and Moral Consideration," 426.
12. Arendt, *Human Condition*, 8.
13. Arendt, *Human Condition*, 7, 20.
14. Her dissertation was later published as *Love and Saint Augustine*. I am very much of the same mind about Arendt's relationship to Augustine as are Joanna Vecchiarelli Scott and Judith Chelius Stark in their interpretive essay accompanying the book. They write, "The themes and modes of discourse Arendt introduces in her dissertation are major 'thought trains' in her subsequent work" (142).
15. My appeal of "basic politics" here follows Arendt's approach but is also indebted to Ober's "basic democracy" in *Demopolis*. As Young-Bruehl notes, Arendt's political thought is organized around "basic experience" (*Why Arendt Matters*, 8).

16. Most prominently in her book *The Human Condition*.
17. Arendt, *Human Condition*, 22.
18. Arendt, *Human Condition*, 2. Of course, we don't escape this fact with human cooperation, community, conviviality, and solidarity either.
19. The importance of communication in human existence is a lesson that Arendt learned from her teacher, mentor, and friend Karl Jaspers. For more on Jaspers and communication, see Gordon, "Karl Jaspers."
20. Arendt, *Men in Dark Times*, 32.
21. Arendt, *Human Condition*, 199.
22. For a wonderful extended meditation on the importance of coming to terms with the world outside our heads, see Crawford, *The World beyond Your Head*.
23. Arendt, *Life of the Mind*, 1:21.
24. Arendt, *On Revolution*, 109–10.
25. Arendt, *On Revolution*, 141.
26. Arendt, *On Revolution*, 139–40.
27. I am touching here on a set of arguments in Arendt's work about human rights, human dignity, political naturalism, and political phenomenology that are both profound and complex. I refer the reader who wants to go deep into these topics to Menke, "The 'Aporias of Human Rights,'" a detailed discussion of Arendt's approach to these challenging topics.
28. Joanna Vecchiarelli Scott and Judith Chelius Stark argue that Arendt's approach to political questions was strongly influenced by her graduate mentor and friend Karl Jaspers: "For him, the task of philosophy is not to set out a complete system of knowledge and reality, but to engage in the process of illumination and disclosure that often reveals oppositions, contradictions, limits, and boundaries, and to share these philosophical reflections through communication" (see their comments in Arendt, *Love and Saint Augustine*, 199–200). As Julia Kristeva, one of Arendt's most eloquent biographers, writes of her thought, "It is neither meticulous nor complete, and it does not place her discourse above the fray." *Hannah Arendt*, 27. The exploratory nature of Arendt's thinking has earned her more than a few critics. Recently, she has been sharply critiqued for some of her positions on what in the middle of the twentieth century was called "the Negro question." See Grines, *Hannah Arendt and the Negro Question*. It is more than justified to say that Arendt struggled to understand and fully appreciate the systemic nature and relentless hold of white supremacy in the United States. This said, claims by some that Arendt was herself a racist psychologize and moralize what was failure in her understanding and perhaps even her sympathy, and neglect the ways in which Arendt expressed appreciation for, even admiration of, the US civil rights movement; see, for example, *On Violence*, 14; and *Thinking without a Bannister*, 355–59.
29. Arendt, "Society and Culture," 280. Arendt's approach to tradition can be compared and contrasted with that of Leo Strauss, one of the most important political philosophers of the twentieth century—who, like Arendt, found himself a refugee in the United States after fleeing Nazi Germany. For both Strauss and Arendt (as well as Martin Heidegger, whose thinking was critical to both Strauss's and Arendt's intellectual projects, though in very different ways), it was crucial that we learn to "read" ancient thought well. However, Strauss approached the classical tradition as the antithesis of modern "historicist" and relativistic philosophy. In other words, the ancient tradition stands for Strauss largely as a counterpoint to modern philosophy. For Arendt, no such stark antithetical relationship between the ancients and the moderns was

possible, as both stand in *relation* to the human world and can be deemed to offer better or worse accounts for it. Strauss's classic work is *Natural Right and History*. For a generous and illuminating discussion of Strauss by an Arendtian, see Zerilli, *A Democratic Theory of Judgment*, 83–116.

CHAPTER ONE

1. The transcript for the second presidential debate, held in St. Louis, Missouri, October 6, 2016, is available at https://www.nytimes.com/2016/10/10/us/politics/transcript-second-debate.html.
2. Dwight D. Eisenhower, "Farewell Radio and Television Address to the American People, January 17th, 1961," Eisenhower Archives, https://www.eisenhower.archives.gov/all_about_ike/speeches/farewell_address.pdf.
3. See Postman, *Amusing Ourselves to Death*.
4. She may not have been escapist, but she did make some dangerous political escapes in her life, above all from Nazi Germany. For a wonderful illustrated account of Arendt's biographical escapes, see Krimstein, *The Three Escapes of Hannah Arendt*.
5. For a useful exercise in comparing and contrasting Postman's and Arendt's approaches to the problems of politics in an age of television, read Postman's *Amusing ourselves to Death*, 125–41, alongside Arendt's *Thinking without a Bannister*, 192–200.
6. Arendt, *Origins of Totalitarianism*, 51.
7. For more on Arendt's worries about the ways we are rendered superfluous in modern life, see Kristeva, *Hannah Arendt*, 4–8.
8. Peter Heinricher, "NFL Protest Letter Justifies Racism," letter to the editor, *News-Gazette* (Champaign, IL), Friday, November 10, 2017. This in fact echoes the title of Harold Lasswell's 1936 classic, *Politics: Who Gets What, When, How?*, and is rampant in liberal thinking of all kinds. As Barber argues in *Strong Democracy*, it makes politics but a form of "zookeeping," where civilians are the animals and the government the zookeepers (20–21).
9. Arendt, *On Revolution*, 268.
10. Robinson, *What Are We Doing Here?*, 85.
11. Kristeva, *Hannah Arendt*, 8.
12. Arendt, *Origins of Totalitarianism*, preface and part 2.
13. Clausewitz, *On War*, 3:121; Bannon quoted in Kimberly A. Strassel, "Steve Bannon on Politics as War." *Wall Street Journal*, November 18, 2016, https://www.wsj.com/articles/steve-bannon-on-politics-as-war-1479513161.
14. Schmitt, *Concept of the Political*, 26–29.
15. McAfee, "Acting Politically," 277.
16. Arendt, *On Revolution*, 268. See also Arendt, *Promise of Politics*, 17. For a rich and challenging discussion of Arendt's approach to politics as a genuine act of freedom rather than politics as rule, see Zerilli, *A Democratic Theory of Judgment*, esp. chap. 7.
17. See Arendt, *Thinking without a Bannister*, 56–68.
18. See, for example, *Aristotle on the Athenian Constitution*, 43.4.
19. Ober, *Demopolis*, 25–26.
20. Arendt, *Human Condition*, 237.
21. Arendt, *On Revolution*, 268.
22. Arendt, *Life of the Mind*, 1:19.
23. Arendt, *Origins of Totalitarianism*, 142n38. It is odd, to be sure, that this definition of politics—one of Arendt's most succinct and clear—came in a footnote. So much of Arendt's work is focused on analysis of the forces and structures and ideologies

that keep us from an authentic political existence. Therefore, though it is odd to find such a clear conception of Arendt's approach to politics relegated to a note, it fits the pattern in her work of focusing, for the most part, not on politics as such but on the things that keep us from politics.

24. Allen, *Talking to Strangers*.
25. Arendt relied on the formula "common world" frequently in her writings. It is different from the notion of "the common good," sometimes associated with republican political thought. The latter is widely criticized by liberals and more Marxist-oriented thinkers. Liberals (in the classical sense) tend toward skepticism of anything "common," and Marxist see "the common good" as ideological tool by which the interests of a few come to dominate those of others, as the few claim their interests serve "the common good." I am not ready in the least to defend "the common good" as an objective, freestanding entity; nevertheless, I don't see how we can also refuse "common goods" (note the plural, and the absence of the article) without opening ourselves up to even grosser forms of ideology and domination. Do we have nothing in common? If we do have things in common, and if among them are common pursuits, goals, or ideals, are these not "common goods"?
26. Zerilli, *Feminism and the Abyss of Freedom*, 30.
27. See Aristotle, *Politics*; and *Nicomachean Ethics*.
28. Arendt, *On Revolution*, 138.
29. Arendt, *On Revolution*, 175. She discusses constitution making at length in *On Revolution* (see esp. 134–38).
30. This sense of the spontaneity of the political is something that Arendt seemed to have gained from her readings of the works of Rosa Luxemburg (1871–1919), a remarkable Polish-born German political thinker and activist who opposed German involvement in World War I and was known as an outspoken critic of Lenin. For more on Arendt's readings of Luxemburg, see Young-Bruehl, *Hannah Arendt*, 293–294, 398–402.
31. Arendt, *Human Condition*, 199.
32. Arendt, *Promise of Politics*, 96.
33. Arendt's relationship to modernity is discussed from different perspectives in both Arnett's *Communication Ethics in Dark Times* and Benhabib's *The Reluctant Modernism of Hannah Arendt*. Arnett sees Arendt as a sharp and categorical critic of modernity; Benhabib sees her as an incisive but ultimately ambivalent critic of modernity.

CHAPTER TWO

1. Adam Villacin, "Shohei Ohtani and Reframing the Way We Think about Sports," *Ringer*, December 24, 2018, https://www.theringer.com/mlb/2018/12/24/18154386/shohei-ohtani-los-angeles-angels-pitching-hitting.
2. See O'Neil, *Weapons of Math Destruction*.
3. Arendt, *Between Past and Future*, 169.
4. See, for example, Donald Trump's presidential nomination acceptance speech at the 2016 Republican National Convention in Cleveland (video and transcript available at https://abcnews.go.com/Politics/full-text-donald-trumps-2016-republican-national-convention/story?id=40786529); and his campaign rally speech at Hilton Head, South Carolina, December 30, 2015 (video available at https://archive.org/details/CSPAN_20151230_160000_Donald_Trump_Campaign_Rally_in_Hilton_Head_South_Carolina; "I'm a doer" section at 12:27).

5. Arendt, *Origins of Totalitarianism*, 142n38.
6. Arendt unabashedly uses the rhetoric of magic and miracle to characterize our modern condition. See *Between Past and Future*, 168–70; *Human Condition*, 246–47; *On Revolution*, 47; and *On Violence*, 86. Arendt's discussion of miracles is closely related to her notion of "natality" and her argument for politics a mode of "beginnings" (in addition to the passage from *Between Past and Future* cited just above, see Arendt, *Human Condition*, 9; and Arendt, *Thinking without a Banister*, 321). These ideas are found in her earliest work on St. Augustine and run throughout her writings. For a helpful overview, see the interpretative essay by Joanna Vecchiarelli Scott and Judith Chelius Stark at the conclusion to Arendt, *Love and Saint Augustine*, 146–48.
7. These are all true political stories. For the story of a black man who talks to Ku Klux Klan members, see Dwane Brown, "How One Man Convinced 200 Ku Klux Klan Members to Give Up Their Robes," National Public Radio, August 20, 2017, https://www.npr.org/2017/08/20/544861933/how-one-man-convinced-200-ku-klux-klan-members-to-give-up-their-robes. For the story of a small town educating undocumented workers, see "Our Town," *This American Life*, https://www.thisamericanlife.org/632/our-town-part-one. For the story of poor farmworkers fighting to win legal protections, see LeRoy Chatfield, "Cesar Chavez: The Farmworker Movement: 1962–1993," Farmworker Documentation Project, UC San Diego Library, accessed May 2019, https://libraries.ucsd.edu/farmworkermovement/.
8. Arendt, *Responsibility and Judgment*, 19. Arendt herself often capitalized *History* when referring to it as a god-like force; I will do the same for that and similar systems in this part of the chapter.
9. See Noble, *The Religion of Technology*, for a well-known discussion of the deification of technology.
10. For a fascinating and incisive mid-twentieth-century discussion of the modern technological creeds, see Ellul, *Technological Society*.
11. Arendt, *Human Condition*, 4. For a similar philosophical diagnosis of the problem of technology—one that certainly influenced Arendt—see Heidegger, "Question Concerning Technology."
12. See Arendt, *Between Past and Future*, 41–90.
13. Arendt, *On Revolution*, 48.
14. For Arendt's discussion of the "irreversible movement" of history in French revolutionary thought, see *On Revolution*, 37–48. For a more general discussion of philosophies of historical movement, see Arendt, *Between Past and Future*, 41–90; and *Origins of Totalitarianism*, 463–470.
15. See Arendt, *Between Past and Future*, 100–101.
16. Arendt, *On Revolution*, 58. See also her discussion of T. E. Lawrence in *Origins of Totalitarianism*, 218–21.
17. If government is a machine for controlling the economy and society, Arendt argued, "politics" is at best a means by which to manipulate the mechanisms of government toward the interests of one group over another. Politics, in the words of Linda Zerilli summarizing Arendt, becomes no more than "an instrumental, means-end activity that entails the micro- and macro-management of social relations." *Feminism and the Abyss of Freedom*, 3.
18. Arendt typically referred to what I am calling Society as either "the social" or "mass society." The former is for her a way of referring to a phenomenon, much in the way she referred to "the political"; the latter is a way of denoting an empirical phenomenon: a giant collective joined together into a common identity by means of mass

media and large-scale logistical and transportation systems. In *Origins of Totalitarianism*, however, she explicitly critiques the concept of "society" as a mechanism that absolves individuals of responsibility; see *Origins*, 79–88.

19. Arendt, *Human Condition*, 29.
20. Arendt, *Promise of Politics*, 68.
21. See also Nussbaum, *Monarchy of Fear*.
22. This was the ideological rational behind so much postwar free market advocacy—above all, that of Friedrich Hayek. See Hayek, *Road to Serfdom*.
23. For an insightful little book on this sort of "scapegoating" in politics, see Roberts-Miller, *Demagoguery and Democracy*. For Arendt's detailed discussion of the scapegoating of Jews in Europe in the years leading up to the Nazi concentration camps, see *Origins of Totalitarianism*, 54–88.
24. This is what political theorists call a "republican" approach to freedom. It assumes that there is no significant distinction to be drawn between "free will" and "political freedom," for both alike, in the words of Philip Pettit, suppose that someone "can be held responsible for what they do in exercise of that freedom. Suppose that someone is said to lack freedom of the will in a certain realm of human activity. That implies straightaway that that they should not be held responsible for what they do. Or suppose that someone is said, not to lack free will as such, but to lack some specific political liberty: say, the liberty to speak out against the government. Again that implies that the person cannot be held responsible—at least not fully responsible—for failing to speak out. In each case there is a tie between the ascription of freedom and the imputation of responsibility." Pettit, *A Theory of Freedom*, 1–2. The correlation between freedom and responsibility is one that Arendt frequently made. See chapter 5 below for more on freedom.
25. Thank you to Dave Tell for putting it this way.
26. Arendt, *Human Condition*, 199.
27. Arendt, *Human Condition*, 3.
28. Zerilli, *Feminism and the Abyss of Freedom*, 23.
29. Crick, *In Defense of Politics*, 151.
30. Arendt, *Origins of Totalitarianism*, 301.
31. Arendt, *On Revolution*, 20, 30; *Thinking without a Banister*, 58. As Arendt noted, "to found" is one meaning of the Greek word *archê*; "to rule" is its other meaning.
32. Arendt, *Promise of Politics*, 95.
33. Arendt, *Promise of Politics*, 95, 108, 116–121.
34. See Arendt, *On Revolution*, 19.
35. See chapter 6 below.
36. Weber, "Politics as a Vocation," 78.
37. Arendt, *On Violence*, 50–51.
38. Arendt, *Promise of Politics*, 111–12.
39. Arendt, *Promise of Politics*, 113.
40. See Allen, *Talking to Strangers*, 56–57.
41. Allen, *Talking to Strangers*, 57.
42. Asen, *Democracy, Deliberation, and Education*, 150–51.
43. For an ancient discussion of the difference between productive, theoretical, and active arts, see Quintilian, *Institutes of Oratory*, 2.18.
44. Arendt, *On Revolution*, 23.
45. This account is based on a lecture given by Lou Turner at the University of Illinois, October 17, 2018.

46. Hunter and Bowman, "Vanishing Center of American Democracy," 19.
47. See Habermas, *Legitimation Crisis*; and O'Gorman, *Iconoclastic Imagination*, chapter 1.

CHAPTER THREE

1. Associated Press, "Paddle-Boarders Surrounded by 15 Great White Sharks Told to 'Exit the Water Calmly' by Police Helicopter," *(London) Telegraph*, May 11, 2017; Daniel Comer, "15 Sharks Surround Paddle Boat in Orange County CA," YouTube video, posted May 12, 2017, https://www.youtube.com/watch?v=Mrwm2H0CfjM&feature=youtu.be.
2. I am here (and elsewhere) indebted not only to Arendt, but to Danielle Allen in *Talking to Strangers*.
3. Arendt, *Life of the Mind*, 1:192.
4. I am in some respects echoing Benjamin Barber in *Strong Democracy*. Barber describes the heart of politics as making decisions or judgments "under the worst possible conditions, when the grounds of choice are not given a priori or by fiat or by pure knowledge" (120–21). However, there is one important way in which my approach differs from Barber's: his language reserves politics for "exceptional" moments when we do not have independent, objective, and valid ways of reaching a decision. I find this "exceptional" approach to politics quite problematic, not the least because it raises the question, Who gets to decide when such conditions apply? It seems to me that this latter question is a political question par excellence. The question of the political is not essentially about exceptional moments *when* we have to make judgments (e.g., when we are without an a priori ground or "foundation"), but about the *ways* in which we make judgments. The same object—say "one person, one vote"—could be approached in a "foundational" way (e.g., according to an a priori principle of mathematical equality) or in a "nonfoundational" political manner (e.g., debates about proportional representation). Hence, *when* something becomes political has nothing to do with its epistemological status, as Barber seems to argue, but rather only with the way in which it is addressed.
5. For a detailed discussion of Arendt's reliance on ancient Greek, particularly Aristotelian, *krinein*, see Marshall, "Origin and Character of Arendt's Theory of Judgment."
6. Arendt, *Crises of the Republic*, 203.
7. Arendt, *On Revolution*, 86, 88.
8. Arendt, *Life of the Mind*, 2:64–74. As Arendt argued in chapter 13 of *Origins of Totalitarianism*, it is in the nature of oppressive, totalitarian power to want to determine or otherwise control not just our actions, but our motives. What we do is not enough; we need to do it for the "right" reason. See also King, *Arendt in America*, 52–53.
9. Arendt, *Origins of Totalitarianism*, 470.
10. Arendt, *Human Condition*, 5.
11. Arendt, *Between Past and Future*, 174.
12. Arendt, *Promise of Politics*, 99–101.
13. Arendt, *Between Past and Future*, 174.
14. Arnett, "Arendt and Saint Augustine." This is all part of her aim to reinvent Kant's approach to aesthetic judgment for political purposes. See Arendt, *Lectures on Kant's Political Philosophy*; and Kateb, "Judgment of Arendt."
15. Kateb, "Judgment of Arendt," 125.
16. Arendt wrote, "I believe that the way in which we say 'This is right, this is wrong,' is not very different from the way we say, 'This is beautiful, this is ugly.' That is, we are now

17. Young-Bruehl, *Hannah Arendt*, xxxi.
18. Arendt, *Promise of Politics*, 167–68.
19. See Zerilli, "'We Feel Our Freedom,'" 162–63.
20. Arendt, *Promise of Politics*, 167–68; emphasis in original.
21. Arendt, *On Revolution*, 221.
22. Arendt, *Lectures on Kant's Political Philosophy*, 43. Arendt elsewhere suggested that empathy can misguide political judgment, as it, ironically, can desensitize us to the plights of others. If how we feel, as opposed to how we think, is our basic guide in judgment, we are dependent on the limited and sometimes dubious range of our feelings and may well find ourselves oblivious to pressing political issues that are staring us in the face. For Arendt's suggestion that something like this happened with slavery in America, see *On Revolution*, 60–62. For a discussion of the political problems with compassion—a close kin of empathy—in Arendt, see Newcomb, "Totalized Compassion."
23. This discussion appeared on Quora, in a post called "What Are the Pros and Cons of Stop and Frisk?," accessed December 21, 2018, https://www.quora.com/What-are-the-pros-and-cons-of-stop-and-frisk. See also "Stop and Frisk," West's Encyclopedia of American Law, accessed December 21, 2018, https://legal-dictionary.thefreedictionary.com/Stop+and+Frisk.
24. Zagajewski, *Two Cities*, 263. (*Zagajewski* is pronounced zah-gah-JEV-ski.) In *Arendt in America*, King draws attention to the importance of "adverbs and adjectives" in Arendt's thought (42).
25. "Judgment in general is the faculty of thinking the particular as contained under the universal." Kant, *Critique of Judgment*, introduction, 17.
26. For the crucial role of narrative not only in Arendt's thought but in her method, see Disch, "More Truth Than Fact."
27. Arendt, *Thinking without a Bannister*, 180–81.
28. Judgments without strict procedures is what Arendt explored under the concept of "reflective judgment" as it was articulated by Immanuel Kant in his *Critique of Judgment*. See Arendt, *Lectures on Kant's Political Philosophy*.
29. Descartes, *Rules for the Direction of the Mind*, rule 2.
30. See Oakeshott, *Rationalism in Politics and Other Essays*, 20.
31. On Arendt's critique of procedures, see Zerilli, "'We Feel Our Freedom.'"
32. My critique of proceduralism here resembles and draws from that of Taylor in *Sources of the Self* (see especially 495–96). Since the 1960s, the most important intellectual defender of proceduralism has been the political philosopher John Rawls. Though his *Theory of Justice* (1971) is his most famous work, it is in his later book *Political Liberalism* (1993) that he offers his most convincing philosophic defense of proceduralism. There Rawls argues for a distinction between our identity as citizens and our personal, private, or everyday identities. To be a citizen in his vision is to take on a quasi-official public role. In his vision of citizenship-as-quasi-official-public-role, you provisionally subordinate your "private" beliefs (for example, your religious beliefs) to agreed-upon public rules, all in the name of political cooperation meant to facilitate achieving democratic social goods. Here Rawls's arguments resemble those of Habermas's concept of the "public sphere" (articulated at length in *The Structural Transformation of the Public* Sphere and volume 2 of *The Theory of Communicative Action*). Rawls and Habermas have been critiqued for taking too much for

granted with regard to what counts as "public" and what counts as "private" (For a critique of Rawls, see Sandel, "Political Liberalism"; for a critique of Habermas, see Fraser, "Rethinking the Public Sphere.") To these critiques, I would add an additional, Arendtian, point: proceduralism, precisely because of its quasi-official approach to citizenship, risks relegating politics to an instrumental means of reaching certain democratic social ends—rather than as integral to the human condition—and thus relegating politics to what I call in the preface an "after-school club."

33. Arendt, *Human Condition*, 45.
34. Arendt, *Origins of Totalitarianism*, 230–31.
35. Arendt, *Life of the Mind*, 1:215.
36. For two quite different but equally thoughtful discussions of the challenges of relating to strangers in the contemporary world, see Allen, *Talking to Strangers*; and Appiah, *Cosmopolitanism*.
37. Arendt, *Between Past and Future*, 221.
38. Disch, "More Truth Than Fact," 666.

CHAPTER FOUR

1. Scott Shane and Alan Blinder, "Secret Experiment in Alabama Senate Race Imitated Russian Tactics," *New York Times*, November 19, 2018, https://www.nytimes.com/2018/12/19/us/alabama-senate-roy-jones-russia.html.
2. See, for example, Glenn Kessler, Salvador Rizzo, and Meg Kelly, "President Trump Has Made 6,420 False or Misleading Claims over 649 Days," *Washington Post*, November 2, 2018, https://www.washingtonpost.com/politics/2018/11/02/president-trump-has-made-false-or-misleading-claims-over-days/?utm_term=.dfaa8a0b8502.
3. Kant, "On a Supposed Right to Lie," 63–67.
4. Bernstein, *Why Read Hannah Arendt Now?*, 78.
5. Max Weber, "Politics as a Vocation," 120.
6. Max Weber, "Politics as a Vocation," 95.
7. Weber was here in many ways simply echoing the assessment of politicians offered more than a century earlier by the German philosopher Immanuel Kant, who declared in his "Toward Perpetual Peace": "I can imagine a *moral politician*, that is, one who interprets the principles of political prudence in such a way that they can coexist with morality, but not a *political moralist*, who fashions himself a morality in such a way that it works to the benefit of the statesman." Kant, "Toward Perpetual Peace," 96; emphasis original.
8. Goffman, "On Face Work," 213–31. Arendt's analogous discussion of what she called "self-presentation" can be found in *Life of the Mind*, 1:23–37.
9. Nyberg, *The Varnished Truth*, 1.
10. "The decisive means of politics is violence," Weber wrote ("Politics as a Vocation," 121). Weber also wrote of the "pragma of violence which no political action can escape" ("Religious Rejections of the World," 336).
11. While in Berlin in the 1930s, Arendt was also arrested and imprisoned for anti-Nazi activities, and she too lied to her interrogators. Unlike Bonhoeffer, who was held in prison for a long time and eventually executed, Arendt was released in a matter of days. Soon after, she escaped to France. For her account of her imprisonment and interrogation, see *Essays in Understanding*, 5–6.
12. Bonhoeffer, *Ethics*, 365.
13. Bonhoeffer, *Ethics*, 365. Note that what Bonhoeffer is expressing here is not "situational ethics," inasmuch as situational ethics is understood as a form of ethical rela-

tivism. On the contrary, Bonhoeffer is arguing for a more robust sense of "absolute truth" (though he rightly steers away from such a phrase)—one that is operative even when a person lies. See O'Gorman, "'Telling the Truth.'"
14. Arendt, *On Revolution*, 94.
15. Arendt, *Crises of the Republic*, 31.
16. Arendt, *Crises of the Republic*, 7–8.
17. For a fascinating documentary on Edward Bernays, see Adam Curtis's *The Century of the Self* (London: BBC, 2002).
18. As she wrote in the preface to the first edition of *The Origins of Totalitarianism* (1953, ix), "Antisemitism (not merely hatred of the Jews), imperialism (not merely conquest), totalitarianism (not merely dictatorship)—one after the other, one more brutally than the other, have demonstrated that human dignity needs a new guarantee which can be found only in a new political principle, in a new law on earth, whose validity this time must comprehend the whole of humanity *while its power must remain strictly limited, rooted in and controlled by newly defined territorial entities.*" This in many respects sums up Arendt's republican political project.
19. Arendt, *Crises of the Republic*, 7.
20. Arendt, *Crises of the Republic*, 7; emphasis added.
21. Arendt, *Origins of Totalitarianism*, 364–88.
22. Arendt, *Origins of Totalitarianism*, 4.
23. Kant, "On a Supposed Right to Lie," 65.

CHAPTER FIVE
1. Plato, *Republic*, VII, 514a–17a.
2. For the *Washington Post* slogan, see https://www.washingtonpost.com.
3. *Nudge: Improving Decisions about Health, Wealth, and Happiness* is the title of a book by the University of Chicago economist Richard Thaler and Harvard University law professor Cass Sunstein.
4. For the *Washington Post* "Fact Checker" tagline, see https://www.washingtonpost.com/news/fact-checker.
5. For Arendt's use of *rhetoric* in this Aristotelian sense, see *Human Condition*, 26. In 1984, the rhetorical scholar Lawrence Rosenfield wrote in the *Quarterly Journal of Speech*, "I think Arendt's work offers the most profound opportunity for the rehabilitation of classical rhetoric of any contemporary thinker." "Hannah Arendt's Legacy," 92. It is interesting, to say the least, that rhetorical studies in the United States continues to neglect Arendt, relatively speaking, even though the field has taken up figures like Martin Heidegger, Michel Foucault, and Emmanuel Levinas with gusto, and even as Arendt's thought has been a major preoccupation of cognate fields. I suspect that one simple if sad reason for this neglect is that Arendt did not use the word *rhetoric* much. (There are no doubt other reasons.) On the crucial role of rhetoric in Arendt's approach to politics, see Marshall, "Origin and Character of Arendt's Theory of Judgment"; Norris, "On Public Action"; Roberts-Miller, "Fighting without Hatred"; Yeatman, "Arendt and Rhetoric"; and Zerilli, "'We Feel Our Freedom.'"
6. Locke, *Essay Concerning Human Understanding*, 452.
7. See Schiappa, "Did Plato Coin *Rhētorikē*?"
8. Aristotle, *Rhetoric*, 1359b10–15.
9. Arendt, *On Revolution*, 77.
10. Plato, *Republic*, III, 414b–c.
11. Arendt, *Lectures on Kant's Political Philosophy*, 43.

12. See Arendt, *On Revolution*, 81.
13. See Arendt's discussion of expertise in the classroom in "The Crisis in Education," *Between Past and Future*, 173–96.
14. "Knowledge is power" is a phrase often mistakenly attributed to Francis Bacon. In fact, it was used by Thomas Hobbes in the 1668 Latin version of *Leviathan*. See Hobbes, *Opera Philosophica*, part 1, chap. 10. That Hobbes is the source is fitting; as I suggest in the next chapter, he was but the first in a long line of engineers posing as political thinkers.
15. Arendt, *Thinking without a Banister*, 309. Arendt's thinking here resembles aspects of Michael Oakeshott's critique of what he calls "Rationalism"—purportedly self-contained and impersonal forms of "technical" or "scientific" knowledge that are frequently seen as the *only* legitimate form of governing knowledge in liberal societies. See Oakeshott, *Rationalism in Politics*, 5–42.
16. Arendt, *Crises of the Republic*, 11–13, and *Essays in Understanding*, 309–11.
17. Arendt's argument here is consistent with decades-old research on "cognitive dissonance" and "consonance"—the idea being that when met with facts or phenomena that don't fit preconceived notions of what should be, we tend to try to make the facts fit our already held conceptions rather than adjust our conceptions. See Festinger, *A Theory of Cognitive Dissonance*.
18. Arendt, *Crises of the Republic*, 17.
19. Hobbes, *Leviathan*, chap. 15.
20. Locke, *Two Treatises of Government*, book 2, chap. 2.
21. See Rousseau, *Discourse on the Origin of Inequality*.
22. Arendt, *Promise of Politics*, 67.
23. Locke, *Two Treatises of Government*, book 2, chap. 6, §67.
24. See Allen, *Our Declaration*.
25. Arendt, *On Revolution*, 21.
26. Arendt, *On Revolution*, 21.
27. This is not to say there are no nonnatural facts on which human equality can rest apart from explicit political constitutions and laws. Jeremy Waldron, in discussing Arendt, suggests that Arendt's concept of "natality"—the innate capacity of each and every human to begin something new in the world—is a suprapolitical basis for human equality in her thought, and this seems correct to me (see Waldron, *One Another's Equals*, 59–60). Yet it is clear that, for Arendt, whatever non- or suprapolitical basis might be claimed for human equality (God, the capacity for speech, reason, etc.) in the modern world, it might as well be moot apart from explicit political structures and commitments.
28. Aristotle, *Rhetoric*, 1.1.5 (1354a). See also Johnstone, "An Aristotelian Trilogy," 1–24.
29. No one makes the case for this sort of rhetoric better than Danielle Allen in *Talking to Strangers*.
30. Arendt, *Thinking without a Banister*, 64.
31. See Aristotle, *Rhetoric*, book 2.
32. Garsten, *Saving Persuasion*, 6.
33. There is a lot more that could be said about the role of coercion in a democracy. For a philosophical discussion, see Pettit, *A Theory of Freedom*.
34. Hawkins et al., "Hidden Tribes," 14.
35. Hawkins et al., "Hidden Tribes," 37.
36. Hawkins et al., "Hidden Tribes," 51.

37. For a philosophical discussion of this "ethic of authenticity," see Taylor, *Ethics of Authenticity*.
38. See Allen, *Talking to Strangers*, esp. chap. 10.
39. Arendt, *Promise of Politics*, 12–14. Arendt tended to not make a distinction between opinions and claims of fact for the simple reason that both need to be attested to in politics. Nevertheless, there is a difference between the statement "All Americans deserve health care" and "The number of uninsured Americans dropped by 3.8 million from January to March 2014." The former might best be called an opinion and the latter a factual claim. Arendt did not belabor this distinction because, in discussing opinion, she was more interested in the status of statements than in their content. For a thorough examination of Arendt's approach to the status of opinion relative to truth in politics, see Enaudeau, "Hannah Arendt: Politics, Opinion, Truth."
40. Benjamin Barber argues that politics is not about truth at all. What makes politics exceptional, he argues, is that it is what we do precisely when there is no truth available. Politics is therefore for Barber the equivalent of what philosophers do when they try to address difficult questions without any pregiven rules or truths. To be sure, when we are disputing whether to go to war, whether to reform health care, or whether to pay public school teachers more, there is no "truth" to be discovered that will settle the matter; agreement, as Barber suggests, can be our only goal. Nevertheless, even in these situations there are truths in the form of facts or logical conclusions that are relevant in reaching agreement, are there not? And there is certainly a place for honesty, integrity, and truth telling. Barber's mistake, from Arendt's perspective, is that he no less than Plato wants to make politics a branch of philosophy. But politics, as Arendt never tired of saying, is simply not philosophy, no matter if it is "foundational" (grounded in pregiven truths) or "nonfoundational" (without any pregiven truths). Rather, politics is a social phenomenon; and like all other kinds of social phenomena, the truth is relevant—and sometimes extremely relevant—without being the only thing that matters. See Barber, *Strong Democracy*.
41. Arendt, *Crises of the Republic*, 6.
42. Arendt, *Crises of the Republic*, 6.
43. Arendt, *Promise of Politics*, 12.
44. Arendt, *Promise of Politics*, 13.
45. Weber, "Politics as a Vocation," 78.
46. Arendt, *Between Past and Future*, 231. Of course, the truth of $2 + 2 = 4$ assumes a system of base 10.
47. On Mike Hugues's adventures, see Jeremy Berke, "A California Man Who Believes the Earth Is Flat Launched Himself Almost 2,000 Feet in the Air in a Homemade Rocket," *Business Insider*, March 26, 2018, https://www.businessinsider.com/mad-mike-hughes-flat-earther-launched-in-homemade-rocket-2018-3/.

    Forcing others to profess or otherwise attest to established knowledge, facts, or truths is something a professor is free to do in the classroom. But students are not full citizens within the bounds of the classroom, and this is precisely the point: to enter into politics is to become a full citizen. A state that would force its citizens to hold a position is a state that would transform the *polis* into a classroom, or a prison—something that cannot be done in a society if that society aspires to be in the least bit free. For Arendt's attempt to work through these complex issues, especially with respect to public education, see Arendt, "The Crisis in Education," in *Between Past and Future*, 173–96.

48. At this point it is helpful to make an important distinction between *individual* opinions and *shared* opinions; or, in more standard parlance, "private" opinions and "public" ones. There is a modern idea, articulated pristinely in the work of Thomas Hobbes, that a political community is nothing but the sum or aggregate of the individuals who make up that community. Therefore, in Hobbes's view, to say that in politics all we have is opinion would be to say that all we have is *individual* opinions. But in fact, most opinions—especially opinions that are used in political debate, judgments, and decisions—are not "individual" at all, but common, shared, or collective. There is a sophisticated philosophical literature here, and plenty of debate (see Taylor, *Philosophical Papers*), but I would appeal to your common sense: What opinions do you possess that are distinctly *your own*? Whatever they are, I bet they fall into the broad category of "taste." You don't like fried onions (though raw ones are fine); you can't stand a pop star's hair; or you think paying more than $150 for a pair of sneakers is absurd. Now consider your opinions about a controversial political or social issue, be it surveillance, college tuition costs, or fracking. If you have any opinions about these issues, I suspect very much that they are not strictly and simply "your own" in the way that an opinion about fried onions might be "your own." Rather, they are shared with some particular or nebulous group of others. In politics, so much of what we count as "my opinion" on an issue (or a politician) are opinions always already formed with seen and unseen others; they are collective before they are individual, rather than the inverse.
49. See Orwell, *1984*.
50. Arendt, *Between Past and Future*, 223–29.
51. Arendt, *Between Past and Future*, 231.
52. Arendt, *Crises of the Republic*, 12.
53. Arendt, *Between Past and Future*, 239–49.
54. Arendt's most thorough discussion of republicanism appears in her book *On Revolution*. For some helpful discussions of Arendt and republicanism, particularly in its American version, see Canovan, *Hannah Arendt*, chap. 6; and King, *Arendt and America*, chap. 10. The leading contemporary political philosopher of republicanism is Philip Pettit; see his *On the People's Terms* and *Republicanism*.
55. Arendt, *Between Past and Future*, 239–49.
56. Arendt, *Between Past and Future*, 243.
57. Arendt, *Promise of Politics*, 93.
58. Arendt, *Human Condition*, 7.
59. Arendt, *Human Condition*, 184.
60. Arendt, *Human Condition*, 26–27. See also Arendt, *On Revolution*, 2.
61. See Hesiod, *Works and Days*, 69–82.
62. Gorgias, "Encomium of Helen," 31.
63. Aristotle, *Politics*, 1.2.

CHAPTER SIX

1. Arendt, *Promise of Politics*, 116.
2. Arendt, *Promise of Politics*, 129.
3. Arendt, *Promise of Politics*, 129.
4. Arendt, *Promise of Politics*, 95; emphasis added.
5. Arendt, *On Revolution*, 11.
6. Arendt, *On Revolution*, 33; *Between Past and Future*, 151–56.

7. See Arendt, *Between Past and Future*, 168–70; *Thinking without a Banister*, 321; *Human Condition*, 9, 246–47; *On Revolution*, 47; *On Violence*, 86.
8. Arendt, *Crises of the Republic*, 5; emphasis original.
9. Arendt, *Crises of the Republic*, 5; emphasis original.
10. Arendt, *Essays in Understanding*, 323. Arendt attempted to work out a theory of the imagination's role in politics by turning to the work of Immanuel Kant. See Arendt, *Thinking without a Bannister*, 387–94; and Arendt, *Lectures on Kant's Political Philosophy*.
11. Arendt, *Eichmann in Jerusalem*, 287–89.
12. I draw the phrase "a world beyond politics" from Manent, *A World beyond Politics?*
13. Arendt, *Between Past and Future*, 153; emphasis original.
14. As Patchen Markell has argued in his book *Bound by Recognition*, one of the more recent manifestations of the idea of freedom as "sovereign" is paradoxically found in "the politics of recognition"—related to what is popularly called "identity politics." The politics of recognition, Markell argues, can center on the "respectful recognition" of one's own (and, in a certain respect, *owned*) identity in ways that contribute a strong sense of one's agency as "the aspiration to be able to act independently, without experiencing life among others as a source of vulnerability, or as a site of possible alienation or self-loss" (12). Markell contrasts this approach with that outlined by Arendt in *The Human Condition*, writing, "In *The Human Condition*, Hannah Arendt offers a different account of the relationship of action to identity. Rather than treating identities as antecedent facts about people that govern their action, Arendt conceives of identities as the *results* of action and speech in public, through which people appear to others and thereby disclose who they are. . . . Arendt makes it clear that identity itself comes into being through the public words and deeds through which actors 'make their appearance' in the world" (13).
15. Walzer, *Revolution of the Saints*. Arendt did not see the English Civil Wars as representing the first modern revolution so much as offering a foretaste of what was to come in America and France. See Arendt, *On Revolution*, 43.
16. Hobbes, *Leviathan*, 146.
17. Berlin, *Four Essays on Liberty*, 122.
18. Hobbes, *Leviathan*, 145.
19. Hobbes, *Leviathan*, 146.
20. Locke argued that all property rights begin in what he took to be the fundamental and undeniable natural right of "men" to "own" themselves; or, as he wrote, "Every man has a *property* in his own *person*." See Locke, *Two Treatises of Government*, chap. 5, §27.
21. Hobbes, *Leviathan*, 88.
22. Arendt, *Between Past and Future*, 164. The matter of boundaries in Arendt's thinking is fraught and, I believe, ultimately unresolved. It is clear that Arendt's conception of political freedom was not strictly a matter of political geography, but of quality of action. Still, she argued for the importance of geopolitical boundaries for the legal protection of rights. She argued that one of the great crises of the modern world is and would be the emergence of what she described as "stateless" people, or what we typically refer to as refugees (*Origins of Totalitarianism*, 277). Certainly, she was right about this. She also argued that the only way for laws to effectively protect peop' for a governing power to supervise and enforce those laws—thus she was d͞ critical of the notion of the "rights of man," and even "human rights " an equally strong commitment to structures of political power (*Or͞* anism, 291–302; *On Revolution*, 98–99). Refugees will have "r͡

only if they are actively given them by a governing power. This said, she was deeply critical of various forms of political exclusion, be they racism or majoritarianism—the sorts of exclusion that "human rights" beyond political borders and boundaries are supposed to prevent or mitigate. What to make of this is well beyond the scope of this book. This said, I read her position as approaching something like the one recently articulated by the political historian Richard Tuck, who argues that, with respect to enfranchisement, "everyone within the boundaries [of a governed territory, or state] should take part in the vote," irrespective of their official status of "resident" or "citizen." Tuck, *The Sleeping Sovereign*, 262–63. Boundaries, Tuck suggests, can be a means of exclusion in a globalized world (and often are); but they can also be a means of equality and inclusion.

23. Arendt, *Origins of Totalitarianism*, 140.
24. Schmitt, *Leviathan in the Theory of Hobbes*, 53–63.
25. Sovereignty is a major concern of Locke's *Two Treatises of Government*.
26. Weber, "Politics as a Vocation," 78; emphasis original.
27. Weber, "Politics as a Vocation," 77.
28. Arendt, *Origins of Totalitarianism*, 140.
29. Here I am indebted, in addition to Arendt, to the insights of Zerilli, *Feminism and the Abyss of Freedom*, 9–16; and Canovan, *Political Thought of Arendt*, 70.
30. That Hobbes tended to ignore what we would today call "international relations" in his philosophy meant that he never really had to address the way the concept of sovereignty could produce, rather than reduce, violence. For Hobbes, the problem of sovereignty was simple: in a given state, there is but *one* sovereign, and so in that state there could be no occasion for a violent clash of sovereign wills. Hobbes never imagined, as far as I know, a single world sovereign; but had he considered the fact that even in his ideal world there would be multiple sovereign states, then he might have seen how his concept of sovereignty could be productive of violence.
31. Schmitt, *Concept of the Political*, 26.
32. Schmitt, *Concept of the Political*, 33.
33. Arendt, *On Revolution*, 35.
34. Arendt, *Between Past and Future*, 143.
35. Arendt, *On Revolution*, 11.
36. Arendt, *Between Past and Future*, 143.
37. Arendt, *Between Past and Future*, 148.
38. Lewis, *Studies in Words*, 111; see also Williams, *Keywords*, 179–180.
39. Lewis, *Studies in Words*, 111.
40. Aristotle, *Politics*, 1331a–b.
41. Quoted in Lewis, *Studies in Words*, 112.
42. Lewis, *Studies in Words*, 113.
43. Lewis, *Studies in Words*, 113.
44. De Sauvigny, "Liberalism, Nationalism, and Socialism," 150–51.
45. De Sauvigny, "Liberalism, Nationalism, and Socialism," 117–18.
46. De Sauvigny, "Liberalism, Nationalism, and Socialism," 115.
47. Arendt does not discuss Milton, but Zera Fink's groundbreaking work on Milton and republicanism, *The Classical Republicans* (Northwestern University Press, 1945), is cited in the bibliography to her *On Revolution*.
48. My argument in this chapter depends on my article in *Advances in the History of Rhetoric*; see O'Gorman, "Milton, Hobbes, and Rhetorical Freedom." My argument

tracks closely with that of Quentin Skinner in *Liberty before Liberalism*. The one place where I differ from Skinner is that I think he significantly underestimates the theological influences, particularly Pauline, on Milton's conception of freedom. I don't address those Pauline elements here in this chapter, but do in "Milton, Hobbes, and Rhetorical Freedom."
49. Arendt, *On Revolution*, 115.
50. See Arendt, *Life of the Mind*, vol. 2.
51. Milton, *Paradise Lost*, bk. 5, lines 224–37.
52. See Hariman, *Prudence*.
53. Hariman, *Prudence*, 8.248.
54. Rosenblatt, *Renaissance England's Chief Rabbi*, 135–57; Oldman, "Milton, Grotius, and the Law of War," 345–50.
55. Grotius, *Rights of War and Peace*, 1.1.8. I have been aided greatly in this discussion of attributive justice in Grotius by Oliver O'Donovan's discussion in *The Ways of Judgment*, 37–40.
56. Grotius, *Rights of War and Peace*, 2.14.2.
57. Victoria Kahn notes, "While Aristotle limits the province of the orator in the *Rhetoric*, he draws several analogies between rhetoric and prudence in the *Nicomachean Ethics*—not so much in terms of the domain of competence . . . as in terms of *the form or activity* of judgment that both involve." *Rhetoric, Prudence, and Skepticism*, 30. Kahn argues that this "implicit, and at times explicit, connection between rhetoric and prudence in the *Ethics*" significantly influenced Quattrocento humanists in their advocacy of rhetoric as a distinct form of human activity, culminating in judgment (30). In contradistinction, as Bryan Garsten argues, "the modern suspicion of rhetoric arises from the . . . impulse to minimize the risks of judgment," since judgment, and even more "justice," is reduced to rules, or—I would add—the abstract equations of "equality." *Saving Persuasion*, 9–10.
58. Grotius, *Rights of War and Peace*, 2.24.7, 2.14.2.
59. Milton, *Paradise Lost*, bk. 5, lines 483–90. See also Philip Pettit's discussion of "discursive freedom" in *A Theory of Freedom*, 65–87.
60. Azoulay, *Civil Imagination*, 99.
61. In *The Human Condition*, Arendt distinguishes between what she calls "action," "work," and "labor." For most of her readers, myself included, these distinctions have been at once illuminating and problematic. For a nice succinct discussion of them, see Bonnie Honig, *Public Things*, 42.
62. Milton, *Paradise Lost*, bk. 1, line 263.
63. Milton, *Paradise Lost*, bk. 5, lines 787–91.
64. Milton, *Paradise Lost*, bk. 2, lines 256–57. Freedom as nonsubmission is structurally analogous to freedom as noninterference, which Pettit argues is at the heart of liberal approaches to freedom, both historically and philosophically. He contrasts this liberal approach to the "more radical" concept of freedom in republican thought, where it is "non-domination"—that is, a condition where there are not sharp asymmetries in political power between people. See Pettit, *On the People's Terms*, 10–11.
65. Milton, *Paradise Lost*, bk. 2, lines 256–57.
66. Milton, *Paradise Lost*, bk. 9, line 762.
67. See Aristotle, *Politics*, 1.3–7.
68. Milton, *Paradise Lost*, bk. 9, lines 1121–31.
69. Milton, *Paradise Lost*, bk. 6, line 178.

70. Milton, *Areopagitica*, 268; emphasis added.
71. Historically, with respect to the *war*, there were two main parties: the king and his army versus Parliament and Parliament's army. However, with respect to the distinct but (of course) closely related *political* conflict, Parliament's army—the New Model Army—quickly became their own entity or party, sometimes cooperating with Parliament, sometimes at odds with Parliament, and also operating as their own relatively independent political force. (This is how Oliver Cromwell and Henry Ireton became political leaders—via the army).
72. Woodhouse, *Puritanism and Liberty*, 26; brackets original; emphasis added.
73. Arendt, *Crises of the Republic*, 75.
74. Arendt, *Crises of the Republic*, 76.
75. Hobbes, *Leviathan*, 145–46.
76. Arendt, *Between Past and Future*, 143.
77. Arendt, *Between Past and Future*, 146.
78. Canovan, *Political Thought of Arendt*, 73–74.
79. The qualitative nature of freedom is at the heart of Arendt's discussion of the *polis* (city) and the *oikos* (household) so central to her arguments in *The Human Condition*. It is not, as some of have concluded, that she sees the home or household as essentially a nonpolitical space of force. Rather, it is that she saw in the ancient Greek distinction between the *polis* and the *oikos* a qualitative differentiation that in turn helped her probe the qualitative nature of human freedom.
80. Arendt, *Promise of Politics*, 129.

CONCLUSION

1. Arendt, *Between Past and Future*, 146.
2. Arendt, *Between Past and Future*, 146.
3. For an attempt to work out a republican theory of social justice, see Pettit, *On the People's Terms*, 75–129, especially: "To be poor is to be lacking in the resources required for being able to function at a basic level in your local society and . . . to live without shame amongst your fellows" (105). This is the core of the republican argument for basic health care, education, and living wages.
4. See Milbank and Pabst, *The Politics of Virtue*.
5. See Arendt's discussion of freedom, virtue, and virtuosity in *Between Past and Future*, 153–54, 169.
6. Arendt, *On Revolution*, 31.
7. Arendt, *On Revolution*, 26–27.
8. For a thoughtful discussion of Arendt's discussion of forgiveness in politics, see Young-Bruehl, *Why Arendt Matters*, chap. 2.
9. Arendt, *Human Condition*, 241.
10. Arendt, *Promise of Politics*, 58. See also Arendt, *Human Condition*, 238–43.

BIBLIOGRAPHY

WRITINGS BY HANNAH ARENDT

Between Past and Future. New York: Viking, 1968.
Crises of the Republic. Boston, MA: Mariner Books, 1972.
Eichmann in Jerusalem: A Report on the Banality of Evil. London: Faber & Faber, 1963.
Essays in Understanding: 1930–1954. New York: Schocken, 1994.
The Human Condition. Chicago: University of Chicago Press, 1958.
Lectures on Kant's Political Philosophy. Chicago: University of Chicago Press, 1982.
The Life of the Mind (combined 2 volumes in 1). New York: Harcourt, 1978.
Love and Saint Augustine. Edited with an interpretive essay by Joanna Vecchiarelli Scott and Judith Chelius Stark. Chicago: University of Chicago Press, 1996.
Men in Dark Times. New York: Harcourt, 1968.
On Revolution. New York: Penguin, 1991.
On Violence. New York: Harcourt, 1969.
Origins of Totalitarianism. New York: Harcourt, 1976.
"Society and Culture." *Daedalus* 89, no. 2 (1960): 278–87.
The Promise of Politics. New York: Schocken, 2007.
Responsibility and Judgment. New York: Schocken, 2003.
"Thinking and Moral Consideration: A Lecture." *Social Research* 38, no. 3 (1971): 417–46.
Thinking without a Banister: Essays in Understanding, 1953–1975. New York: Schocken, 2018.

OTHER SOURCES

Adams, John. *The Works of John Adams.* Vol. 10. Boston: Little, Brown, 1856.
Allen, Danielle. *Our Declaration: A Reading of the Declaration of Independence in Defense of Equality.* New York: Norton, 2014.
———. *Talking to Strangers: Anxieties of Citizenship since Brown vs. Board of Education.* Chicago: University of Chicago Press, 2006.
Appiah, Kwame Anthony. *Cosmopolitanism: Ethics in a World of Strangers.* New York: Norton, 2006.
Aristotle. *Aristotle on the Athenian Constitution.* Translated by Frederic Kenyon. London: George Bell, 1907.
———. *Nicomachean Ethics.* Translated by Joel Sachs. Newburyport, MA: Focus, 2002.
———. *Politics and the Constitution of Athens.* Edited by Stephen Everson. Translated by Benjamin Jowett. New York: Cambridge University Press, 1996.

———. *Rhetoric*. Translated by W. Rhys Roberts. New York: Modern Library, 1954.
Arnett, Ronald C. "Arendt and Saint Augustine: Identity Otherwise Than Convention." In *Augustine for the Philosophers: The Rhetor of Hippo, the Confessions, and the Continentals*, edited by Calvin L. Troup, 39–57. Waco, TX: Baylor University Press, 2014.
———. *Communication Ethics in Dark Times: Hannah Arendt's Rhetoric of Warning and Hope*. Carbondale: Southern Illinois University Press, 2013.
Asen, Robert. *Democracy, Deliberation, and Education*. University Park, PA: Penn State University Press, 2015.
Azoulay, Ariella. *Civil Imagination: A Political Ontology of Photography*. New York: Verso Books, 2012.
Barber, Benjamin. *Strong Democracy: Participatory Politics for a New Age*. Berkeley: University of California Press, 1984.
Barry, Norman P. *On Classical Liberalism and Libertarianism*. London: Macmillan, 1986.
Benhabib, Seyla. *The Reluctant Modernism of Hannah Arendt*. New York: Rowman and Littlefield, 2003.
Berlin, Isaiah. *Four Essays on Liberty*. New York: Oxford University Press, 1970.
Bernstein, Richard J. *Why Read Hannah Arendt Now?*. Medford, MA: Polity, 2018.
Bertier de Sauvigny, G. de. "Liberalism, Nationalism, and Socialism: The Birth of Three Words." *Review of Politics* 32, no. 2 (April 1970): 147–66.
Bonhoeffer, Dietrich. *Ethics*. Edited by Eberhard Bethge. Translated by Neville Horton Smith. New York: Macmillan, 1955.
Browne, Stephen Howard. "Arendt, Eichmann, and the Politics of Remembrance." In *Framing Public Memory*, edited by Kendall R. Phillips, 45–64. Tuscaloosa, AL: University of Alabama Press, 2004.
Canovan, Margaret. *Hannah Arendt: A Reinterpretation of Her Political Thought*. New York: Cambridge University Press, 1992.
———. *The Political Thought of Hannah Arendt*. New York: Harcourt Brace Jovanovich, 1974.
Clausewitz, Carl von. *On War*. Vol. 3. Translated by J. J. Graham. London: Kegan Paul, Tranch, Trubner, 1908.
Crawford, Matthew. *The World beyond Your Head: On Becoming an Individual in an Age of Distraction*. New York: Farrar, Straus, and Giroux, 2016.
Crick, Bernard. *In Defense of Politics*. 4th ed. Chicago: University of Chicago Press, 1992.
Descartes, Rene. *Rules for the Direction of the Mind*. Translated by Harold H. Joachim. London: Allen and Unwin, 1957.
Deudney, Daniel. "Publius before Kant: Federal-Republican Security and Democratic Peace." *European Journal of International Relations* 10, no. 3 (2004): 315–56.
Disch, Lisa J. "More Truth Than Fact: Storytelling as Critical Understanding in the Writings of Hannah Arendt." *Political Theory* 21, no. 4 (1993): 665–94.
Ellul, Jacques. *The Technological Society*. New York: Vintage, 1964.
Enaudeau, Corinne. "Hannah Arendt: Politics, Opinion, Truth." *Social Research* 74, no. 4 (2007): 1029–44.
Festinger, Leon. *A Theory of Cognitive Dissonance*. Stanford, CA: Stanford University Press, 1957.
Fraser, Nancy. "Rethinking the Public Sphere: A Contribution to the Critique of Actually Existing Democracy." *Social Text* 25/26 (1990): 56–80.
Garsten, Bryan. *Saving Persuasion: A Defense of Rhetoric and Judgment*. Cambridge, MA: Harvard University Press, 2009.
Goffman, Erving. "On Face Work." *Psychiatry* 18, no. 3 (1955): 213–31.

Gordon, Ronald D. "Karl Jaspers: Existential Philosopher of Dialogical Communication." *Southern Communication Journal* 65, nos. 2 & 3 (2000): 105–18.

Gorgias. "Encomium of Helen." In *The Norton Anthology of Theory and Criticism*, edited by Vincent B. Leitch et al., 30–33. New York: W. W. Norton, 2001.

Grotius, Hugo. *Rights of War and Peace*. Indianapolis: Liberty Fund, 2005.

Habermas, Jürgen. *Legitimation Crisis*. Translated by Thomas McCarthy. Boston: Beacon Press, 1975.

———. *The Theory of Communicative Action, Volume 2: Lifeworld and System: A Critique of Functionalist Reason*. Translated by Thomas McCarthy. Boston: Beacon Press, 1987.

———. *The Structural Transformation of the Public Sphere*. Translated by Thomas Burger. Cambridge, MA: MIT Press, 1989.

Hariman, Robert, ed. *Prudence: Classical Virtue, Postmodern Practice*. State College, PA: Penn State University Press, 2003.

Hawkins, Stephen, Daniel Yudkin, Miriam Juan-Torres, and Tim Dixon. *Hidden Tribes: A Study of America's Polarized Landscape*. New York: More in Common, 2018. https://www.moreincommon.com/hidden-tribes.

Hayek, Friedrich. *The Road to Serfdom*. Vol. 2, The Collected Works of F. A. Hayek, edited by Bruce Caldwell. Chicago: University of Chicago Press, 2007.

Heidegger, Martin. "The Question Concerning Technology." In *The Question Concerning Technology and Other Essays*, edited by Martin Heidegger, 3–35. Translated by William Lovitt. New York: Harper, 1977.

Henry, P. J., and Jaime L. Napier. "Education Is Related to Greater Ideological Prejudice." *Public Opinion Quarterly* 81, no. 4 (2017): 930–42. https://doi.org/10.1093/poq/nfx038.

Hesiod. *Works and Days, Theogony and the Shield of Heracles*. Translated by Hugh G. Evelyn-White. New York: Dover, 2006.

Hobbes, Thomas. *Leviathan*. New York: Penguin, 1982.

———. *Opera Philosophica Quae Latine Scripsit Omnia: In Unum Corpus Nunc Primum Collecta Studio Et Labore Gulielmi Molesworth*. https://archive.org/details/operaphilosophi03molegoog/page/n8.

Honig, Bonnie. *Public Things: Democracy in Despair*. New York: Fordham University Press, 2017.

Huddy, Leonie, Lilliana Mason, and Lene Aarøe. "Expressive Partisanship: Campaign Involvement, Political Emotion, and Partisan Identity." *American Political Science Review* 109, no. 1 (2015): 1–17. https://doi.org/10.1017/S0003055414000604.

Hunter, James Davidson, and Carl Desportes Bowman. "The Vanishing Center of American Democracy." Charlottesville: University of Virginia Advanced Studies in Culture Foundation, 2016.

Iyengar, Shanto, Gaurav Sood, and Yphtach Lelkes. "Affect, Not Ideology: A Social Identity Perspective on Polarization." *Public Opinion Quarterly* 76, no. 3 (2012): 405–31. https://doi.org/10.1093/poq/nfs038.

Johnstone, Christopher. "An Aristotelian Trilogy: Ethics, Rhetoric, Politics, and the Search for Moral Truth." *Philosophy & Rhetoric* 13, no. 1 (1980): 1–24.

Kahn, Victoria. *Rhetoric, Prudence, and Skepticism in the Renaissance*. Ithaca, NY: Cornell University Press, 1985.

Kant, Immanuel. *Critique of Judgment*. Translated by J. H. Bernard. London: Macmillan, 1914.

———. "On a Supposed Right to Lie Because of Philanthropic Concerns." In *Grounding for the Metaphysics of Morals*, translated by James W. Ellington, 63–67. Indianapolis: Hackett, 1993.

———. "Toward Perpetual Peace: A Philosophical Sketch." In *Toward Perpetual Peace and Other Writings on Politics, Peace, and History*, edited by Pauline Kleingeld, translated by David L. Colclasure, 67–109. New Haven, CT: Yale University Press, 2006.

Kateb, George. "The Judgment of Arendt." In *Judgment, Imagination, and Politics: Themes from Kant and Arendt*, edited by Ronald Beiner and Jennifer Nedelsky, 121–38. New York: Rowman and Littlefield, 2001.

King, Richard H. *Arendt and America*. Chicago: University of Chicago Press, 2015.

Krimstein, Ken. *The Three Escapes of Hannah Arendt: A Tyranny of Truth*. New York: Bloomsbury, 2018.

Kristeva, Julia. *Hannah Arendt*. Translated by Ross Guberman. New York: Columbia University Press, 2001.

Lasswell, Harold. *Politics: Who Gets What, When, and How*. New York: Whittlesey, 1936.

Lewis, C. S. *Studies in Words*. 2nd ed. New York: Cambridge University Press, 1967.

Locke, John. *An Essay Concerning Human Understanding*. Edited by Roger Woolhouse. New York: Penguin, 1997.

———. *Two Treatises of Government*. New York: Cambridge University Press, 1988.

Manent, Pierre. *A World beyond Politics? A Defense of the Nation-State*. Translated by Marc LePain. Princeton, NJ: Princeton University Press, 2006.

Markell, Patchen. *Bound by Recognition*. Princeton, NJ: Princeton University Press, 2003.

Marshall, David L. "The Origin and Character of Hannah Arendt's Theory of Judgment." *Political Theory* 38, no. 3 (2010): 367–93.

McAfee, Noëlle. "Acting Politically." In *From Voice to Influence: Understanding Citizenship in a Digital Age*, edited by Danielle Allen and Jennifer S. Lights, 273–92. Chicago: University of Chicago Press, 2015.

Menke, Christoph. "The 'Aporias of Human Rights' and the 'One Human Right': Regarding the Coherence of Hannah Arendt's Argument." *Social Research* 74, no. 3 (2007): 739–62.

Milbank, John, and Adrian Pabst. *The Politics of Virtue: Post-Liberalism and the Human Future*. New York: Rowman and Littlefield, 2016.

Milton, John. "Areopagitica: A Speech of Mr. John Milton for the Liberty of Unlicenc'd Printing, to the Parliament of England." In *The Prose of John Milton*, edited by J. Max Patrick, 265–345. New York: New York University Press, 1968.

———. *Paradise Lost*. New York: Penguin, 2000.

Newcomb, Matthew J. "Totalized Compassion: The (Im)Possibilities for Acting out of Compassion in the Rhetoric of Hannah Arendt." *JAC* 27, no. 1/2 (2007): 105–33.

Noble, David F. *The Religion of Technology: The Divinity of Man and the Spirit of Invention*. New York: Penguin, 1999.

Norris, Andrew. "On Public Action: Rhetoric, Opinion, and Glory in Hannah Arendt's *The Human Condition*." *Critical Horizons* 14, no. 2 (2013): 200–224.

Nussbaum, Martha. *The Monarchy of Fear: A Philosopher Looks at Our Political Crisis*. New York: Simon and Schuster, 2018.

Nyberg, David. *The Varnished Truth: Truth Telling and Deceiving in Ordinary Life*. Chicago: University of Chicago Press, 1993.

Oakeshott, Michael. *Rationalism in Politics and Other Essays*. Indianapolis: Liberty Fund, 1991.

Ober, Josiah. *Demopolis: Democracy before Liberalism in Theory and Practice*. New York: Cambridge University Press, 2017.

O'Donovan, Oliver. *The Ways of Judgment*. Grand Rapids, MI: Eerdmans, 2005.

O'Gorman, Ned. "Milton, Hobbes, and Rhetorical Freedom." *Advances in the History of Rhetoric* 18, no. 2 (2015): 162–80.
———. *The Iconoclastic Imagination: Image, Catastrophe, and Economy in America from the Kennedy Assassination to September 11*. Chicago: University of Chicago Press, 2016.
———. "'Telling the Truth:' Dietrich Bonhoeffer's Rhetorical Discourse Ethic." *Journal of Communication and Religion* 28, no. 2 (2005): 224–48.
Oldman, Elizabeth. "Milton, Grotius, and the Law of War: A Reading of Paradise Regained and Samson Agonistes." *Studies in Philology* 104, no. 3 (2007): 340–75.
O'Neil, Cathy. *Weapons of Math Destruction: How Big Data Increases Inequality and Threatens Democracy*. New York: Crown, 2016.
Orwell, George. *1984*. New York: Penguin, 1977.
Pariser, Eli. *The Filter Bubble: How the New Personalized Web Is Changing What We Read and How We Think*. New York: Penguin Press, 2011.
Pettit, Philip. *On the People's Terms: A Republican Theory and Model of Democracy*. New York: Cambridge University Press, 2012.
———. *Republicanism: A Theory of Freedom and Government*. New York: Oxford University Press, 1997.
———. *A Theory of Freedom: From the Psychology to the Politics of Agency*. New York: Oxford University Press, 2001.
Pew Research Center. *Political Typology Reveals Deep Fissures on the Right and Left*. Washington, DC: Pew Research Center, 2017. https://www.people-press.org/2017/10/24/political-typology-reveals-deep-fissures-on-the-right-and-left/.
———. *A Wider Ideological Gap between More and Less Educated Adults*. Washington, DC: Pew Research Center, 2016. http://www.people-press.org/2016/04/26/a-wider-ideological-gap-between-more-and-less-educated-adults/.
Plato. *Republic*. Translated by Joel Sachs. Newburyport, MA: Focus, 2007.
Postman, Neil. *Amusing Ourselves to Death: Public Discourse in the Age of Show Business*. New York: Penguin, 1985.
Quintilian. *The Institutes of Oratory*. Translated by Donald A. Russell. Cambridge, MA: Harvard University Press, 2002.
Rawls, John. *Political Liberalism*. New York: Columbia University Press, 1993.
———. *A Theory of Justice*. Cambridge, MA: Harvard University Press, 1971.
Roberts-Miller, Patricia. *Demagoguery and Democracy*. New York: Experiment, 2017.
———. "Fighting without Hatred: Hannah Arendt's Agonistic Rhetoric." *JAC* 22, no. 3 (2002): 585–601.
Robinson, Marilynne. *What Are We Doing Here?* New York: Farrar, Straus, and Giroux, 2018.
Rosenblatt, Jason P. *Renaissance England's Chief Rabbi: John Selden*. New York: Oxford University Press, 2006.
Rosenfield, Lawrence. "Hannah Arendt's Legacy." *Quarterly Journal of Speech* 70, no. 1 (1984): 90–96.
Rousseau, Jean-Jacques. *Discourse on the Origin of Inequality*. Indianapolis: Hackett, 1992.
Sandel, Michael. "Political Liberalism." *Harvard Law Review* 107 (1994): 1765–94.
Schiappa, Edward. "Did Plato Coin Rhêtorikê?" *American Journal of Philology* 111, no. 4 (1990): 457–70.
Schmitt, Carl. *The Concept of the Political*. Expanded ed. Translated by George Schwab. Chicago: University of Chicago Press, 2007.
———. *The Leviathan in the State Theory of Thomas Hobbes: Meaning and Failure of a Political Symbol*. Translated by George Schwab and Erna Hilfstein. Chicago: University of Chicago Press, 2008.

Skinner, Quentin. *Liberty before Liberalism*. New York: Cambridge University Press, 1998.
Spohr, Dominic. "Fake News and Ideological Polarization: Filter Bubbles and Selective Exposure on Social Media." *Business Information Review* 34, no. 3 (2017): 150–60.
Strauss, Leo. *Natural Right and History*. Chicago: University of Chicago Press, 1953.
Taylor, Charles. *The Ethics of Authenticity*. Cambridge, MA: Harvard University Press, 1992.
———. *Philosophical Papers: Volume 1, Human Agency and Language*. New York: Cambridge University Press, 1985.
———. *Sources of the Self: The Making of Modern Identity*. Cambridge, MA: Harvard University Press, 1989.
Thaler, Richard, and Cass Sunstein. *Nudge: Improving Decisions about Health, Wealth, and Happiness*. New Haven, CT: Yale University Press, 2008.
Tuck, Richard. *The Sleeping Sovereign: The Invention of Modern Democracy*. New York: Cambridge University Press, 2015.
Waldron, Jeremy. *One Another's Equals: The Basis of Human Equality*. Cambridge, MA: Harvard University Press, 2017.
Walzer, Michael. *The Revolution of the Saints*. Cambridge, MA: Harvard University Press, 1965.
Weber, Max. "Politics as a Vocation." In *From Max Weber: Essays in Sociology*, edited and translated by H. H. Gerth and C. Wright Mills, 77–128. New York: Oxford University Press, 1946.
———. "Religious Rejections of the World and Their Directions." In *From Max Weber: Essays in Sociology*, edited and translated by H. H. Gerth and C. Wright Mills, 302–61. New York: Oxford University Press, 1946.
Williams, Raymond. *Keywords: A Vocabulary of Society and Culture*. Rev. ed. New York: Oxford University Press, 1985.
Woodhouse, Arthur Sutherland Pigott, ed. *Puritanism and Liberty: Being the Army Debates (1647–9) from the Clarke Manuscripts with Supplementary Documents* (the "Putney Debates"). Chicago: University of Chicago Press, 1951.
Yeatman, Anna. "Arendt and Rhetoric." *Philosophy Today* 62, no. 2 (2018): 471–92.
Young-Bruehl, Elisabeth. *Hannah Arendt: For the Love the World*. New Haven, CT: Yale University Press, 2004.
———. *Why Arendt Matters*. New Haven, CT: Yale University Press, 2006.
Zagajewski, Adam. *Two Cities: On Exile, History, and the Imagination*. Translated by Lillian Vallee. Athens: University of Georgia Press, 2002.
Zerilli, Linda M. G. *A Democratic Theory of Judgment*. Chicago: University of Chicago Press, 2016.
———. *Feminism and the Abyss of Freedom*. Chicago: University of Chicago Press, 2005.
———. "'We Feel Our Freedom': Imagination and Judgment in the Thought of Hannah Arendt." *Political Theory* 33, no. 2 (2005): 158–88.

INDEX

action, 47, 50–51, 74–75, 79, 102, 130, 131, 134. *See also under* Arendt, Hannah
Adams, John, xiv
"Allegory of the Cave," 92–96, 109, 136
Allen, Danielle, 49
Arendt, Hannah: and action, 5, 10–13, 25, 33, 36–37, 38, 43, 46, 52, 56–57, 71, 111, 118, 127; and anarchy, 48; and automation, 36; and "banality of evil," 5; and civil disobedience, 132–33; and the "common world," 10, 74, 151n25; concept of politics, 8–12, 27, 38, 48; and democracy, 13, 94, 95, 100, 104–6; and economy, 49; and equality, 12, 13; and experts (*see* experts); and facts, 88, 90, 98–99, 105–6, 109–11; and forgiveness, 141–42; and freedom, 11, 12, 13, 25, 49, 114–15, 118, 125, 130, 136–37, 142; and history, 40–41; and the human condition, 6, 8–9, 40, 46, 100; and human nature, 8–9; and human rights, 12–13, 149n27, 161n22; and identity, 161n14; and imagination, 116 (*see also* political imagination *and under* judgment); and judgment, 57, 60–62, 65, 75; and lying, 86–91, 98; and miracle, 21, 36, 38, 49, 152n6; and natality, 152n6; and opinion, 64, 104–9, 159n39; and plurality, 6, 25–26, 63, 100, 110–11; and political power, 12; and public happiness, xi; and republicanism, xiv, 89; and "rule of nobody," 71; and the "social," 42–43, 152n18; and sovereignty, 122–24; and "space of appearances," 11, 20, 77, 94; and speech, 30, 33, 47, 57, 108, 111, 125; and technology, 40, 50; and thinking, 5, 10; and totalitarianism, 5, 22, 37, 47, 88–91, 94, 98, 109, 111, 154n8, 157n18; and violence, 13, 48, 111, 133–34
Aristotle, 29–30, 32, 33, 95–96, 101, 102, 106, 113, 126, 129, 131, 163n57
authoritarianism, 13, 22, 24, 25, 28, 43–45, 98, 99, 103, 104, 108–9, 110–11

Bannon, Steve, 23
Barber, Benjamin, 147n3, 150n8, 154n4, 159n40
Berlin, Isaiah, 120
Bernays, Edward, 88
Bonhoeffer, Dietrich, 82

Canovan, Margaret, 134
Clausewitz, Carl von, 22
Clinton, Bill, 86
Clinton, Hillary, 16, 53
Constitutions, 29–33, 48, 50–51, 66–67, 89, 101, 132, 151n29, 158n27

Darwin, Charles, 21–22
democracy, xiv, 13, 24–25, 32, 46, 51, 75, 89, 92–94, 101, 102–3, 140, 147n3, 148n15. *See also under* Arendt, Hannah
demagoguery, 37, 44–45
Descartes, René, 70

economy, 41–42, 117. *See also under* Arendt, Hannah

electoral-entertainment complex, 16–18
English Civil Wars, 118–19
equality, 2, 99–101, 154n4. *See also under* Arendt, Hannah
experts, 92–99, 103, 104, 139

"face work," 79
facts, 86, 88, 89, 90, 104, 159n39. *See also under* Arendt, Hannah
fact-checking, 77, 83, 94
fear, 43–44
freedom, 2–3, 24, 29, 46, 48, 54, 107, 110, 113, 110–39. *See also under* Arendt, Hannah
free speech, 108, 112, 131–33

Goffman, Erving, 79
Gorgias, 112
Grotius, Hugo, 129–30

Habermas, Jürgen, 53–54, 155n32
Hesiod, 112
Hobbes, Thomas, 21–22, 99–100, 115, 118–28, 131, 133–36, 158n14, 160n48, 162n30

Jaspers, Karl, 149n28
Jefferson, Thomas, xi
Jesus, 142
Jones, Doug, 77
judgment, 57–64, 105; and adjectives, 66–67; and imagination, 66–69, 96; and stories, 69. *See also under* Arendt, Hannah

Kant, Immanuel, 67–68, 77, 91, 156n7, 161n10
Kristeva, Julia, 21, 149n28

law, 29–31, 50, 61, 81, 95, 100, 103, 106, 121, 132–33, 161n22
liberalism, xii–xiii, 9, 71–73, 119–22, 148n1
Locke, John, 8–9, 21–22, 94, 99–100, 106, 119, 121, 129–30, 161n20
Luxemburg, Rosa, 151n30

Machiavelli, 140
Milton, John, 115, 118–19, 127–34

Nash, Diane, 133
Nyberg, David, 80

Ohtani, Shohei, 35
opinion, 64–65, 70, 73–74, 104–9, 159n39, 160n48. *See also under* Arendt, Hannah
organized lying, 87–89, 90
Orwell, George, 109

persuasion, 102–6, 111–13
Plato, 19, 50, 92–96, 106, 109, 136
political imagination, 30, 114–18
politicians, 17, 23, 78–81, 83; as celebrities, 18; cynicism about, xii, 53, 54; and lying, 76, 77, 83–88, 90, 156n7
politics: as art, 49–50; and citizenship, 32–33; defined, 3, 4, 12, 27, 29; and governing, 30–32; and lying, 76, 82–83, 85–91; and polarization, 3; and power, 97; and rule, 24–25, 50; as showbusiness, 18–21; and speech, 47; and truth, 76, 82–83, 85–91, 106–9; as war, 22–24. *See also under* Arendt, Hannah
populism, 7, 43–46. *See also* demagoguery
Postman, Neil, 18, 20
proceduralism, 70–74, 155n32
progressivism, 41
publicity, 110

republicanism, xiii, 110, 153n24. *See also under* Arendt, Hannah
resentment, 3
rhetoric, 94–95, 96, 101–6, 107, 111, 130, 131, 157n5
Rousseau, Jean-Jacques, 99

Schmitt, Carl, 23–24, 122, 124, 130
sovereignty, 121–24, 130, 134, 161n14, 162n30
speech, 82, 101, 102, 107, 108, 112, 126, 128, 131. *See also under* Arendt, Hannah

Taylor, Charles, 155n32
technology, 116–17. *See also under* Arendt, Hannah
totalitarianism, 66–67, 108, 115. *See also under* Arendt, Hannah
Trump, Donald, 4, 16, 22, 53

violence, 81, 106, 112–13, 117–18, 123, 156n10. *See also under* Arendt, Hannah
virtue, 139–41

Weber, Max, 78–79, 81, 83, 85, 106, 123, 156n7

Zagajewski, Adam, 66–67
Zerilli, Linda, 47, 147n7, 152n17